Function Point Analysis

BOB BARNES
BAKER BARNES ASSOC
INC.
6/01

Addison-Wesley Information Technology Series
Capers Jones and David S. Linthicum, Consulting Editors

The information technology (IT) industry is in the public eye now more than ever before because of a number of major issues in which software technology and national policies are closely related. As the use of software expands, there is a continuing need for business and software professionals to stay current with the state of the art in software methodologies and technologies. The goal of the Addison-Wesley Information Technology Series is to cover any and all topics that affect the IT community: These books illustrate and explore how information technology can be aligned with business practices to achieve business goals and support business imperatives. Addison-Wesley has created this innovative series to empower you with the benefits of the industry experts' experience.

For more information point your browser to
http://www.awl.com/cseng/series/it/

Sid Adelman, Larissa Terpeluk Moss, *Data Warehouse Project Management*. ISBN: 0-201-61635-1

Wayne Applehans, Alden Globe, and Greg Laugero, *Managing Knowledge: A Practical Web-Based Approach*. ISBN: 0-201-43315-X

Michael H. Brackett, *Data Resource Quality: Turning Bad Habits into Good Practices*. ISBN: 0-201-71306-3

James Craig and Dawn Jutla, *e-Business Readiness: A Customer-Focused Framework*. ISBN: 0-201-71006-4

Gregory C. Dennis and James R. Rubin, *Mission-Critical Java™ Project Management: Business Strategies, Applications, and Development*. ISBN: 0-201-32573-X

Kevin Dick, *XML: A Manager's Guide*. ISBN: 0-201-43335-4

Jill Dyché, *e-Data: Turning Data into Information with Data Warehousing*. ISBN: 0-201-65780-5

Dr. Nick V. Flor, *Web Business Engineering: Using Offline Activites to Drive Internet Strategies*. ISBN: 0-201-60468-X

David Garmus and David Herron, *Function Point Analysis: Measurement Practices for Successful Software Projects*. ISBN: 0-201-69944-3

Capers Jones, *Software Assessments, Benchmarks, and Best Practices*. ISBN: 0-201-48542-7

Capers Jones, *The Year 2000 Software Problem: Quantifying the Costs and Assessing the Consequences*. ISBN: 0-201-30964-5

Ravi Kalakota and Marcia Robinson, *e-Business 2.0: Roadmap for Success* ISBN: 0-201-72165-1

David S. Linthicum, *B2B Application Integration: e-Business-Enable Your Enterprise* ISBN: 0-201-70936-8

Sergio Lozinsky, *Enterprise-Wide Software Solutions: Integration Strategies and Practices*. ISBN: 0-201-30971-8

Patrick O'Beirne, *Managing the Euro in Information Systems: Strategies for Successful Changeover*. ISBN: 0-201-60482-5

Mai-lan Tomsen, *Killer Content: Strategies for Web Content and E-Commerce*. ISBN: 0-201-65786-4

Bill Wiley, *Essential System Requirements: A Practical Guide to Event-Driven Methods*. ISBN: 0-201-61606-8

Bill Zoellick, *Web Engagement: Connecting to Customers in e-Business*. ISBN: 0-201-65766-X

Function Point Analysis

Measurement Practices
for Successful
Software Projects

David Garmus
David Herron

Addison-Wesley

Boston • San Francisco • New York • Toronto • Montreal
London • Munich • Paris • Madrid
Capetown • Sydney • Tokyo • Singapore • Mexico City

The publisher offers discounts on this book when ordered in quantity for special sales. For more information, please contact:

Pearson Education Corporate Sales Division
One Lake Street
Upper Saddle River, NJ 07458
(800) 382-3419
corpsales@pearsontechgroup.com

Visit us on the Web at www.awl.com/cseng/

Library of Congress Cataloging-in-Publication Data

Garmus, David.
    Function point analysis : measurement practices for successful software projects / David Garmus and David Herron.
        p. cm. — (Addison-Wesley information technology series)
    Includes bibliographical references and index.
    ISBN 0-201-69944-3
    1. Computer software—Development. 2. Function point analysis.
I. Herron, David (David E.)   II. Title.   III. Series.

    QA76.76.D47.G36 2000
    005.1'4—dc21   00-060558

ISBN 0-201-69944-3
Text printed on recycled paper
1 2 3 4 5 6 7 8 9 10—MA—0403020100
First printing, November 2000

To Don Buchanan

His courage and faith have been an inspiration to all who know him.

Contents

CHAPTER 10   **CALCULATING AND APPLYING FUNCTION POINTS**   **161**

CHAPTER 11   **CASE STUDIES IN COUNTING**   **173**

CHAPTER 14 **COUNTING AN OBJECT-ORIENTED APPLICATION** 231

CHAPTER 15 **TOOLS** 243

Foreword

In the mid-1970s, IBM commissioned an engineer named Allan Albrecht and his colleagues to explore software measurements and metrics. The motives for this assignment were the growing importance of software within IBM, coupled with the problems and limitations of "lines of code" metrics.

After more than a year of research and discussion, Albrecht and his team formulated the first version of the metric now known as "function points." Function point metrics were intended to be independent of the amount of code in software applications. Further, function point metrics were intended to be useful for analyzing the entire life-cycle of software projects from early requirements through many years of maintenance and enhancement.

After several years of usage within IBM, it was decided by IBM executives to make function point metrics available to customers and to the software industry as a whole. In October of 1979, Albrecht presented a paper on "Measuring Application Development Productivity" in Monterey, California at a conference jointly sponsored by IBM and two IBM customer associations called SHARE and GUIDE. This was the first external publication of function point metrics to the software industry.

Usage of function point metrics began to spread among IBM customers and then among other companies that were interested in software measurements. By 1984 function point usage had become so widespread that a non-profit association was created called "The International Function Point Users Group" or IFPUG for short. IFPUG has grown every year since its creation and has become the largest software measurement association in the world. There are now scores of affiliated organizations in many countries.

Function point metrics would not have spread spontaneously among so many companies and countries if they did not provide substantial benefits to users. The primary benefit of function point metrics is that they have given the software industry the ability to carry out serious economic studies.

As this book is published at the dawn of the twenty first century, function point metrics have become the standard for studying many important topics associated with software, including but not limited to:

- Productivity baselines and benchmarks
- Quality baselines and benchmarks
- Process improvement economics
- Outsource contracts
- Litigation analysis

Although function point metrics are powerful, successfully applying function point metrics is not a trivial undertaking. Accurate counting of function point metrics requires training. Most function point studies today involve function point analysis carried out by practitioners who have successfully passed a certification examination administered by IFPUG or one of the equivalent organizations in other countries.

The authors of this book, David Garmus and David Herron, have long been associated with IFPUG and with function point training. This book teaches and discusses the latest version of the IFPUG counting rules, which is Version 4.1 as of the end of calendar year 2000.

Learning to use function points is easiest if there are practical examples and case studies. The book also includes many examples of how function point analysis can be applied to various kinds of software applications such as object-oriented projects, client-server projects, and real-time projects.

This book is joining an expanding library of recent books that either explain function point analysis or use function point analysis to provide benchmark and baseline data for software projects. No fewer than 15 books have been published within the past 10 years on aspects of function point analysis. Over this same time span, more than 100 journal articles have appeared on function point analysis, including even articles in mainstream journals such as Scientific American.

As this book points out, almost all of the international software benchmark studies published over the past 10 years utilize function point analysis. The pragmatic reason for this is that among all known software metrics, only function points can actually measure economic productivity or measure the defect volumes found in software requirements, design, and user documentation as well as measuring coding defects.

As more and more information becomes available using function point metrics, the value of function point metrics themselves is steadily increasing. A metric with no empirical data is of little value. Now that IFPUG function points have been applied to thousands of software projects, they have become the de facto standard for software economic studies.

Although no one claims that function point metrics are perfect and have no problems of their own, it can be stated that no better metrics than function points exist for software economic and quality studies.

Capers Jones
Chief Scientist, Software Productivity Research (an Artemis company)

Preface

Writing this book has been a process, a journey, and a wonderful learning experience.

We have been immersed in the world of function points and software metrics for more than ten years. We both are proud of our accomplishments and contributions to the advancement and utilization of the function point methodology. We recognize a responsibility, as experts in this field, to communicate our experiences and to express our opinions in such a way that others can gain from what we have observed, learned, and practiced. You could say that we believe and that we are extending the wisdom of the message. We have also found our writings to be an opportunity for continued learning. While writing this book, we had the good fortune to receive comments and constructive criticisms from a significant number of book reviewers and industry experts. Their thoughtful comments and contributions have given us greater insight into the software community views of software measurement and management and, in particular, function points. We thank all of you who participated in the review process.

Our second book was in many ways easier, but in some ways more challenging, than the first. We endeavored to write a book that was significantly better than the first. We achieved success with our first book, but we knew that there was so much more to share. The process of writing becomes easier once you understand that it is a process similar to developing software. Our challenge was to identify the content that would serve a diverse audience while not losing sight of the most important audience, the practitioner. After all, it is the practice, not the theory, of function points that will sustain this valuable software management methodology.

Acknowledgments

Considering everything that went into this book, it is difficult to remember and to include all of those individuals who contributed to the content and substance.

We must first recognize our loved ones, who have given us the space and have had the patience to take on a little extra on the home front, while we sat at the dining room table with papers spread about and pounded away on our laptops. We say a special thanks to our wives, Caren Garmus and Mary Herron; and to our children, Alexander, Elizabeth, Joshua, and Jason Herron; and Kim Garmus and Danelle Hughes. In this wonderful age of electronics, we have become very portable; our efforts in writing this book have traveled with us to various family home sites including those of our parents, Paul and Mary Garmus and Mildred Herron. We thank all of them for their support and their assistance.

Of course without the opportunity to practice these methods and techniques, we would not have had very much to write about. We have been blessed with a number of wonderful clients over the years, and we would like to recognize those companies that have allowed us to apply our trade. They contributed in large part to the writings in this book. They include ADP, AMS, AT&T, Agilent, aligne, Ameritech, Andersen, Bellcore, Blue Cross & Blue Shield of Michigan, Boeing, Booz Allen & Hamilton, CACI, Cigna, Citicorp, Computer Associates, Condor, CSC, DCI, Dean Witter, Delta Air Lines, Diasorin, DFAS, DLA, Dun & Bradstreet, Dupont, EDS, Ernst & Young, Federal Reserve Bank, Fidelity Investments, Ford, Geneer, General Accident Ins., General Motors, haht Software, Harleysville Insurance, IBM, IMR Global, IRS, JP Morgan, Lockheed Martin, Lucent Technologies, MasterCard, Merrill Lynch, MST, NASD, Ortho Clinical Diagnostics, Perot Systems, Pitney Bowes, Price Systems, Prudential Insurance, Ralston Purina, Revenue Canada, ROLM, Rubin Systems, SCT, Safeguard Scientifics, Software Quality Engineering, Smith Barney, Software Productivity Centre, Software Productivity Consortium, Software Quality Solutions, Target, Technology Transfer, Texas Instruments, USAA, U.S. Air Force, U.S. Coast Guard, U.S. Navy, and Viasoft.

Each company is made up of people; we have met many wonderful people in our quest to bring function points to the market. Of course, we have met some real jerks along the way, but that has made life more interesting. Our special thanks to all those relationships that we have built and enjoyed.

The most helpful people are the people that we have engaged to work as part of The David Consulting Group. Many of these loyal and professional metric specialists have been with our group for a number of years and have helped us to grow and have grown with us as individuals in their own right. To say we are proud to be associated with them would be an understatement. Our heartfelt thanks to our current DCG consultants, Don Buchanan, Koni Thompson, Eric Buel, Ray Boehm, Mike Cunnane, Richard Desjardins, Andy Sanchez, Janet Russac, Charlie Colpitts, and Jim Glorie; our past DCG consultants, Jacqueline Jones and Mary Bradley; our part-time DCG consultants, Mark Schilling, Marianne Goldberg, and James Nowin; and our administrative assistant, Jennifer Pannell.

A special thanks and recognition are due to Koni Thompson for her significant contribution to the chapter on Counting Advanced Technologies and to Janet Russac for her review efforts.

Of course, we are forever indebted to the International Function Point Users Group, its members, board, committees, and affiliates for the dedication to the software measurement field. We are honored by our roles in this organization.

We save the best for last. As we said in the beginning, it has been a learning experience. We continue to be amazed by how blessed we have been. The good fortune that has come to us is totally attributable to our Lord God. We give thanks to Him every day, and we pray for His continued blessing and presence in our lives. We pray that His blessings be upon all of you as well.

Introduction

This is our second book to be published on the topic of function points and software measurement practices. Since the writing of our last book, there have been some important advancements in the function point methodology and in the software industry. This book is primarily about the function point methodology and the use of function points in managing the development and deployment of software. We have incorporated the latest changes to the function point methodology, and we describe how this sizing methodology applies to the latest technologies in the software development environment. In addition, we include chapters detailing the applied use of function points in estimating software development projects and the use of function points in conjunction with software measurement programs.

The intent of this book is to provide a comprehensive presentation on the function point methodology to the practitioner. Toward that end we have included and further defined the rules and guidelines as prescribed by the International Function Point Users Group (IFPUG), following the latest release (4.1) of the Function Point Counting Practices Manual (CPM).

In addition, we would like this book to be read by nonpractitioners. Some individuals in the software industry are either unaware of function points or have a misconception about the effective use of function points. It is to this group that we have addressed several chapters on the use of function points—focusing particularly on how they may be used to manage the software development environment more effectively. We have even been so bold as to address the issue of function points and their value to the executive.

We have learned some valuable lessons from our first publishing experience. Many readers were kind enough to express their sentiments regarding the usefulness of the content of our first book. In particular, function point practitioners found the information to be extremely helpful as a guide to counting and a useful tool as a reference manual. However, some individuals were critical of the chapters focusing on topics related to software measurement, such as baselining and estimating. They felt that these topics were too broadly covered—that we did not go into the depth required to address the topics properly. We have listened.

Used as a sizing metric, function points are only the tip of the software metrics iceberg. There is such a wide variety of topics related to software measurement and process management that it would not be feasible to incorporate all of them into one publication. Some of the related topics, such as baselining and estimating, could fill an entire book by themselves. However, these are important topics that have a strong relationship with function points, so we can't ignore them either; therefore, we have taken a different approach. We address these topics specifically in terms of their relationships to function points. We are not trying to write a book that encompasses everything about project estimation (for example), but we do want our readers to understand that function point analysis can play a key role in improving the effectiveness of project estimation.

Basic Counting Rules

The content of this book is centered around the primary chapters dealing with the function point methodology. As stated earlier, these chapters (6 through 10) provide the reader with all of the counting rules and guidelines as presented in IFPUG's CPM 4.1. Together with the rules and guidelines, we present detailed examples and case studies to aid the reader in understanding how to apply the methodology. Numerous examples and a variety of counting scenarios are presented in Chapters 7 and 8, on data and transactional functions, respectively.

Advanced Counting

Along with the basic counting rules, we have included a new chapter on counting advanced technologies (Chapter 12). With the advent of data warehousing, client-server environments, and Web-based technology, we felt it necessary to provide the reader with insights into how function points can be applied in these new environments.

Preparing for Certification

Perhaps the single most popular section of our first book was the chapter on preparing for the CFPS (Certified Function Point Specialist) exam. A significant number of people who had used our book to prepare for the IFPUG certification exam found it extremely helpful. Therefore, in Chapter 16 we provide an entirely new exam, which is based on the latest release of the Counting Practices Manual (4.1).

What's Different?

Software Measurement

As stated earlier, software measurement is one of those broad subjects that covers so many different topics that any one of them could justify a book of its own. Rather than attempting to create an all-encompassing condensed chapter on the broad topic of software measurement, we decided to take a different approach. It is not enough to create a how-to guide on establishing a software measurement program; success is in the execution. Successful execution depends on several key elements. Chapter 1, Software Measurement, drives home three key points: (1) A software measurement program must satisfy the unique needs of the different audiences it is intended to address, (2) there are two key components in an effective software metrics model (quantitative and qualitative), and (3) a world-class program should have certain proven and effective characteristics.

Function Points and the Executive

Function point analysis is usually successful in organizations in which senior management believes that measurement is necessary to improve and be competitive; however, many senior managers are still unaware of the benefits or the necessity of measurement. It is to this audience that we offer Chapter 2, Executive Introduction to Function Points, which focuses on the senior IT executive. As of this writing, it is safe to say that most senior executives running IT shops today are uneducated regarding the effective and practical use of software metrics and function points. We don't expect that all senior executives will pick up this book and read it cover to cover; however, if we can compel them to read only one chapter, Chapter 2 is the one they should read.

Function Point Utilization

To make this a truly useful book on the topic of function points, we had to present a practical view of function points and discuss how they are typically used in software shops. In Chapter 4, Using Function Points Effectively, we examine three of the more common uses of this popular software-sizing metric: (1) project estimating, (2) application development and maintenance outsourcing, and (3) performance baselining. We have taken great care to present some unique and practical ideas on how function points can be used.

Chapter 3, Measuring with Function Points, presents some detailed measures that use function points as the base metric. Although not a comprehensive list of all possible function point and function point–related measures, it does detail the more common measures used by organizations today.

Automation

Everyone wants to know about tools and how they can purchase a software product that automatically does everything, including the actual counting of function points. If such a product existed, there would not be much need for a book describing how to manually count function points. Unfortunately, no such software tool exists; however, a wide variety of tools use function points in one form or another. We did not conduct an exhaustive search of all tools that reference or use function points. That research would have taken an investment in time that would have far outweighed the value gained. Instead we narrowed our focus to just those tools that are strictly function point repository tools and function point–based project-estimating tools. In addition, we discuss how to select a tool and the features that are important.

Industry Benchmarking Data

During the past few years there has been an increase in interest in achieving the capacity to compare one organization's level of performance with another, or one technology with another. Many companies are looking for data sources that can provide benchmark data. Function points are a key normalizing metric in many of these benchmark data sources. Where are these data sources, and do they provide the data that most companies require? In Chapter 5, Software Industry

Benchmark Data, we take somewhat of a controversial view of the current state of data reliability and the source of data that your organization needs.

This book is intended to be used primarily as a reference manual and as a learning guide. But just as important is our intent to raise the level of awareness and understanding with regard to the function point metric. We take the position that the business of developing software is relatively low on the industry maturity scale when compared to other professions, such as accounting, medicine, and manufacturing. All of these industries have a standard set of metrics that is incorporated into the business model. We predict that the same will eventually hold true for software development.

The International Function Point Users Group

Critical to the ongoing success of function points as a viable software metric is the work that is being accomplished by the International Function Point Users Group (IFPUG). Since 1986, IFPUG has continued to grow in members and in its importance to the software measurement community. Today IFPUG enjoys a membership of thousands of individual, corporate, educational, and institutional members from more than 30 countries.

IFPUG is a not-for-profit, member-run user group. IFPUG's mission is to be a recognized leader in promoting and encouraging the effective management of application software development and maintenance activities through the use of function point analysis and other software measurement techniques. For more information, contact IFPUG at http://www.ifpug.org, e-mail: ifpug@ifpug.org, phone (United States): 609-799-4900, or fax: 609-799-7032. IFPUG serves to facilitate the exchange of knowledge and ideas for improved software measurement techniques and seeks to provide a composite environment that stimulates the personal and professional development of its members. IFPUG typically meets twice a year, once in the spring and then again in the fall. The spring conference is dedicated to training programs and committee meetings. The fall program is devoted to both committee work and training programs, but it also typically includes a two-and-a-half-day user conference and vendor showcase.

Committee work is the core of IFPUG. The two most visible committees are the Counting Practices Committee and the Certification Committee. The Counting Practices Committee is responsible for maintaining the current counting guidelines, *Counting Practices Manual.* The Certification Committee is responsible for establishing and enforcing the certification guidelines. Other critical committees that generate guidelines for either counting or using function points, include New Environments, IT Performance, and Management Reporting.

Internationally, IFPUG is represented in numerous countries supported by members that include the following:

- Australian Software Metrics Association (ASMA)

  asmavic@ozonline.com.au
- Austria Function Point Users Group (FPUGA)   Gerald.Rehling@debis.at
- Brazilian Function Point Users Group (BFPUG)

  mauricioaguiar@yahoo.com
- Denmark Function Point Users Group (DANMET)   eh.kmd.dk
- Germany: Deutschsprachige Anwendergruppe für
- Software-Metrik und Aufwandschätzung (DASMA)

  73752.542@compuserve.com
- Italian Users Group on Function Points (GUFPI)

  mancini@ogrouptec.com
- Japan Function Point Users Group (JFPUG)

  nishiyama.s@rdc.east.ntt.co.jp
- Netherlands Software Metrics Users Association (NESMA)

  www.nesma.nl/english
- South African Software Metrics Association (SAMA)   bram@iafrica.com
- UK Software Metrics Association (UKSMA)   pr_rule@compuserve.com

The health and well-being of function points is directly related to the ongoing effectiveness of IFPUG. Its challenge is to continue to enhance the counting methodology and to raise the level of awareness among professions that are not function point literate.

Function point analysis is a method that has been misused and misunderstood in the past. The use of function points provides the software project manager, the IT organization, and the business user with a key piece of information about software that can be used to improve the effectiveness of how they design, develop, and deploy software. It is not currently in use in every IT shop, but it is available for those who understand its value.

Alternative methods of sizing software have been introduced over the past ten years. Capers Jones' Feature Points and Boeing's 3D Function Points have been two of the more popular and long-lasting variations on function points. Neither method has gained much popularity or widespread utilization. Several other sizing methods, such as Mark II and Demarco's Bang Metric, have a limited but consistent following. And new methods are still being introduced. As recently as 1998 the Common Software Measurement International Consortium (COSMIC) introduced COSMIC FFP as a new measurement for the functional size of software. The basic principles of the method were established, drawing on the best features of the existing IFPUG, Mark II, NESMA, and FFP VI methods; on the ISO standard on functional size measurement; and on new ideas. The first formal definition of the method was released in October 1999. It is too early to tell whether or not this method, still in its infancy, will provide any additional benefit to the software community at large.

Understandably, this book isn't for everyone involved in software, but it is for everyone who wants to improve his or her software development environment through the effective utilization of software functional metrics.

About the Authors

David Garmus is an acknowledged authority in the sizing, measurement, and estimation of software application development and maintenance. He has more than 25 years of experience in managing, developing, and maintaining computer software systems. Concurrently, he served as a university instructor, teaching courses in computer programming, system development, information systems management, data processing, accounting, finance, and banking. He received his B.S. from UCLA and an M.B.A. from Harvard University. Mr. Garmus is President of the International Function Point Users Group (IFPUG) and a member of the Counting Practices Committee. He previously served IFPUG as Chair of the Certification Committee, as Chair of the New Environments Committee, and on the Board of Directors as Director of Applied Programs. His e-mail address is dcg_dg@compuserve.com.

David Herron is an acknowledged authority in the use of metrics to monitor the impact of Information Technology (IT) on the business, on the advancement of IT organizations to higher levels on the SEI Capability Maturity Model, and on the governance of outsourcing arrangements. He assists clients in establishing software measurement, process improvement, and quality programs and to enhance their project management techniques. He has more than 25 years experience in managing, developing, and maintaining computer software systems. He serves as a Cutter Consortium Expert Consultant. He attended Union College and Northeastern

University. Mr. Herron is Chair of the IFPUG Management Reporting Committee, a member of the IFPUG IT Performance Committee, and a member of the American Society for Quality. His e-mail address is dcg_dh@compuserve.com.

Together, as the principals and founders of The David Consulting Group, they are recognized authors and lecturers who have addressed audiences worldwide on functional measures, software process improvement, and outsourcing. They co-authored *Measuring the Software Process: A Practical Guide To Functional Measurement,* published by Prentice Hall in 1996, and have contributed numerous articles to such periodicals as *Software Development, Data Manager, Software Testing & Quality Engineering, Methods & Tools,* and *CrossTalk.* They maintain a Web site at www.davidconsultinggroup.com.

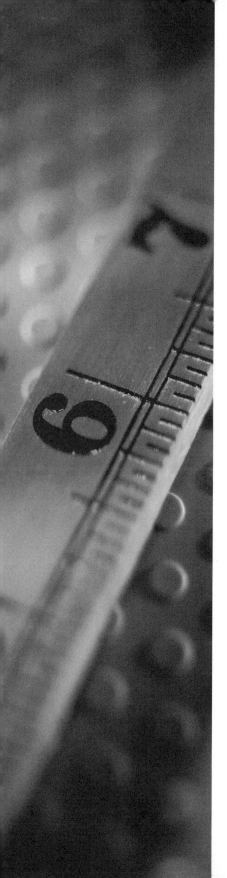

CHAPTER ONE

Software Measurement

Introduction

Much has been written about the benefits of software measurement and the failure of software measurement programs. Industry publications often contain first-person accounts of the value gained from utilizing a specified set of software measures, or they provide the reader with a cookbook approach to successful implementation of a software measurement program. Seldom do we read about a fully executed measurement program that is delivering all the benefits to the organization that industry experts promise. This reality is underscored by our own real-world observations during numerous consulting engagements. On many occasions we have been introduced into a situation in which we have encountered software measurement programs that would not be considered robust enough to be delivering true benefit to the organization. So the question remains: If software measurement is beneficial and relatively easy, why aren't more companies incorporating measurement into their development practices, and why aren't all the touted benefits of measurement being realized?

Part of the answer lies in the fact that the business of software development is a relatively young profession, and the lack of measurement is simply a reflection of the maturity level of the software profession. When we examine other professions, such as accounting, law, manufacturing, or medicine, which all have been around for a much longer period of time, we see that they have established measures and standards that have become part of the business. However, the business of

veloping software is maturing, and software measurement is slowly being recog-
zed as part of the process. The increased role of measurement and its impor-
nce to the industry can be observed in such instances as the development of
...ernational standards such as ISO 9001.

Because we are in the early stages of a maturing profession, the fundamental
issue surrounding the expansion and utilization of software measurement as a viable
tool in the development process is the need to raise the level of awareness among
software practitioners, project managers, and others. Professionals in the software
measurement business need to be the Johnny Appleseeds of our profession and
spread the good news beyond the inner circles of software metrics practitioners.

In an effort to raise that level of awareness, we are using this chapter to
advance the reader's understanding of software measurement, the fundamental
elements of good software measurement practices, and the definition of a world-
class software measurement program.

The Need for Software Measurement

Before we can explain why software measurement is needed, we should identify
who needs software measurement. The *who* will direct our response in answering
why it is needed. Typically we categorize software measurement activities into
three tiers (see Figure 1-1).

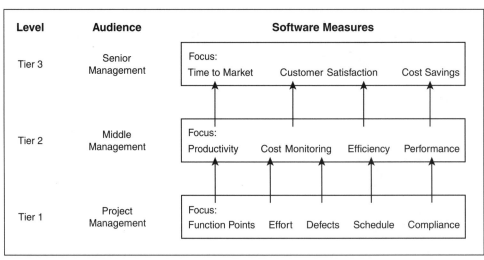

Figure 1-1 Categories of software measurement activities

First, there is the obvious and common use of measurement at the software project level, tier 1. This is where the action is. The project manager is responsible for controlling the software project and therefore needs the proper tools and methods available to manage and control the project environment. Contained within a complete project management tool kit is software metrics.

The key measurement activity that project managers require is the ability to accurately estimate and control the software deliverable. These tasks require some very well-defined measures, including size of the deliverable (function points), schedules, defects, project-related costs (effort), compliance to standards, and management of change requests.

The benefit is limited for the project manager who is simply using these measures in a reactive form of project control. Project forecasts, based on measurement data, that anticipate schedule delays, cost overruns, and poor quality need to be part of the value-added equation that a good software measurement program supplies. Today, most organizations are content simply to capture these data points, review them on a weekly basis, see where the project has been, and make sure it is tracking in the right direction. This approach is similar to steering a ship by looking out from the stern of the boat.

The proactive measurement program, on the other hand, captures these data points and records them in a metrics repository with other essential project profile data. The metrics analyst develops models that are used by the project manager on future projects to forecast outcomes and to steer the project from the bow rather than the stern. In summary, the need for metrics at the project manager level is based on the ability to proactively manage project deliverables using a database of historical metrics data.

The second level of software measurement activity includes those metrics required by middle management, tier 2. These are the division or business unit leaders, the individuals typically responsible for multiple project deliverables. They share the needs of the project managers, but they are more focused on overall performance rather than on day-to-day project outcomes.

The measures that provide value to middle management include productivity, cost monitoring, software process efficiency, and performance. What middle managers usually don't measure is whether the application actually works. Naturally they want it to be fit for use, to install cleanly, and to run properly through the first several production cycles. They are usually focused on delivery and possibly turning the system over to a maintenance group that will manage the long-term health of the system; however, they should also be concerned with the effective functioning of the application, so we may want to add defects to the list of appropriate measures for middle managers.

This middle level of measures is executed on a project-by-project basis; however, these measures are viewed at a collective or overall performance-based level. The overall monitoring of the department or business unit is measured by its percentage of projects that are completed on time, on budget, and so on. Process capability profiles, measuring organizational performance, are created and reviewed. This review presents an excellent opportunity to recognize general, across-the-board process strengths and weaknesses, and it directs process improvement initiatives in the right direction. Activities are baselined at this level as well, and this baselining is used to track trends in performance. In summary, the measurement needed at this level is one of overall performance as indicated by aggregated measures of project performance.

The third tier is for senior management. Senior managers include the chief information officers (CIOs), chief executive officers (CEOs), and chief operating officers (COOs). Do they care about software metrics? That's not a fair question, because they probably aren't aware of what constitutes a software metrics arsenal (remember what we said earlier about the level of awareness within the software industry). The real question is, Do they need information to run their business? The answer is, absolutely. That information should be provided to them in a software metrics format for quantitative decision making.

CEOs and other senior executives have long desired to understand and quantify the contribution of their information technology (IT) organizations to the business. Today, more than ever, IT is recognized as an integral part of an organization's business strategy. IT performance measures, which have been used in the past to show productivity and quality performance results, must now evolve into a more sophisticated, business-oriented measure. CIOs will be required to demonstrate their contribution to the business using this new form of measurement.

Basic Software Measurement Elements

The basic elements of an effective software measurement model can be captured in two words: "quantitative" and "qualitative." An effective software measurement program must have both elements in order to be complete. If you think you have a complete software measurement program, and it consists of quantitative software metrics but does not contain any qualitative values, then you have only half of what you need.

To help you understand what we mean by "qualitative" and "quantitative," we present a very simple and yet effective model for software measurement (see Figure 1-2).

Software Measurement Model: Quantitative and Qualitative Elements

Quantitative data includes factors such as the functional size of the software deliverable, the work effort required to deliver or support that software, the overall schedule duration or time required to produce the software, the number of defects, the labor cost of the project, and the time to market.

Performance productivity levels are calculated on the basis of these quantitative data points. Common expressions of performance levels include productivity and quality ratings relative to size. When measuring the size of software in function points, we would express a productivity result as the number of function points produced per person-month or as the number of hours per function point. This measure of productivity becomes one of several measures that allows us to create profiles of organizational performance and to compare our performance to industry standards.

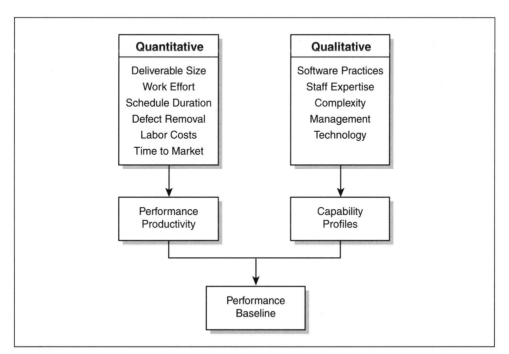

Figure 1-2 Software measurement model

When we measure software systems or software projects, we establish what is commonly referred to as a baseline. This baseline provides us with a variety of performance-level project data points based on varying degrees of productivity and quality performance. Not all projects within an organization will demonstrate the same rate of performance.

As depicted in Figure 1-3, collecting data on multiple projects results in a display of various productivity levels. The vertical axis measures the total size (function points delivered); the horizontal axis, the rate at which each project delivered the function points. This delivery rate is a measure of performance.

It is important that we recognize and acknowledge the varying degrees of performance and ultimately understand the causes of the variations in performance. This is where the qualitative data becomes so critical. Qualitative data describes how we build and maintain our systems and can be used to analyze the variances in performance.

Referencing our model once again, we see that the qualitative data is expressed in terms of the software process we use, the skill levels of our staff, the level of automation in our development environment, and the nature of the business environment. These factors are often referred to as influencers. Depending on the assessment method used, any number of influencers ultimately affect the productivity and quality levels of our software development performance.

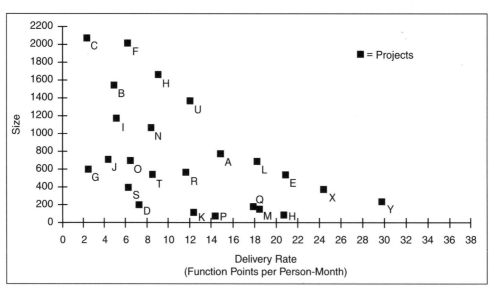

Figure 1-3 Delivery rate versus project size

Several assessment methodologies have realized a certain level of popularity and acceptance in the software industry. One such technique is the Capability Maturity Model (CMM) assessment methodology, developed originally for the U.S. Department of Defense, at the Software Engineering Institute (SEI) in Pittsburgh, Pennsylvania, and initially led by Watts Humphrey. This model is represented by five evolutionary steps, each level contributing to successive levels of maturity. Associated with each level are key process areas. These five levels define the scale for measuring the maturity of an organization's software process capability. The five levels and the associated key process areas are shown in Table 1-1. Note that there are no key process areas associated with level 1. Level 1 is characterized as ad hoc and sometimes chaotic. Few processes are defined, and success often depends on individual efforts.

This model focuses on the qualitative aspect of process assessment. Although it subscribes to the use of software measures, the Capability Maturity Model itself does not utilize any quantitative measures directly associated with the SEI maturity level ratings. In other words, advancing from one level to the next only suggests levels of improvement in productivity and/or quality; it does not quantify

Table 1-1: The Capability Maturity Model (CMM)

Level	Description	Key Process Areas
5	Optimizing	Process change management
		Technology innovation
		Defect prevention
4	Managed	Quality management
		Process measurement
3	Defined	Peer reviews
		Intergroup coordination
		Software product engineering
		Integrated software management
		Training program
		Organization process definition
		Organization process focus
2	Repeatable	Software configuration management
		Software quality assurance
		Software subcontract management
		Software project tracking
		Software project planning
		Requirements management
1	Initial	

anticipated levels of performance. Such quantitative measures would have to be gathered in parallel to the CMM model in order to quantify possible improvements realized by progressing up the CMM scale.

In terms of effectively capturing and analyzing qualitative data, the CMM performs very well. In our opinion, the shortfall of the CMM process is that it provides no direct quantitative measurement of the resulting assessment. We assume that if we move up the maturity scale—for example, from a level 2 rating to a level 3 rating—we will quantitatively increase our level of performance productivity and quality, but without quantitative measures we really never know for sure.

This CMM is what we refer to as a static process assessment model. The assessment process and resulting recommendations for improving that process require that an organization begin at a base level of predescribed process areas. The organization must satisfy all the requirements at one level before progressing to the next stage of maturity. The fundamental flaw in this presentation is most often found in its execution. Organizations may ignore isolated achievements in certain key process areas at the higher levels and sacrifice those potential strengths by requiring the organization to concentrate on lower levels of performance.

We can compare the static SEI/CMM model with a more dynamic model for process improvement. The use of a more dynamic model for process improvement would allow an organization to quantitatively and qualitatively examine its current performance, identify areas of inadequacy and areas of proficiency, and focus on improvement where it would be most beneficial. The dynamic model does not have a particular predefined path to software maturity. Instead, it begins the process of improvement by allowing an organization to seek its own level of strengths and weaknesses and then plan improvement strategies based on recognition of our own best practices.

The assessment model depicted in Figure 1-2 suggests that software practices are to be evaluated on the basis of both quantitative and qualitative data. From the collected data we derive performance levels and current process capabilities. Using this data, we can identify and quantify current proficiencies and inadequacies and ultimately identify opportunities for software improvements. As those improvements are identified, we update our current practices while continuing to measure.

We have performed many of these types of process performance assessments using our own proprietary assessment method and set of questions (see Appendix A). The method of collection involves interview and survey sessions, with each of the project teams participating in the assessment. Data is collected on key influencers, such as project management capabilities, requirements and design effectiveness, build and test practices, skill levels, and other contributing environmental factors. Individual projects are analyzed, and project profiles are created. This data is also analyzed in the aggregate and may be used as the basis for determining overall organization process improvements (see Appendix D).

The results are somewhat predictable. Typical influencers include skill levels, effective use of front-end lifecycle quality practices, tool utilization, and project management. These results parallel, in part, the findings from the International Software Benchmarking Standards Group (ISBSG) database analysis, which revealed that language complexity, development platform, maximum team size, and application are significant factors influencing productivity.

KEy

World-Class Measurement Program

As organizations pursue alternatives to improve their efficiency in managing the design, development, and deployment of software, they eventually recognize the need for measurement. During the late 1990s we observed a variety of metric program installations and have concluded that there are four metric program profiles that may be used to characterize the nature of programs currently being executed in the software industry. Each profile can be described by a set of attributes, which alternatively may be used to indicate the level of measurement program maturity. The four levels of metrics maturity are entry, basic, industry leader, and world-class.

Entry Level

Typically at the entry level a management group or a development team has recognized the basic benefits of measuring software. The philosophy "if you can't measure, you can't manage" has been accepted, and basic measures are being collected on a limited basis throughout the organization.

Typical attributes of a start-up level include the following:

- The metrics definition within the lifecycle methodology is limited.
- Partial or no formal metrics data collection is in place.
- Measurement terms and definitions (e.g., release duration, start date, end date, actual start date, actual end date) are not consistently understood.
- Data integrity is poor.

- Data collection activity and due dates are limited or inconsistent.
- The level of commitment from senior management is not recognized.
- The responsibility for collection, review, analysis, and reporting of the data is undefined.
- Benefits derived from using software metrics are not clearly stated.

Basic Level

At the basic level the organization has recognized and communicated the need for measurement. Frequently the measurement program is linked to or executing in parallel with a particular process improvement award or strategy (e.g., International Standards Organization, Malcomb Baldrige National Quality Award, Software Engineering Institute's Capability Maturity Model) or its own software process improvement initiative.

Typical attributes of a basic level include the following:

- Use of metrics has been documented in the lifecycle methodology process.
- Formal metrics collection processes are in place; however, compliance is not monitored.
- Measurement terms have been defined and documented.
- The accuracy and integrity of the data are more reliable but at times still questionable.
- Data collection and reporting procedures are defined and adhered to.
- Management commitment to the measurement program results in the allocation of limited resources for collection, review, analysis, and reporting of the data.
- Measurement is generally viewed as a positive activity; however, the data remains underutilized.
- Measurement data may be stored in a common repository.

Industry Leader Level

The organization has integrated metrics into its software development process. The organization has realized the benefits and added value of the measurement program and has begun to socialize the process at an enterprise level.

Typical attributes of an industry leader level include the following:

- Lifecycle methodology incorporates the use of metrics and is being followed by the majority of the organization.

- Formal metrics collection processes are in place, and compliance is monitored.
- The definitions of measurement terms (e.g., release duration, start date, end date, actual start date, actual end date) are commonly understood; the measures collected have been identified and defined.
- The accuracy and integrity of the data are reliable, and the data is being used by the organization for business decisions.
- Data collection, reporting, and analysis are consistent for the development team and throughout the organization.
- Management is committed to the measurement program, and resources are allocated for collection, review, analysis, and reporting of the data. Metrics support business decisions.
- There is a formal reward for teams supporting the metrics initiative.
- Measurement data is stored in a common repository that is accessible throughout the organization.

World-Class Level

The organization has established an effective measurement process that enables the assessment of current productivity and quality levels of performance. The organization uses the metrics to identify opportunities for development and to support productivity and quality improvement. IT can demonstrate and quantify its contribution to the business.

Typical attributes for a world-class level include the following:

- The organization has a vision to be a world-class leader in the areas of application development and support performance.
- The organization has a mission statement to implement a standard set of process metrics.
- A common set of measurements has been employed, focusing on size (through function points), cost, cycle time, and quality measurements such as defects and customer satisfaction.
- The organization uses the measures and metrics to achieve high standards in the areas of development, support performance, and product delivery and reliability.
- Measures are an integrated part of the work process, collected in real time and through automation where possible.
- Measurement data supports the needs of the business.

- Benchmarks with other organizations are based on industry data. The organization is aware of sources of benchmarking data (benchmarking consortiums, ISBSG, and so on).
- The organization participates in activities to support and promote benchmarking.
- The organization tracks and reports trends of data over time, and it establishes baselines of performance and goals for improved performance in various categories.
- Management has developed policy statements and fully supports the process.
- Procedures have been institutionalized within the organization.
- A separate organization is responsible for the collection, analysis, and reporting of data.
- Employees are trained on the goals, definitions, and process of the program.
- There is a organizationwide awareness of the metrics program—its benefits and uses.
- Development teams receive regular feedback about the data they have submitted.
- Development teams participate in the review of the measurement process.
- There is a high degree of integrity in the data, validated by regularly scheduled audits.

Establishing a World-Class Measurement Program

A world-class measurement program ensures that the monitoring and achievement of key business drivers is effectively managed through the collection, analysis, and reporting of select software metrics. As part of the transformation from the current state of metrics activity to a world-class position, an organization must execute a series of activities that lead to the creation of a metrics positioning statement.

Using a goal-question-metric paradigm, the metrics team must ensure that the correct goals are identified in order to validate the appropriate suite of measures in support of an organization's business drivers. Once identified, these goals are validated through a series of questions that ensure that the correct measures and metrics collected will effectively measure that strategic goal. The result is a metrics positioning statement, which describes how the identified metrics support strategic business goals.

Once the positioning statement is finalized, an evaluation process is executed that will identify the gaps in the current measurement program relative to a world-class program. This approach includes a discovery phase and a gap analysis phase.

- **Discovery phase.** Data regarding current metrics activities is collected during the discovery phase through interviews with IT directors, product managers, and project managers. In addition, information is gathered regarding current business initiatives.
- **Gap analysis phase.** This phase incorporates the results of the data collected and analyzed during the discovery phase and compares those results to a world-class metrics program profile. By examining a list of measurement program attributes and contrasting current performance levels to world-class performance levels, the metrics team creates a report that describes the differential between the two.

The gap analysis is used to develop the framework for a world-class measurement program. In addition, the metrics team considers two other components to shape and direct the measurement program: current business goals and fundamental measurement program building blocks.

Fundamental measurement program building blocks are the basic measurements that should be included in even the simplest of programs. Basic measures include labor effort and cost, duration, and defects. Accountability and responsibility for the program need to be clearly communicated. In addition, every measurement program should document the measurement process, which includes the collection, analysis, and reporting of data.

The result is a well-focused and customized world-class measurement program framework.

Discovery Phase

The assessment conducted during the discovery phase is based on information gathered from the project and application teams via interviews and questionnaires. All questionnaires are reviewed and analyzed at an aggregate, organizational level. A sample questionnaire and possible responses are summarized in Table 1-2. A rating for each response is based on the following scale:

- **Sporadic.** Demonstrates *minimally achieved* performance of the tasks and activities; data may be partially gathered.

- **Partial.** Demonstrates performance of the tasks and activities *achieved by the team;* data may be gathered by a few teams, or even at an organization level, but the thoroughness and usability of data are lacking.
- **Consistent.** Demonstrates performance of the tasks and activities *achieved in the organization;* data may be gathered throughout the organization.
- **Consistent and improving.** Demonstrates performance of the tasks and activities *achieved with effective utilization;* data is gathered and used effectively throughout the organization.

Table 1-2: Sample Metrics Program Initial Assessment

Questionnaire	Rating Scale[a]			
	S	P	C	CI
PROCESS				
1. Is a formal, documented lifecycle methodology being followed?				
2. Are metrics included as an activity or task within the methodology?				
3. Do the software methodology activities address development, enhancement, and support?				
4. Is there a formal metrics collection process with documented definitions?				
5. Is a particular process improvement award or strategy being pursued?				
6. Is the measurement collection process monitored for consistency and compliance?				
7. Is there a process for ensuring accuracy of the data being collected?				
8. Does the vision or mission statement include or support metrics?				
9. Do teams receive feedback on the data they submit?				
10. Are any measurement collection processes automated?				
11. Are there policy statements that support the process?				
12. Have the procedures been institutionalized within the organization?				

[a]S = sporadic; P = partial; C = consistent; CI = consistent and improving.

Qualifying Notes:

	Rating Scale[a]			
Questionnaire	S	P	C	CI
13. Do development teams receive regular feedback about the data they submit?	▬			
14. What is the level of integrity of the data submitted?	▬▬			
ORGANIZATION				
1. Are there resources for collecting, reviewing, analyzing, and reporting data?	▬▬▬			
2. How supportive of the existing program do you perceive management to be?	▬▬▬▬▬			
3. Do you have a separate metrics team for metrics activities?	▬▬▬			
4. What training has the team received to assist it in its role?	▬▬▬			
5. What is the experience level regarding collection, review, analysis, and reporting?	▬			
AWARENESS				
1. Have the metrics and definitions been identified to everyone on your team?	▬▬			
2. Are awareness programs offered that describe the measurement program?	▬▬▬			
3. Are teams rewarded for supporting the metrics initiative?	▬▬			
4. Is the measurement program at a team, organization, or enterprise level?	▬▬			
5. Is there a common set of metrics that everyone supports?	▬▬			
6. Is there an awareness of the benefits and uses of the metrics being collected?	▬▬▬			
7. How supportive of the measurement program are the business users?	▬			
8. Have your primary business needs for measurements been identified?	▬▬			
9. Do your current metrics support known business drivers?	▬▬▬			

[a]S = sporadic; P = partial; C = consistent; CI = consistent and improving.   *(continued)*

Qualifying Notes:

Table 1-2: Sample Metrics Program Initial Assessment (*cont.*)

Questionnaire	Rating Scale[a]			
	S	**P**	**C**	**CI**
10. Does your team gather unique metrics?	▬▬▬	▬		
11. Are metrics compared with those of other teams or organizations?	▬▬			
12. Are metrics being used for process improvement planning?	▬▬▬	▬		
13. Are you benchmarking your data with industry values?	▬▬	▬		
14. Does the organization participate in activities to support benchmarking?	▬▬▬	▬		
15. Is the organization tracking and reporting trends in data over time?	▬▬			
DATA GATHERING: APPLICATION DEVELOPMENT AND ENHANCEMENTS				
1. Project size: estimated and actual?	▬▬	▬		
2. Business value: net present value?	▬▬	▬		
3. Duration: estimated and actual?	▬▬▬	▬		
4. Delivery on plan or slippage percentage?	▬▬▬			
5. Cost, labor, other: estimated and actual?	▬▬▬			
6. Costs versus value?	▬▬▬			
7. Effort, by phases, by tasks: estimated and actual?	▬▬▬			
8. Costs by nonproject activity, and overtime?	▬▬▬			
9. Staffing head count: actual and at peak staffing?	▬▬▬			
10. Defects (type, severity level, origin, phase where found)?	▬			
11. Productivity rates?	▬			
12. Inspection defects?	▬			
13. Estimating data?	▬			
14. Reuse by modules and artifacts?	▬			
15. Process compliance?	▬			
16. Current project SEI rating?	▬			
17. Project success factors and obstacles to success?	▬▬			
18. Customer satisfaction?	▬▬			
19. Project characteristics?	▬▬			
20. Canceled projects?	▬▬			
21. Changes in scope?	▬▬	▬		

[a]S = sporadic; P = partial; C = consistent; CI = consistent and improving.

Qualifying Notes:

Questionnaire	Rating Scale[a]			
	S	P	C	CI
DATA GATHERING: PRODUCTION SUPPORT				
1. Application size?	▪			
2. Application availability?	▬▬			
3. Usage availability?	▬▬			
4. Failure rate?	▬▬			
5. Frequency of failures?	▬▬▬			
6. Costs, labor, equipment, and others?	▪			
7. Effort, and support effort for maintenance?	▬▬▬			
8. Production defects, severity 1 and 2?	▬▬			
9. Production defects, severity 3 and 4?	▬▬▬▬			
10. Number of customer requests received and repaired during a period?	▬▬▬			
11. Customer satisfaction?	▬▬			
12. Application characteristics?	▬▬▬			
13. Time to acknowledge failures?	▬▬			
14. Time between failures?	▪			

[a]S = sporadic; P = partial; C = consistent; CI = consistent and improving.

Qualifying Notes:

Gap Analysis Phase

On the basis of the results from the discovery phase, a gap score is derived according to the levels of observed or demonstrated performance for the key categories outlined in the questionnaire. This section correlates the data gathered from the project team interview process (shown in Table 1-2), assesses the maturity level on the basis of those findings, and consolidates and displays the results, as shown in Table 1-4. We use the matrix shown in Table 1-3 to map the initial assessment to a metrics maturity level of entry, basic, industry leader, or world-class.

The data is summarized to the organization level. For example, if only a small percentage of the teams interviewed responded to a particular attribute question, then the organization overall would be rated as partially satisfying that particular attribute.

Table 1-4 shows the maturity level for each of the world-class measurement program attributes, as well as the gap (dotted line) between the actual maturity

Table 1-3: Matrix for Assessing Measurement Program Maturity Level

Assessment Level	Key Attribute	Metrics Maturity Level
Sporadic	Minimally achieved	Entry
Partial	Achieved in team	Basic
Consistent	Achieved in organization	Industry Leader
Consistent and improving	Effective utilization achieved	World-class

Table 1-4: Gap to World-Class Attributes

World-Class Measurement Program Attributes	Metric Gap Analysis			
	Entry	Basic	Industry Leader	World-Class
Has a vision to be a world-class leader in development.				
Has a mission statement that includes the use of metrics.				
Has a common set of measurements focusing on quality.				
Uses the measurements to achieve high standards in quality.				
Measurements are an integrated part of the work and the software development methodology.				
The measurement data collection process is automated as much as possible.				
Measurement data supports all business needs, development, and support.				
Organization has policy statements to endorse the use of metrics that are supported by management.				

World-Class Measurement Program Attributes	Metric Gap Analysis			
	Entry	Basic	Industry Leader	World-Class
Organization provides regular feedback to teams about their data.				
Data within the metrics program has a high degree of integrity.				
Metrics focus supports the organization's development needs.				
Organization has a separate team responsible for the metrics data.				
Employees have an awareness of the metrics program benefits.				
Procedures have been institutionalized within the organization.				
Organization participates in benchmarking support activities.				
Organization tracks and reports trends of data over time.				

level and world-class. By studying the results of this gap analysis, the organization can determine the actions to be taken in order to achieve an industry leader or world-class position.

Summary

Software measurement will have the greatest impact when the measures contribute value-added information to the organization and serve as a useful management tool. For example, the on-time delivery of software is managed through the use of rigorously collected and analyzed data required by a project manager, and it is a significant data point of information at the senior management level.

The more meaningful application of software metrics is their use as a proactive management tool. Start-up measurement activities typically involve the reporting of what has happened (reactive) up to that point in the lifecycle of a project or a process. The proactive position means that measurement data is mature enough to be used as a means to forecast future outcomes.

Regardless of how a measurement program is organized, it should consist of two complementary components: qualitative data and quantitative data. Quantitative data includes the reporting of actual measurement results, such as cost analysis, productivity, defect density, and time to market. These values are used to show trends, set performance levels, and compare to benchmark data points.

Qualitative data complements the quantitative data by contributing information about the attributes or characteristics of the development environment. This information can be used in a stand-alone format to perform a risk analysis, or the data can be compiled to the aggregate level to indicate general organizational process strengths and weaknesses. When coupled with quantitative data, the qualitative information provides insights into the factors that have contributed to high or low yields of productivity and quality performance.

Measurement programs can generally be categorized into four classes: entry, basic, industry leader, and world-class. The attributes of each level are definable and can be used to evaluate current program practices. The result is an assessment of the organization's overall program maturity level.

CHAPTER TWO

Executive Introduction to Function Points

Introduction

Senior executives, including chief executive officers (CEOs), chief financial officers (CFOs), and chief information officers (CIOs), have long desired to understand and to quantify the contribution of their Information Technology (IT) organization to the business. Today more than ever, IT is recognized as an integral part of an organization's business strategy. IT performance measures, which have been used in the past to show productivity and quality performance results, must now evolve into a more sophisticated, business-oriented measure. CIOs find it increasingly necessary to demonstrate their contribution to the business using a new form of measurement.

A 1999 survey of CEOs revealed that their primary critical success factors included data management, new technologies, business reengineering, increased profitability, corporate growth, and customer service. The CEOs interviewed agreed that IT plays a critical role in their organizations' ability to gain a competitive advantage in the marketplace and in reducing expenses. To ensure high performance in these critical success areas, IT managers are challenged to find new ways to measure and demonstrate IT value to the business.

Historical Perspective

The use of software measurement has evolved fairly slowly and has experienced limited support within most IT organizations. Frederick Brooks, in his book *The Mythical Man-Month*

(1975, Addison-Wesley), was among the first to bring our attention to the idea of measuring IT productivity. Unfortunately, the message seemed to be that measurement was not an easy task and accuracy was certainly not one of the results.

The next significant milestone in measuring software delivery performance came in the early 1980s, when function point analysis was introduced by Allan Albrecht of IBM. The value-added and practical use of the function point methodology was based on the ability to measure the size of the functionality being delivered to an end user and to use this size to estimate the cost of delivery more effectively. Over the years, function point analysis has proven to be a consistent and well-accepted sizing metric. When used in conjunction with other measures, such as time to deliver, level of effort, and project costs, it can be of significant value to the IT manager in providing accurate measures for productivity and quality.

From a historical perspective the use and acceptance of IT measures has occurred in phases. The first phase included measures relating to hardware operational performance such as response time, down time, availability, and so on. These measures are relatively common today and include industry-accepted operational performance benchmarks that are generally accepted and used by various operational benchmarking vendors, such as Meta, Gartner Group, and Compass America.

The second phase along the evolution path included the use of software process performance indicators. Here we see measures such as rate of delivery, time to market, duration, cost per function point, cost per defect, and defects delivered. Similar to the operational measures, these values demonstrate the ability of the IT organization to perform. They produce results that demonstrate productivity and quality performance and are often used to measure the output of IT. Here, too, the software process performance measures can be used to perform benchmark comparisons to industry data. As a result, IT can demonstrate its ability to produce software quickly, economically, and with high quality. What these measures do not reveal is the contribution of the software deliverable to the business. Is it the right software, and does it fit the intended use?

The third (and current) phase in the evolution of software metrics is in the area of business value measures. The challenge has now been placed on the IT organization to demonstrate—in fact to measure—its contribution to the business; however, the challenge is not that of IT alone. The business must work together with the IT organization to effectively develop the measures that will have the greatest meaning to the organization. IT production costs and the size of the delivered functionality will certainly play a role, but a new set of measures must be introduced. This third stage of software metrics needs to include elements that are external to IT. They need to be business-oriented metrics created and evaluated relative to their ability to measure and report on business impacts (see Figure 2-1).

To be effective, these business-focused measures should support the need for information about key business issues. Issues such as technology impact, performance gains, increased profitability, and customer satisfaction must be clearly stated as priorities. Once these priorities are established, the metrics analysts can begin the task of identifying how each will be measured. Not all measures will map directly to stated business priorities. Often a combination of measures and indicators will be utilized to track the overall achievement of the strategic business drivers.

	Level 1	Level 2	Level 3
Service-Level Metrics	Technology Focused	Customer Focused	Business Focused
Accountability	Internal IT	Internal Customer	Senior Manager
Purpose	IT Efficiency	Impact on Organization	Impact on Business
Business-Related Metrics	- - - - - - - - - -	- - - - - - - - - -	Cost Reduction Increased Profitability Revenue Generation
Customer-Related Metrics	- - - - - - - - - -	Customer Satisfaction Throughput Responsiveness Timely Delivery Quality	
Technology Metrics	Up Time Responsive Time Availability Delivery		

Figure 2-1 Evolution of service-level metrics

Once the business drivers are identified, success factors can be defined and the metrics to support those success factors can be identified. As an example, we can expect that an organization wants to improve its overall competitive advantage and gain a larger share of the market. The factors that would be influenced by IT and contribute to the success of this goal may be identified as timely delivery of the product (software), accuracy or quality of the deliverable, and increased customer satisfaction. From this set of success factors, detailed metrics can be developed to enable senior management to monitor the progress. Of course the proof of success will be in the attainment of a larger market share. It is important to realize that IT is a contributor to the success of the business, but not the sole contributor. Many other factors, unrelated to IT, also help influence an organization's ability to gain a larger share of the market.

In some instances, strategic business drivers will be described in more generalized terms, such as "realizing gains through technology." In such cases, the more generic the description of the business driver, the more generic the measure. In fact, some business strategies, as stated, may not be directly measurable at all. An organization may decide, for example, that to "realize gains through technology" it must purchase commercial off-the-shelf (COTS) solutions. The process of selecting and installing COTS solutions is measurable; however, the measures are not business-oriented measures as much as they are IT performance measures. Even applying function point analysis techniques to determine the amount of functionality actually delivered and consumed is not likely to have a direct correlation to how the business is performing as a result of the COTS solution.

The industry is learning that to have a deliverable that is measurable, the description of that deliverable must be clearly defined. Once defined, measures can be applied to evaluate success. If IT is a contributor to that success, then its contribution can be measured. The measures may be a combination of internal productivity and performance of delivery, as well as business-related measures such as the consumption rate of delivered functionality. As these measures evolve, we will see a greater emphasis on measurement and more intelligent and informed decisions for the effective use of IT resources.

Currently a handful of techniques, old and new, are being used to meet the IT measurement challenge. Balanced Scorecards and return on investment (ROI) calculations are two of the more prevalent forms of measurement vehicles that are commonly used to measure and monitor IT performance. Both have been used with moderate degrees of success. However, they do not provide a very fundamental and necessary measure: cost per unit of work. If you consider IT as a manufacturer of software with a front-end design and a back-end support service of the manufactured product (software), then there should be a basic unit-of-work measure.

Balanced Scorecard

Robert S. Kaplan and David P. Norton of the Harvard Business School developed the Balanced Scorecard in 1992. The purpose of the Balanced Scorecard is to evaluate and report on combined operational and financial measures of an organization for the purpose of monitoring the overall performance effectiveness. The Balanced Scorecard report provides the CEO with a view of the organization from several perspectives. The Balanced Scorecard includes financial measures plus specific operational measures, including internal processes, customer satisfaction, and organizational ability to learn.

The scorecard is not supposed to be used as a fixed list of measures, but more as an evolving mechanism for monitoring and managing the changing business environment. The scorecard concept may be used at the corporate, division, and business unit levels and across functional areas such as finance, operations, human resources, and information technology.

The Balanced Scorecard concept has been adapted to meet the needs of many IT organizations. The basic elements of financial and operational measures are populated with values that relate directly to the IT department. Financial measures may include information on revenue and costs such as monitoring within-budget project performance, operational costs (hardware expenditures), portfolio management costs, and return on investment. The customer elements measured may include customer satisfaction, on-time project completion, service-level agreement performance, throughput, and help desk performance. Operational indicators may include system availability, outages, response time, production abends, software development productivity, and business case development (percentage of projects). People-oriented measures may include elements dealing with the staff, such as hiring, staff optimization, employee retention, compensation, and employee satisfaction.

Return on Investment

One of the more common financial measures incorporated into the Balanced Scorecard and as a stand-alone financial calculation is return on investment

(ROI). ROI is used as a measure of how dollars are being invested. It is calculated as follows:

$$\frac{\text{Total benefits } - \text{ total cost of investment}}{\text{total cost}} \times 100$$

The resulting ROI value is then compared to a standard rate of return to evaluate the potential benefit of the investment.

When using a return-on-investment analysis, organizations should consider the intangible benefits as well as the tangible benefits. It is not always possible or easy to quantify all benefits. Measuring resource reductions, reduced handling costs, or lower inventory may be obvious; however, benefits from improved employee satisfaction or customer satisfaction are not always as easy to quantify.

In most organizations, how IT actually is doing differs from how the business thinks IT is doing. Communicating value can sometimes depend more on the CIO's ability to demonstrate the qualitative benefits or the effectiveness of IT above and beyond the cost efficiencies associated with any given IT strategy. In 1993, Nolan, Norton & Co. of Boston conducted a study on the impact of IT on the business. The CEOs least satisfied with their information technology investment characterized success in terms of cost efficiency only. CEOs who viewed information technology success in terms of how effectively IT met business goals, as opposed to merely how efficient it was, tended to feel they had received either all or most of the benefits of their investments.

The key to success is a mutual understanding between business and IT management relative to the business benefits resulting from technology. CIOs need to focus on demonstrating IT effectiveness rather than just return on investment. Effectiveness metrics examine whether the right things are being done for the right business functions. Effectiveness is often seen in more qualitative terms, such as improved customer service or improved competitive positioning.

Unit of Work

Often missing from a Balanced Scorecard or ROI calculation is the fundamental metric: unit of work. To be effective, a unit of work must be based on a deliverable that is meaningful to the intended audience. The audience in this case includes both IT and the business. So the ideal unit-of-work measure will demonstrate value to both parties. In support of IT, the unit of work should provide the IT organization with the ability to monitor its progress with respect to meeting the required deliverables that support the software solution being provided to the customer. On the business side of the equation, the unit of work needs to measure business value received from the software solution. Users need to receive the deliverable they asked for.

A unit-of-work metric should enable the CIO to measure productivity and business value of the software deliverable on a level playing field. Regardless of the economic or presentation techniques used to display IT performance, such as ROI and Balanced Scorecards, establishing a cost per unit of work should be a fundamental element of a manager's financial tool kit.

The unit-of-work measure will characteristically normalize the technical delivery of the software and demonstrate the dollar value of functionality being delivered to the end user. The establishment of a unit-of-work measure should also not leave itself open to be challenged for its consistency or level of accuracy.

Accountability for the unit-of-work measure must be a shared responsibility. The IT organization performs a function within the organization. That function is appropriately viewed as a service. The service provides software solutions to the organization. These solutions consist of functional software that enables business operations and technology advancement to increase the productivity of the workforce. The user has the responsibility of defining how to perform the business functions and identifying those functions that will have the greatest impact on the business. IT and the customer must collaborate on creating advanced solutions that will serve the greater whole (the company). IT should not have the sole responsibility of identifying the total technical and business solution.

The key is to develop a unit of work that is meaningful to both parties. IT needs to be concerned with costs, schedules, and functionality of the software being developed. IT knows that its ability to deliver will be influenced by myriad factors, including the complexity of the technology it will deploy, the availability of skilled resources, the tools and methods used for deployment, and the time constraints under which it must operate. Therefore, the unit of work will be influenced by all these factors, but it cannot be altered by these factors. The unit of work must remain constant. For example, using the number of source lines of code as a unit of work is faulty because it is influenced by technology and by the skill levels of the people writing the code.

For the business, the unit of work must perform in an equally meaningful way. It must be able to identify the functionality that is being presented. As a user specifies the desired functionality required to run and support the business, the unit of work must measure that functionality in a very direct way. The user asks for one widget, and that is exactly what is measured. To put it into a technical deliverable perspective, the user asks for the ability to view an online report, and that is precisely the unit of work that is measured.

Function Points

Function points are an effective, and the best available, unit-of-work measure. They meet the acceptable criteria of being a normalized metric that can be used consistently and with an acceptable degree of accuracy.

The fundamental practice of function point analysis centers around its ability to measure the size of any software deliverable in logical, user-oriented terms. Function point analysis does not concern itself directly with technology platforms, development tools, or generated lines of code. It simply measures the functionality being delivered to an end user.

The function point method evaluates the software deliverable and measures its size on the basis of well-defined functional characteristics of a software system. It accounts for data that is entering a system—external inputs (logical transaction inputs, system feeds); data that is leaving the system—external outputs and external inquiries (online displays, reports, feeds to other systems); data that is manufactured and stored within the system—internal logical files (logical groups of user-defined data); and data that is maintained outside the system but is necessary to satisfy a particular process requirement—external interface files (interfaces to other systems) (see Figure 2-2). In addition, the impacts of general system complexities associated with system and processor constraints, distributed data processing, logical and algorithmic complexity, and several other variables are also assessed.

Once completed, the function point size of an application or a new development project can be communicated in various ways. As a stand-alone value, the functional size of a system can give a quick estimate of how large the overall software deliverable will be. When the function point value is segmented into a more detailed display, it can communicate to end users the functional value of specific components of the system. Finally, organizations that have reached a certain level of software measurement maturity may use function points to predict outcomes and monitor program progress.

In a common scenario, an organization that has established function points as a unit-of-work measure has amassed a database of system sizes and other relevant

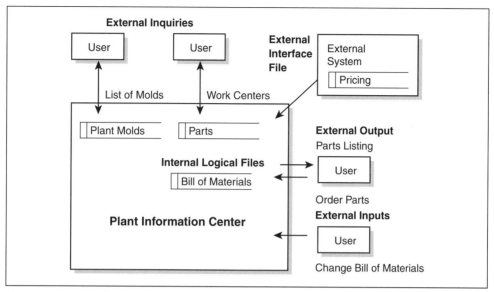

Figure 2-2 Functional characteristics of a software system

measures and has been able to baseline a cost per function point, or a cost per unit of work. The more mature organization knows its dollar cost per unit of work and is now highly leveraged to use that information in making more informed decisions.

As requests come in for additional system enhancements and new development products, the organization uses the function point method to determine the cost of the deliverable, manage expectations of the end user, and manage the delivery of the software product. On the basis of the stated requirements, the business analyst is able to analyze all of the business functionality and assign it a function point value. This value can be converted into a cost per function point, and the cost for the total system is then effectively derived. Using this as a whole number, the savvy CIO can express the cost of the proposed software deliverable in terms that the user can best understand. The cost per function point can be broken down and displayed by logical business function groups, and the user can readily see the cost for the specific business functions that have been requested.

As the project is managed and the scope of work changes according to new requirements being introduced into the system, the CIO can continue to use function points as a unit-of-work measure and communicate to the user the exact nature of the scope change and the specific costs associated with that particular scope change (see Figure 2-3).

CIOs need to work with business managers to define and understand which measures will be used most effectively. A combination of Balanced Scorecard techniques, along with traditional ROI measures and a value-added unit-of-work measure, can collectively form the basis of an effective IT performance-monitoring device. To ensure that this robust selection of metrics is used effectively and efficiently, some key elements must be present—for example, defining value, time to market, accountability.

Defining Value

For an IT project to be successful, expected business outcomes must be agreed on and completely understood. Once these objectives have been defined, a plan must be formulated that describes the processes contributing to the attainment of those outcomes. For instance, increases in sales depend on higher customer satisfaction. Customer satisfaction depends on successful interaction with the company. How do customers interact with the company? Does the help desk handle problems effectively? Are easy-to-use Web sites available to the customer?

By examining the current processes and technology that support the customer-related processes, an IT organization can baseline current levels of performance. From a quantitative perspective the organization can identify efficiencies in operations where cost saving can be realized; in addition, it can identify qualitative improvements that may result in even higher levels of operating effectiveness.

Change in Scope	FP Size	Additional Effort (staff-months)	Additional Cost ($000)	Additional Schedule (calendar months)
New Vendor Function	100	7	100	2.0
Graphical Displays	20	1.2	20	.4
Banking System	20	1.2	20	.4
Mandatory Changes	10	.6	10	.2
Total	150	10	$150	3.0

Figure 2-3 Evaluating the cost of changes in scope

For IT to provide real value, the solution has to add measurable improvement to the business. By establishing a baseline of performance, we can easily measure and monitor the progress of improvement initiatives.

Time to Market

One of the more effective approaches to making sure the business fulfills its project commitments is to keep project duration to a minimum. James Martin first introduced the notion of creating project deliverables not exceeding 12 months in duration. Many organizations today have reduced that figure to 6 to 9 months. Clearly some initiatives are necessarily going to take longer than 9 months, but deliverables (value to the user) can be sliced into "bite-sized" chunks that can be delivered in shorter time frames.

Accountability

Ultimately, building a business case isn't up to the CIO. Technology isn't a driver; it is an enabler. The user should be committed to deriving benefit from the project and be able to build the appropriate business case.

The key to holding operating units accountable for results is to make sure you know what they hope to accomplish. The CIO needs to be involved in early stages of the strategic planning process and needs to help determine the business unit's financial goals and which processes in the operation will drive the activity. The CIO can then recommend how technology can facilitate increased performance of those processes and thereby contribute to the bottom line. It is a collaborative effort that puts the responsibility for justification where it belongs: on people who will use the technology rather than on the technology itself.

The most important step is to make sure that the business manager not only commits to hard-dollar results from implementing the IT initiative, but incorporates those numbers into the next year's fiscal budget.

Summary

The use of software metrics has evolved over the past 25 years from a project-centric view to a contribution-to-the-business view. To ensure added business value, IT needs to align itself with the business, the users of the technology. A CIO's responsibility is to partner with the business and to help build a convincing case for how the IT initiative will support the business operation in meeting its goals. Then, through the use of measurement-reporting techniques such as Balanced

Scorecard reporting and ROI, performance can be measured, monitored, and managed to ensure delivery of value.

CIOs should be applying the same capital investment formulas for IT projects that are used for any other investment the company makes. A quarterly review of the Balanced Scorecard, along with ROI analysis for each strategic initiative, will help IT focus on those projects that represent return opportunity. Calculating a cost per unit of work based on function points will further enhance an organization's financial analysis and allow for improved decision making at the CIO level.

CHAPTER THREE

Measuring with Function Points

Introduction

The use of function points and related metrics is commonly incorporated into a division- or organizationwide measurement and process improvement program. As discussed in Chapter 1, these programs vary widely among companies and even within organizations. Some programs contain the most basic of measures—for example, cost, delivery, and quality. The more sophisticated and mature programs have a greater variety of measures and invest in a greater number of resources to support measurement activities.

The framework of a successful measurement program is fairly typical of most internal program initiatives. The program must have commitment from senior management; it must have meaningful and clearly stated goals and objectives. The processes, policies, roles, and responsibilities should all be clearly documented and enforced. And most importantly, the program must continuously be improved to provide the organization with value-added data needed to perform.

In Chapter 1, we discussed the basic principles of successful software measurement. A software measurement program should deliver value-added information to a variety of individuals and functions within the organization. The basic elements of a software measurement program include quantitative data (e.g., function points) and qualitative data (e.g., customer satisfaction).

This chapter will focus on how function points fit into a measurement program. We will describe the measures commonly used to support the definition, development, deployment, and maintenance of software. And we will answer the following questions: If I had function points, what would I do with them? and How would I use function points with other metrics to effectively manage my software development and maintenance environment?

In addition to identifying specific function point measures, we will discuss the importance of other key elements, such as a function point repository, analysis of measurement data, and measurement reporting. It is important to remember that no single measure tells the whole story. Software measurement is effective only when the metrics are used and analyzed in conjunction with one another.

Function Points in the Lifecycle

Because it is neither practical nor of particular value to identify every known function point–related measure, we will focus on a selection of key metrics that we have seen used effectively within numerous client organizations. To put this list of primary metrics in the proper context, we have divided the function point measures into four categories: productivity, quality, financial, and maintenance. In each case we identify the meaning of the measure, how it can be used, and how it is calculated.

The function point size serves as a normalizing metric. For example, two systems are monitored for defects, and system A is found to have twice as many defects as system B. An immediate assessment is that system B has higher quality than system A. Without a sizing metric, however, there can be no practical point of comparison. If we added function points to the scenario and realized that system B is one-fourth the size of system A, we would view system A as possessing higher quality than system B. System A would have fewer defects per functionality maintained.

Function Point Measures

Productivity

Hours per function point is an industry-accepted unit-of-work measure. It measures the number of hours required to develop one function point. It is most often used as a measure of productivity, which is usually evaluated at a project level. It should never be used as a measure of individual performance. This metric is calculated as follows:

$$\frac{\text{Total number of project hours}}{\text{Number of function points delivered}}$$

The total number of hours and the number of function points represent values for a specific project. The total number of hours recorded for a project most often includes all effort associated with the project. This value can vary significantly among departments, organizations, and industries. When performing comparative analysis, the metrics analyst must ensure that the total number of hours recorded for a project is consistent when making comparisons either internal or external to the organization.

This measure is often used to represent productivity for various categories—new development, enhancements, or different technologies. For example, an organization may show varying rates of productivity for new development versus enhancements or for client-server productivity versus mainframe productivity.

Frequently this measure is displayed as function points delivered per person-month. However, using person-months as a measure is problematic because no industry standards define a person-month. Using an hour as the metric permits greater consistency.

Information technology productivity is the overall productivity of the IT department. It is commonly used as a baseline measure in outsourcing contracts. IT productivity represents an overall level of performance, but it does not take into consideration the mix of work involved. For example, overall IT productivity for an organization that does very little new development but maintains mostly legacy systems, will have a significantly different value from that of an organization that develops new client-server and Web-based applications. The measure is calculated as follows:

$$\frac{\text{Total function points}}{\text{Total IT work effort}}$$

This measure can be used effectively at the senior management level to monitor overall productivity. During the contractual life of an outsourcing arrangement, this value may be used to track improvement trends. Such tracking assumes that the mix of work does not change significantly from one year to the next.

Rate of delivery is an industry-accepted measure that measures calendar time to deliver the required software solution to the end user. It is often used as a service-level measure to demonstrate how quickly an organization introduces functionality into use. It is frequently described as a time-to-market measure. The measure is calculated as follows:

$$\frac{\text{Number of function points}}{\text{Elapsed calendar time}}$$

Elapsed time is usually defined as calendar time in months. It represents the time from the introduction of requirements through software installation. When using this measure for comparative analysis, one should ensure that elapsed time is consistently sized within the organization. In some companies, elapsed time begins with project start activities prior to requirements and ends when the system is fit for use (but not necessarily installed). Elapsed time should also exclude dead time, any period during which project development has been temporarily stopped.

Delivered functionality and **developed functionality** are often used as contrasting measures; they indicate how much functionality was actually delivered to the end user in relation to the rate of productivity of the developed functionality. For example, a software solution may contain portions of functionality that can be satisfied through the purchase of a commercially available software package. The remainder of the functionality must be developed in-house. The organization should receive credit for the total functionality delivered; consequently, it would count the functionality associated with both the software developed in-house and the purchased software. However, when productivity levels are being calculated, the development level of effort is unknown for the packaged software, and the productivity rate can be calculated only for the in-house developed software. The measures are calculated as follows:

$$\frac{\text{Total cost}}{\text{Total functionality delivered}} \qquad \frac{\text{Total development effort hours}}{\text{Total functionality developed in-house}}$$

The functionality developed, when it involves installation of a purchased package, should include the functionality associated with any interfaces necessary to link the purchased product to the existing systems. The functionality developed should also include any changes, deletions, or additions of functionality that are necessary to the purchased software.

The advantage of measuring the total functionality delivered is that the organization can then demonstrate to its users all functionality being provided, and it can understand the total functional value that will require maintenance support.

Quality

Functional requirement size measures the total number of functions requested by the end user expressed in terms of function points. As a meaningful metric it may have limited value to the end user, but the developer should be able to use this value as an important input parameter to any one of several estimating models. The calculation derives the functionality (function points) required by a requesting user organization.

The use of this metric can ultimately benefit both the developer and the requesting end user. Imagine a scenario in which the developer seeks to ensure an understanding of the functional requirements. The developer engages the end user in an interactive session by creating a context diagram or another vehicle to communicate a common understanding of the requested deliverables. Using a diagramming technique and the function point components of input, output, inquiries, data stores, and interfaces, the analyst and the end user discuss the functionality in terms they both understand. At the conclusion of the session, the analyst has the basic information required to perform a high-level function point sizing.

Completeness is a measure of the functionality delivered versus the functionality originally requested. This measure can be used in several different ways, so the organization must present a clear definition of how it is to be used to ensure its continued effectiveness. As the title implies, we are measuring the completeness of the deliverable: Did the user receive all functionality requested? Because function points operate in numeric terms, the simple comparison would be as follows: Did the user receive the 100 function points requested? However, the problem here is obvious: Did the 100 function points delivered represent the same 100 function points originally requested?

We can apply the measure better by not only identifying the value (function points) of the promised deliverable, but also demonstrating that the same functions were requested. We can do this by comparing the set of five original data and transactional functions to the delivered set. The basic measure compares the number of functions delivered to the number of functions expected and agreed on.

The term "agreed on" is the key to making an "apples to apples" comparison. The question that most often arises with this measure is, How do I compare what was delivered to what was originally requested if it is constantly changing? Rate of change is another measure, which we will address next. This measure is a true completeness measure; therefore, the beginning point of comparison is based on the final agreed-on requirements.

Rate of change measures the amount of functional specification change that occurs during the development process. It can be used to track "scope creep" (added functionality) within a project for purposes of more effectively managing project costs and schedules. It may also be used to determine the effectiveness of the requirements process. We calculate this measure by counting function points during each primary milestone deliverable, commencing with the functional requirements.

Change can be tracked through the various phases of the development lifecycle. As the scope of the project expands, the project manager can use this information to substantiate increases in budgeted project dollars and/or schedule extensions.

Defect removal efficiency measures the total number of defects found prior to delivery of the software in comparison with the total number of defects found both before and after delivery. The function point metric is not part of this equation, but it is typically used hand in glove with this measure—for example, defects per function point. Defect removal efficiency is a true measure of both the quality of a system and the effectiveness of quality practices executed during the development of the system. This measure is calculated as follows:

$$\frac{\text{Total number of defects found prior to delivery}}{\text{Total number of defects}}$$

The total number of defects found usually represents a specified period after delivery. The period after delivery is often one quarter, but many organizations include periods up to one year.

There can be some interesting and useful variations in the application of this measure. Defect removal efficiency can be calculated by lifecycle phase, or by comparison of front-end development defect removal efficiencies to back-end defect removal efficiencies. Typically, defect removal efficiency measures include the most severe defects, severity levels 1 and 2.

Defect density measures the number of defects identified across one or more phases of the development project lifecycle and compares that value to the total size of the application. It can be used to compare density levels across different lifecycle phases or across different development efforts. It is calculated as follows:

$$\frac{\text{Number of defects (by phase or in total)}}{\text{Total number of function points}}$$

Test case coverage measures the number of test cases that are necessary to adequately support thorough testing of a development project. This measure does not indicate the effectiveness of the test cases, nor does it guarantee that all conditions have been tested. However, it can be an effective comparative measure to forecast anticipated requirements for testing that may be required on a development system of a particular size. This measure is calculated as follows:

$$\frac{\text{Number of test cases}}{\text{Total number of function points}}$$

Volume of documentation can be used to measure or estimate the number of pages produced or anticipated in support of the development effort. Pages per function point value can be derived for any of the documents produced during the development lifecycle. This measure is calculated as follows:

$$\frac{\text{Number of pages (per document)}}{\text{Total number of function points}}$$

Like test case coverage, this measure should not be considered a measure of quality.

Financial

Cost per function point identifies the cost for each function point developed. This measure is usually applied at the project or organizational level. At the project level, cost per function point is calculated and compared to a baseline organizational value. An overall cost per function point is calculated for the entire organization and establishes the baseline. Cost per function point may also be used to compare the cost of developing an internal solution to the cost of purchasing a commercial package solution, or to compare internal cost to an external industry (benchmark) cost. The metric is computed as follows:

$$\frac{\text{Total cost}}{\text{Total function points}}$$

The ability to compare an organization's internal cost per function point to industry averages or best-in-class benchmarks depends on a consistently applied cost basis. Project cost usually consists of total project labor, project-related tools, project-related travel and living expense, and a fully defined burden rate (which includes overhead costs).

Repair cost ratio is used to track the costs to repair applications that are operational. It is commonly used as a monitoring metric for newly installed applications. During the first six months of operation this measure should include all fixes and all costs of repair for the newly installed system. The metric is calculated as follows:

$$\frac{(\text{Total hours to repair} \times \text{cost per hour})}{\text{Release function points}}$$

The measure may be used to monitor required systems fixes. It can be applied prior to installation to monitor project expenses directly related to the repair of defects. The function point component of the equation usually represents the total number of function points for the release; however, it can be modified to represent only those function points associated with each repair. Many outsourcing arrangements use this measure as a basis for tracking maintenance support service levels on a repair-by-repair basis.

Portfolio asset value is used to track the value of an organization's entire portfolio of systems software. It can be used to gain a better understanding of the potential replacement costs for legacy systems. It is calculated as follows:

$$\text{Cost per function point} \times \text{Total function points}$$

Maintenance

Maintainability is the measure of effort (cost) required to maintain an application. The metric is used to monitor maintenance cost on an application-by-application basis. It is most often applied to core business applications or to applications that have demonstrated a high cost of maintenance. It is calculated as follows:

$$\frac{\text{Maintenance cost}}{\text{Application function points}}$$

Some maintenance activities do not directly relate to size (function points). Outsourcing arrangements often refer to this category of costs as zero function point maintenance. For example, the required maintenance repair does not generate any new or changed functionality and cannot be measured in function points; however, a cost is incurred to accomplish the repair. The organization should establish a policy on accounting for this zero function point maintenance. Most often the cost is either accounted for as general maintenance expense or charged on a full-time equivalent (FTE) basis.

Reliability is a measure of the number of failures an application experiences relative to its functional size. This measure can be used to track system performance and to monitor possible service-level measures associated with the application. It is calculated as follows:

$$\frac{\text{Number of production failures}}{\text{Total application function points}}$$

Assignment scope is a measure of the number of FTE resources required to support an application. This measure may be used to monitor resource levels required to adequately support an application being maintained in production. As an application increases in functional size during its life span (see the discussion of growth rate below), the resources required to support the application are expected to increase. The measure is sometimes referred to as maintenance assignment scope. Assignment scope is one of several measures that should be used to identify the potential for increased resource requirements. It is calculated as follows:

$$\frac{\text{Total application function points}}{\text{Number of full-time resources required to support the application}}$$

As with most of the measures defined here, this measure should not be used as a single source of information. For example, staffing levels do not equate to quality of support. Each of these measures must be viewed and analyzed in conjunction with other measures.

Rate of growth measures the growth of an application's functionality over a specified period of time. Rate of growth can be used by the IT department to monitor the rapid growth of applications or conversely as a means to determine when an application has reached maturity and its rate of growth has diminished. This measure can also be used to monitor the portfolio rate of growth. This information is essential for budgeting resources. Rate of growth is calculated as follows:

$$\frac{\text{Current number of function points}}{\text{Original number of funtion points}}$$

Portfolio size is a measure of the organization's portfolio of function points. This metric is often used for budgeting purposes or in conjunction with outsourcing arrangements. Outsourcing an organization's application development and maintenance activities requires sizing of the organization's suite of applications. Levels of service can be based on the total number of function points, which must be serviced by the third-party vendor. Portfolio size is the total number of function points for all applications in the organization's portfolio.

Backfire value is a computed function point value based on the total number of lines of code and the complexity level of the programming language. It was initially used for quickly sizing an organization's portfolio. Recently it has become less useful as more advanced (and complex) languages have been introduced. Because of the nature of these newer languages, it has become difficult to statistically establish meaningful backfire values. Many sources of backfire data have not updated their ratios of function points to lines of code to reflect changes in the function point methodology and the rules for counting; another complication is the lack of a consistent standard for counting lines of code, so using the backfire values for comparative purposes can be very problematic. The backfire value is the number of lines of code factored by a language complexity multiplier to derive the number of function points.

Stability ratio is used to monitor how effectively an application or enhancement has met the expectations of the user. The measure is based on the number of changes that were required during the first 60 to 90 days of production. The changes may be categorized as original requirements versus enhancements, or they may be viewed as one total sum. Stability ratio is calculated as follows:

$$\frac{\text{Number of changes}}{\text{Number of application function points}}$$

We have examined numerous function point measures classified into four different categories. Table 3-1 shows some of the same measures relative to their use in the systems development lifecycle. This view of the measures is further evidence of the varied use of the function point metric.

Table 3-1: Use of Function Point Measures in the Systems Development Lifecycle

Measure	Phase of Development					
	Require-ments	Design	Build	Test	Implemen-tation	Mainte-nance
PRODUCTIVITY						
Hours per function point	X	X	X	X	X	
Rate of delivery	X	X	X	X	X	
Delivered and developed functionality					X	
QUALITY						
Functional requirement size	X					
Completeness					X	
Rate of change	X	X	X	X	X	
Defect density	X	X	X	X	X	
Test case coverage				X		
Volume of documentation					X	
FINANCIAL						
Cost per function point					X	
Repair cost ratio						X
MAINTENANCE						
Maintainability						X
Reliability					X	X
Assignment scope						X
Rate of growth						X
Stability ratio						X

Using Function Point Measurement Data Effectively

Most complaints about (ineffective) measurement programs stem from the failure to properly report collected measurement data. There are three key ingredients to successful communication of measurement results:

1. Establishing a metrics repository
2. Consistently reporting results
3. Analyzing (not just reporting) the data

Establishing a metrics repository serves several purposes. It organizes the data in an orderly fashion for greater flexibility in sorting and accessing the data. It also stores historical data, which is useful for trend analysis and monitoring rates of change. Repositories can be created through internally developed spreadsheets or database applications. They should be centrally maintained with secured access. Several commercially available tools have frameworks for building a measurement repository. The repository is usually a secondary capability of the tool. Unless the tool is used in a different capacity, the purchase of the tool for the primary use of a repository framework is ill-advised.

Consistently reporting measurement results seems like an obvious deliverable from the measurement program, but time and time again we have observed organizations in which proper identification and collection of measurement data were used with only limited effectiveness because results were not reported properly.

We observed firsthand an example of improper reporting several years ago when we were engaged to audit a well-established measurement program at one of the larger U.S. commercial banks. We were familiar with the measurement activities being conducted at this particular bank from relationships we had formed with members of its metrics team. A request to audit the bank's measurement program came to us via a senior vice president who had recently been appointed to oversee the metrics initiative. Our audit revealed some very advanced and sophisticated measurement activity, which was supported by formalized and well-documented data collection processes. However, we uncovered a major flaw in the reporting of the measurement data.

The reporting process had not taken into account the requirements of the various business units that were receiving the reports. The reports contained a wide variety of statistically correct measurement tables and graphs, but the recipients of the report had little to no use for the data and the formats that were contained within the report. This was not a case of not reporting, but rather a case of reporting the wrong information, perhaps to the wrong audience.

Analysis of the data is another major weakness we have observed in the industry. Actually, the problem may be more correctly stated as simply reporting the data and not analyzing it at all. If a manager received a periodic report indicating the number of function points produced, together with the effective rates of productivity and growth, that information could be useful. However, further analysis could significantly enhance that information. For example, further analysis of the reported function points could show a trend toward increased development within certain technical environments, with commensurate increases in productivity. This enhanced information would certainly be useful for future strategic direction setting. The analysis of the data could also result in projections of anticipated future growth rates and identify the need to shift budget dollars to support anticipated growth trends.

Depending on the organization, analysis of measurement data could range from basic statistical process control–based analysis to a much more advanced statistical analysis of the data, depending on the ability of the intended audience to understand the reported data. The key ingredient is to take a proactive view of the data being analyzed. It is interesting and useful to review the past, but value is added when current business can be managed with the ability to forecast outcomes on the basis of accurate reporting.

Developing a Measurement Profile

Documenting the policies and procedures that support a measurement program is another key ingredient in the success of that program. At a minimum, a measurement program should have a documented profile for each of its measures. The profile defines each measure and describes its use and benefit to the organization. A sample profile is shown in Figure 3-1.

Available Industry Comparisons

Function point measures have many internal uses; however, one of the biggest advantages is the availability of function point–based industry data. Industry data allows organizations to measure and compare themselves with other similar industries. In recent years there has been a great deal of interest in industry best practices. This information often reveals levels of qualitative improvement that

Measurement Profile

Metric: Cost per function point

Purpose: To measure cost for application development and
                 enhancements

Definitions: **Cost** is the total of labor hours, regular and overtime (paid and
                 unpaid), charged to the project by all team members
                 (management, technical, and support).

                 Size is the number of function points delivered on a project.

Data Elements Required:

                 Project hours

                 Size of project in function points

Formula: Hours will be used only as the cost basis to report projects that
                 require less than a total of three FTE effort months.

                 Function points per person-month will be used as the cost
                 basis to report projects that require three or more FTE effort
                 months.

Description of Collection Procedure:

                 Labor hours are reported on a weekly basis.

                 Function points are counted at acceptance, upon scope
                 changes, and at delivery.

Frequency of Collection:

                 Project delivery

Commencement Date:

                 Reporting of data will begin July 1, 2000.

Figure 3-1 Sample metric profile

can be achieved by execution of a prescribed set of tools, techniques, and
methodologies. The base size for all this information is function points.

Any organization interested in measuring itself against the competition or in
learning from industry best-practice experiences is well advised to begin a rigorous program of function point and measurement data collection.

Summary

Function points are often described as the cornerstone metric of most software measurement programs. They have a wide range of use, both across the development lifecycle and in their ability to display measured views of data with a technical and business orientation.

It is important to remember that no single view of data gives a complete picture. The function point measures must be used together with each other and with other related measures.

The key ingredients to a successful measurement program include the following:

- A well-defined set of measures that are properly documented
- A metrics repository that is centrally located and secured
- The ability to effectively report the results and properly analyze the metrics data

In addition, a metrics profile should be developed for each measure. This profile is an efficient way to communicate critical information about the measure and to promote consistent use of the measure.

Finally, the greatest value in utilizing function point measures is as an industry indicator of performance. Many sources of data can be accessed for purposes of comparing internal rates of performance to external industry benchmarks.

Using Function Points Effectively

Introduction

This chapter describes common uses of the function point metric by the software development organization. To demonstrate the versatility of the function point metric, we have selected three scenarios; each one represents the use of the metric at a different level in the organization. Function points are used at the project manager level to improve the overall accuracy of estimating the time and cost of projects. At the IT management level, function point analysis is the key normalizing metric in establishing performance benchmarks used to identify and track improvements. Finally, function points are often used at the organizational level as the base metric for establishing quantifiable service levels (seen primarily in outsourcing arrangements).

In each of these scenarios, function point analysis has its greatest value when used in conjunction with other metrics. For example, simply knowing the average size of your software deliverable (expressed in function points) is of little value; however, by incorporating other data points, such as deliverable cost, duration, and defects, you can create and report on value-added measures such as the cost per function point, time to market, and defect density.

It is true that the function point metric is not a panacea for software development ills; however, it does afford the development team and IT management an opportunity to measure and evaluate key elements in the development environment in order to make more informed decisions.

Project Manager Level: Estimating Software Projects Using Function Points

Accurately estimating a project deliverable is a management task that many project managers feel ill equipped to perform effectively. However, by using a well-defined estimating process along with an effective estimating model, project managers can significantly improve their ability to estimate a set of software deliverables. An effective project-estimating process provides a project manager with the capability to

- Produce a reasonably accurate estimate of the effort required and the final completion date of the project
- Properly set expectations and raise the level of awareness of the project team and the end users about the potential risks and predicted outcomes
- Estimate intermediate milestones, so that problems can be corrected early
- Determine the impact of additional or changed requirements
- Assess the impact of likely risks on the project schedule

In addition to helping project managers to achieve more accurate estimates, the proper techniques and tools will produce insights into the various risks that may affect the success of the project. For example, an estimating tool can sort through and assess the factors that will contribute to high or low yields of product quality and reveal to the project manager those risks that could produce results that are not acceptable in terms of desired quality. Of course, the capacity to deliver an accurate estimate will always depend on how well the requirements are defined. But the lack of a well-defined requirement is no excuse for not estimating.

Four primary elements are required for accurate estimating:

1. A basic understanding of the requirements
2. An ability to accurately size the deliverable
3. An assessment of the complexity of the deliverable
4. A characteristic profile of the organization's capacity to deliver

Figure 4-1 depicts a common estimating model. We will refer to this model as we further describe the estimating process.

A well-defined user requirement is the primary input used as the basis for producing a realistic estimate. Typically, however, end users require an estimate of the cost and delivery date well before they have clearly defined the user requirement. Therefore, we will explore the role that function point analysis plays in both scenarios: (1) well-defined requirements and (2) high-level user requests.

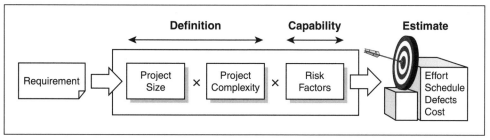

Figure 4-1 An estimating model

A well-defined requirement takes many forms. It may be a formal document that describes the functionality being requested. It may be in the form of use cases or a combination of text and diagrams. In any event, the key is to have a clearly defined set of functional requirements that are accurate and understood by both the development and the user organizations. Using such a document as a starting point makes it relatively easy to identify the functional components that make up the function point count.

By example, let's examine a sample requirement displayed in textual format, use case format, and context diagram format. Our requirement states that the user needs the following capabilities: to add a new order, to initiate a change request to an order, and to check the status of an order. In addition, a regional report will be generated and an order notification report will be distributed. The use case diagram representing this requirement is shown in Figure 4-2.

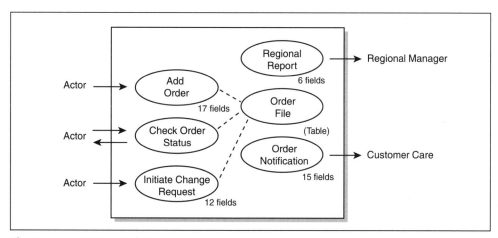

Figure 4-2 Use case diagram

A context diagram format gives us another view of the requirement. We use the diagram to identify data and transactional function types, as shown in Figure 4-3.

The complexity for each function type is computed, and a value adjustment factor of 1 is assumed. The resulting calculation is as shown in Table 4-1. This example has the advantage that a great deal of detailed information is available.

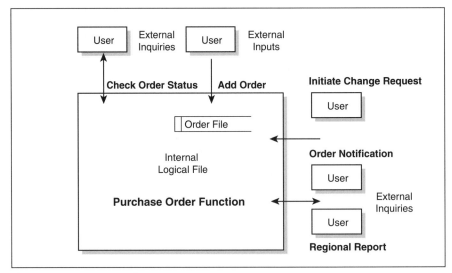

Figure 4–3 Context diagram

Table 4-1: Calculating the Function Point Count

Function	Type[a]	Value
Check order status	EQ	3
Add order	EI	4
Initiate change request	EI	3
Order notification	EQ	3
Regional report	EQ	3
Order file	ILF	7
Total unadjusted function point count		23
Value adjustment factor		1.00
Adjusted count		23

[a]EI = external input; EQ = external inquiry; ILF = internal logical file.

Now let's examine a scenario in which we do not have a well-defined requirement. Perhaps we know the high-level functionality being requested, but we don't have enough detailed information to properly compute the data element types (DETs), record element types (RETs), and file types referenced (FTRs) (these types are covered in Chapters 7 and 8). In this case we will have to make some basic assumptions. If we know all the data and transactional function types, we can assume average weightings and apply those values to derive our function point count (see Table 4-2).

When we haven't identified all of the functionality, our capacity to derive an accurate estimate is significantly reduced. Here we may deploy a function point ratio–based method using data points from either our own historical benchmark data or from a well-known and reliable industry data source. Using a function point ratio–based method, we define at least one of the five function types and then apply the relative value and compute a function point count. For example, if we know how many internal logical files (ILFs) are present, and if our historical database of information suggests that ILFs typically account for 25 percent of the total function point count, we can compute an approximated count as follows: We have one ILF (order file), which we have evaluated as average, for a value of 10 function points. So the total value of the ILFs is 10. A value of 10 is 25 percent of 40; therefore, the total unadjusted function point count is equal to 40.

Table 4-2: Calculating the Function Point Count

Function	Type[a]	Value
Check order status	EQ	4
Add order	EI	4
Initiate change request	EI	4
Order notification	EQ	4
Regional report	EQ	4
Order file	ILF	10
Total unadjusted function point count		30
Value adjustment factor		1.00
Adjusted count		30
[a]EI = external input; EQ = external inquiry; ILF = internal logical file.		

Obviously the more information we have available to us, the more accurately we can size the deliverable. But even with partial or incomplete data, we should be able to use the function point method as the basis for calculating deliverable size.

Once the size has been properly determined, the next element we need to satisfy is project complexity. Project complexity factors include such things as logical algorithms, mathematical algorithms, data relationships, functional size, reuse, code structure, performance, memory, security, and warranty (see Appendix C). In other words, we must consider the proposed or required technical solution in the estimating equation.

After the size and complexity have been defined, the estimating model evaluates the organization's capacity to deliver the defined product by assessing a variety of risk factors (see Figure 4-1) that influence the development organization's ability to deliver software in a timely and economical fashion. Risk factors may include the software processes to be used, the skill levels of the staff (including user personnel), the automation to be utilized, and the influences of the physical environment (e.g., development conditions) and the business environment (e.g., competition and regulatory requirements). In fact, numerous factors influence our ability to deliver high-quality software in a timely manner (see Appendices A and B). Categorized in Table 4-3 are some examples of influencing factors that must be evaluated in order to produce an accurate estimate.

The selected risk factors are assessed to determine the impact they will have on the organization's ability to design, develop, and deploy software. The analysis of these risk factors requires a historical baseline of data, collected over an extended period of time and statistically evaluated to determine the causal effect each factor has on the development lifecycle.

Naturally, most organizations do not have this data readily available. Alternatives include the use of third-party tools that require you to input responses to a series of questions and then match your responses to preexisting profiles that have a corresponding rate of delivery (see Appendix D).

In an ideal environment, with all variables identified, what should be an acceptable level of accuracy from this model? Typically, organizations establish an accuracy rating that scales the level of accuracy depending on where in the lifecycle the estimate is performed. For example, after completion of the requirements document, the level of accuracy expected is lower than the level of accuracy expected after detailed design. Once an organization has established an effective estimating practice, it can reasonably expect accuracy levels of ±50 percent after requirements and ±10 percent after detailed design.

Table 4-3: Risk Factors That Influence the Delivery of Software

MANAGEMENT	DEFINITION	DESIGN
• Team dynamics	• Clarity of stated requirements	• Formal process
• Morale	• Formal process	• Rigor of the review
• Project tracking	• Customer involvement	• Design reuse
• Project planning	• Experience levels	• Customer involvement
• Automation	• Business impact	• Development staff experience
• Management skills		• Automation

BUILD	TEST	ENVIRONMENT
• Code reviews	• Formal testing methods	• Newness of the technology
• Source code tracking	• Test plans	• Automated process
• Code reuse	• Development staff experience	• Adequate training
• Data administration	• Effectiveness of test tools	• Organizational dynamics
• Computer availability	• Customer involvement	• Certification
• Staff experience		
• Automation		

IT Management Level: Establishing Performance Benchmarks

Baselining an organization's performance level has become a standard industry practice, particularly in companies whose IT organizations are required to track and improve their delivery of products and services relative to improved time to market, cost reduction, and customer satisfaction. Creation of an IT performance baseline (often referred to as benchmarking) gives an organization the information it needs to properly direct its improvement initiatives and mark progress.

Performance levels are commonly discussed in terms of delivery—for example, productivity, quality, cost, and effort. In each of these categories, function points are used as the denominator in the metrics equation. By using function points as the base measure, the organization benefits in two ways. First, because function points are applied in a consistent and logical (not physical) fashion, they are considered a normalizing metric, thus allowing for comparisons across technologies, across business divisions, and across organizations—all on a level playing field. Second, there is an extraordinary amount of industry baseline data, which can be used to compare performance levels among various technologies and industries and compare internal baseline levels of performance to best-practice performance levels.

Noted in Table 4-4 are some examples of industry data points for productivity levels. These data points are from the International Software Benchmarking Standards Group (ISBSG), one of the numerous sources of industry benchmark data. The ISBSG data displayed in Table 4-5 depicts similar rates by business area.

Table 4-4: ISBSG Industry Data

Function Point Size	Mainframe	Client-Server	Packaged Software	Object-Oriented
225	9.1	11.4	7.6	12.5
400	10.4	13.0	8.7	14.3
625	12.2	15.2	10.1	16.7
875	14.6	18.3	12.2	20.1
1,125	18.3	22.8	15.2	25.1

Note: All values are expressed in hours per function point as a rate of delivery.

Table 4-5: Rates of Delivery by Business Area

Business Area	Rate of Delivery[a]
Accounting	11.3
Manufacturing	6.3
Banking	12
Telecommunications	2
Insurance	27.4
Engineering	8.1

[a]Expressed in hours per function point.

The data points shown in Tables 4-4 and 4-5 make obvious the advantage of using function points. Representative industry performance data using function point–based measures and data points is available for organizations to use as the basis of their cost and performance comparisons to industry averages and best practices.

For the organization that has been engaged in the collection and analysis of its own metrics data, creating baseline information similar to the industry views displayed in Tables 4-4 and 4-5 is a relatively easy task. However, most organizations do not have the advantage of readily available metrics data; therefore, they need to create a baseline of performance data from the ground up. Fortunately, a baseline can be developed relatively economically, depending on the level of systems documentation and project management data available.

The baselining process includes the quantifiable measurement of productivity and quality levels. Performance is determined by the use of measurements collected from a representative sampling of projects. The selection of projects is commonly based on unique criteria:

- The project was completed or undergoing development during the previous 18 months.
- The labor effort to complete the project amounted to more than six staff-months.
- The project represents similar types of projects planned for future development.
- The primary technical platforms are represented.
- The project selection includes a mix of technologies and languages.

Project data is collected (when available) on the function point size of the deliverable, level of effort, project duration, and number of defects. These measures are analyzed, and performance levels are established on a project-by-project basis. These data points can then be used to create a quantitative baseline of performance (see Figure 4-4). In Figure 4-4, data points for all projects are recorded during the baselining process. These data points create one view of an organizational baseline. The data points include an expression of functional size and rate of delivery. For our purposes, rate of delivery is expressed in terms of function points per person-month.

Figures 4-5 and 4-6 have sorted the baseline projects relative to the type of development. Figure 4-5 shows all enhancement projects; Figure 4-6, all new development projects. Note the difference among the various views for a baseline project of 400 function points. The advantage of looking at this baseline data

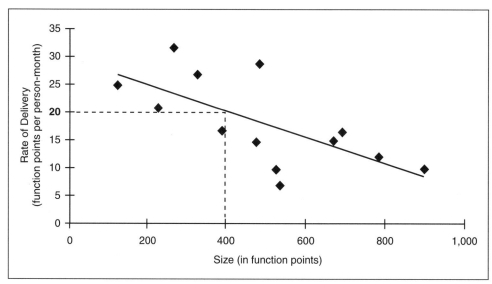

Figure 4-4   Rate of delivery

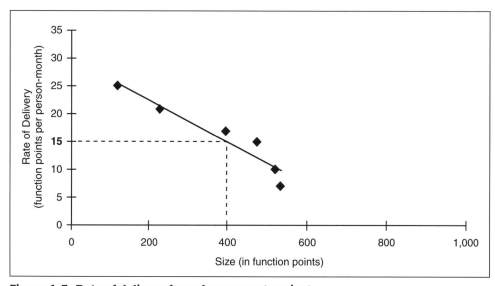

Figure 4-5   Rate of delivery for enhancement projects

from different viewpoints is to better understand the impact of different development types on performance levels. It would not be reasonable to expect future enhancement projects to perform at the same rate of delivery as new development projects.

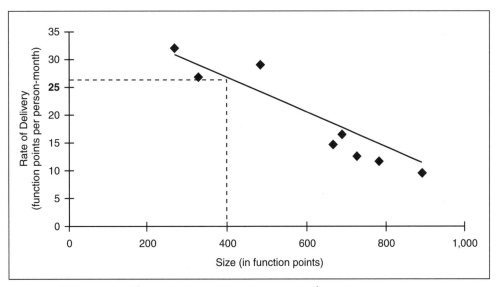

Figure 4-6 Rate of delivery for new development projects

Obviously project size and complexity are contributing factors that influence productivity. However, numerous other factors also affect the capacity of an organization to define, develop, and deploy software. Assessing an organization's capacity to deliver represents the qualitative portion of the benchmarking process. A capacity analysis reveals the influence of current software practices on performance levels. Using the information from the capacity analysis, it is possible to recommend improvements in current practices, to suggest new practices, and to emphasize existing practices that have already demonstrated positive influence on productivity (see Appendix D).

For example, we can observe from Figures 4-4 through 4-6 that our capacity to deliver is influenced by size and type of development. If we hold these two variables constant while analyzing our baseline data, we can observe that there are still variations in performance data.

Figure 4-7 shows data from several projects that are closely related in size. Four data points fall in the range of 400 to 550 function points. Their corresponding rates of delivery are from 8 to 18 function points per person-month. That is a significant difference in performance. The challenge now becomes one of determining the contributing factors that caused these projects to perform at different levels.

We have completed many of these types of process performance assessments on the basis of our own proprietary assessment method (see Appendix A). The method of collection consists of selected interview and team survey sessions with

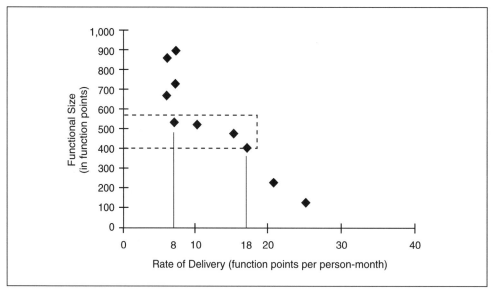

Figure 4-7   Rate of delivery by functional size

each of the project teams. Data is collected on key influence factors, such as project management capabilities, requirements and design effectiveness, build and test practices, skill levels, and other contributing environmental factors. Individual projects are analyzed, and project profiles are created. This data is also analyzed in aggregate and may be used as the basis for determining overall organization process improvements.

The results are somewhat predictable. Typical influence factors include skill levels, effective use of front-end lifecycle quality practices, tool utilization, and project management. These findings parallel, in part, those of the ISBSG database analysis, which revealed that language complexity, development platform, methodology, and application type were significant factors influencing productivity.

Analysis of the qualitative data leads an organization to the discovery of certain process strengths and weaknesses. As performance profiles are developed and contrasted to quantitative levels of performance, key software practices that are present in the higher-performing projects tend to be missing from the lower-performing projects. These practices differentiate between success and failure.

The real value of the benchmarking activity results from identifying performance levels, analyzing process strengths and weaknesses, monitoring process improvements, and comparing to industry data points. There is much to be learned

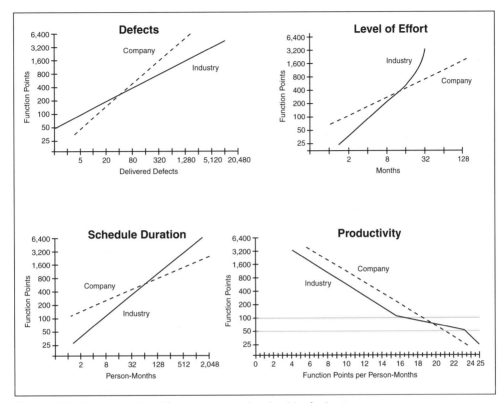

Figure 4-8 Common baseline measures tracked by industry

from comparisons to industry data. An IT organization can see at a glance the overall effectiveness of its performance in contrast to industry benchmarks. In addition, there is an opportunity to identify industry best practices and evaluate how these best practices will affect your organization's performance levels. Common industry measures that are benchmarked include defects, productivity, level of effort, and schedule duration (see Figure 4-8).

Industry Best Practices

IT organizations are often seeking information relative to best-in-class practices. They want to know the current best practices in the industry. On the one hand this need to know is a positive trend as the industry begins to recognize the value of software measurement and its ability to provide useful information to the IT organization and to the business. On the other hand it still has the feeling of an organization looking for a magic cure-all.

An IT organization can best position itself by incorporating the use of internal benchmarking practices and utilizing data points representing industry best practices. Only then can IT be assured of where it is and where it is going.

Organization Level: Establishing Service-Level Measures

Service-level measures are most commonly associated with outsourcing arrangements. They are established as a means to measure the performance of an external provider of software services. In addition, as organizations become increasingly sensitive to the needs of their customers and as IT goals and objectives become more aligned with business performance and customer satisfaction levels, internal service-level measures are becoming more popular.

Function points play a key role in the establishment of application development and maintenance (AD/M) service-level metrics. There are three typical outsourcing scenarios in which function points can play an important role: single projects or applications, application maintenance, and the outsourcing of an entire AD/M environment. The decision to outsource a particular project rather than an entire development shop will, of course, vary significantly. Some of the typical reasons for outsourcing include the following:

- To allow companies to focus on "core competencies"
- To convert relatively fixed allocated costs to direct variable costs
- To take the IT function to the next level of capability
- To improve time to market
- To facilitate best-practice implementation of new applications
- To change the culture and reskill the IT function
- To convert legacy system resources to new development resources

An effective set of measures is mandatory to monitor performance trends and improvements. These measures should link to and provide information on performance as it relates to stated organization goals and objectives.

Project and Application Outsourcing

Outsourcing of a project or application involves contracting a third-party vendor to perform the work, either on- or off-site. The completion of the contract results in the delivery of the project or application software.

For service levels to be established in the case of a project or application scenario, three basic questions need to be answered: (1) What is the outsource provider's responsibility? (2) What standards or development practices are required? and (3) What defines the "goodness" of the deliverable? Answers to these questions will guide us in outlining and defining which service levels are most appropriate.

First, defining the areas of responsibility provides an opportunity to define handoff or touch points where deliverables are passed between the provider and the customer. The most obvious handoff point is the final deliverable, but other handoff points may include specifications, design, test plans, test cases, code, and so on. Each handoff point is an opportunity for measuring the level of service. What will be delivered to the provider, and what will the provider in turn deliver?

Function point analysis has an obvious role here. For example, the initial deliverable to the provider may be a requirements document. Here's an excellent opportunity to size the requirement and to establish a service level that measures the size of the final deliverable. As scope changes are introduced, they will be sized by function points, thereby identifying to both the provider and the customer a specific quantification of the end deliverable.

Second, knowing what standards or development practices are required typically leads to the establishment of one or more compliance-related service-level measures. The opportunity to use function points is limited in this aspect of the outsourcing arrangement. However, there may be a desire to monitor productivity, measured in function points per unit of time or cost. The proper use of development tools and techniques during the development process will, of course, influence productivity, and the function point–related metric can be used to measure the effectiveness of the selected tools and techniques.

Finally, the "goodness" of the deliverable is the most basic of the service-level measures. Here function points would usually be the denominator in a variety of metrics equations measuring such things as rate of delivery, duration, cost, and quality.

Maintenance Outsourcing

The outsourcing of selected applications to be maintained by a third-party vendor requires a much different set of measures from those used in the project or application outsourcing arrangement. The key elements involved when one is considering the measurement of a maintenance outsourcing arrangement include the following:

- Monitoring customer expectations
- Maintaining an acceptable response time

- Limiting bad fixes
- Managing the volume of fixes
- Monitoring the decrease or increase in application functionality
- Establishing effective handoffs
- Ensuring application expertise
- Monitoring smooth customer interfacing

All of these factors are measurable, although not all of them require the use of function points. Let's examine several situations and see how function points play a role.

Monitoring customer expectations is an opportunity to use function points as a means to monitor the growth of the entire application portfolio, as well as to maintain an overall view of the costs associated with each application. Figures 4-9 and 4-10 depict these views graphically.

Monitoring the increase or decrease of functionality in any given application allows the development organization to monitor the cost of functionality supported.

As Figure 4-11 shows, a maintenance assignment scope is established for each application. The maintenance assignment scope defines how many resources are being used to support each application's functionality. This service-level measure

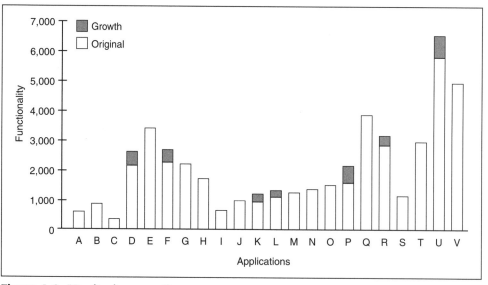

Figure 4-9 Monitoring growth

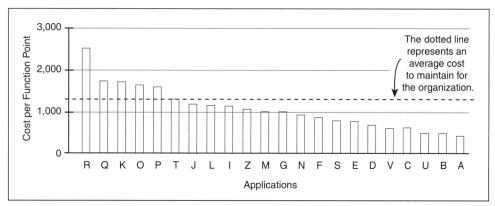

Figure 4-10 Monitoring cost

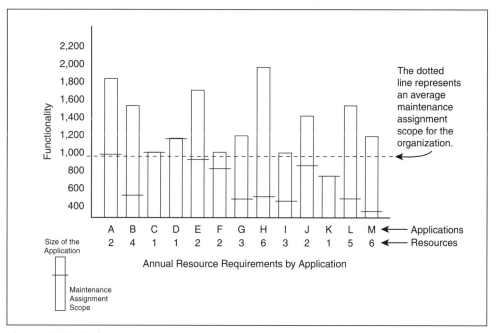

Figure 4-11 Maintenance assignment scope

may be established at the beginning of the contract and monitored throughout the life of that contract. The maintained application baseline count should be updated periodically, along with a measure of resources being expended to maintain the application.

AD/M Outsourcing

The final outsourcing scenario we will review is the outsourcing of an entire application development and maintenance department. Such outsourcing usually extends over multiple years and may be linked to a much larger outsourcing initiative, which could include the outsourcing of the entire IT organization. Once again we observe a much different measurement dynamic from what we encountered with the first two scenarios.

In this scenario the customer continues to monitor the management and performance of individual projects and the maintenance of the application portfolio. However, usually a much higher or broader performance view is taken when the service-level measures for an entire IT department are being considered.

The issues driving AD/M outsourcing engagements include the following:

- Assessing the impact of new technology
- Increasing profitability
- Reducing costs
- Improving customer service
- Improving time to market
- Increasing financial control

Service-level measures that are formulated to support an AD/M outsourcing arrangement are usually multi-layered. The contract may require a primary set of service-level measures that measure overall performance on an organizationwide basis. In addition, the contract may require a set of service-level measures to monitor specific project deliverables.

This scenario is similar to an agreement you might have with a contractor building your house, in which there are specific measures relative to the details of the house such as room dimensions, electrical capacities, and the like. However, the overall performance is more likely to be monitored as time to market, final cost, and overall quality of workmanship.

A well-defined process should be followed to establish the proper service-level measures for an AD/M arrangement. This process requires the customer to understand the goals and objectives of the outsourcing arrangement, identify measures that will monitor the performance or the achievement of those goals, and determine the proper level of service to expect initially and on a continuing basis.

The goals and objectives of the outsourcing initiative are developed at a senior management level and documented in a strategic business document. The identified business drivers express the expected outcomes of the outsourcing arrangement in terms of increased profitability, market positioning, and improved service. The challenge is to derive a set of service-level measures that will effectively monitor how these elements are affected—positively or negatively—by the activities being executed at the software development level.

In addition to defining or discovering the business drivers, it is critical to consider the performance of the software practices within the development organization itself. For example, any existing problems with the ability to deliver clearly stated and accurate requirements need to be identified when service-level measures are being established. The introduction of a third-party provider that has taken over the existing development staff will not immediately improve the development organization's ability to provide clear requirement specifications.

Through analysis of the business drivers and the performance considerations of the development environment, a set of applicable metrics is derived (see Figure 4-12). For each service-level metric identified, a metric profile is created. Each profile includes a definition of the metric, its stated purpose, the data elements required, and the formula to calculate.

The next step in the process is to establish the actual values or levels of performance that must be assigned to each service-level metric. We must determine reasonable values for the established service levels. If we have established time to market as a service level, we need to determine the proper interval of time to be

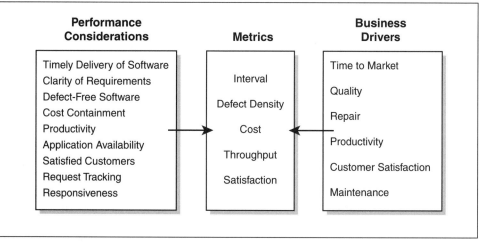

Figure 4-12 Metrics derived by analysis of business drivers and performance considerations

expected. If cost is going to be measured, what is a reasonable cost? When quality is integrated into the set of service measures, what are the defect density levels? We can determine these values best either by establishing organizational performance benchmarks or by relying on industry data.

Summary

The effective use of function points centers around three primary functions: estimating, benchmarking, and identifying service-level measures. For each of these functions, function points are used in conjunction with other measures and other informational data points.

Critical to the success of any estimating model is the sizing element. The size measure is an extension of the definition. Utilizing function points enables the project manager to size the required deliverable accurately and consistently, and function points enable that size to be expressed to end users in terms they are more likely to understand—for example, inputs, outputs, interfaces, and so on.

The use of function points as part of a comprehensive baseline performance measurement initiative demonstrates the versatility and many uses of function points. Specifically, function points permit an organization to compare internal performance levels in a more consistent fashion. In addition, the use of function points allows for a wide range of comparison opportunities outside of the organization. An ever-increasing amount of industry performance data uses function points as the base measure. An organization that can express its productivity in terms of function points can compare those performance values with industry-related benchmarks and determine the relative position of its performance. In addition, some industry data goes a step further in that it can identify and quantify best-practice performance levels.

Finally, when function points are incorporated into the service-level metrics for an application development outsourcing arrangement, their value to the organization increases. They have often been described as the currency or unit of work that is at the core of the service-level metrics. Once again we can see the dual role that function points can play in servicing both the IT organization and the business community. In the case of outsourcing, the business is paying for functionality delivered. That functionality can be quantified best by the function point metric.

CHAPTER FIVE

Software Industry Benchmark Data

Introduction

The need for accurate, reliable information on the most effective and productive tools and methods for designing, developing, and deploying software is on the rise within the software industry. Often referred to as best practices or best-in-class data, this information is available in a variety of formats through various benchmark service providers. Industry data can provide significant value to IT organizations that need benchmarks as points of reference for monitoring and comparing average and best-in-class industry performance levels.

Historically, industry benchmark data for application development environments has been available to the public through technical writings, trade publications, and research articles from a handful of measurement gurus, including Capers Jones and Howard Rubin. In the past this data typically represented a broad spectrum of development environments, tools, and methods. Valuable from the general standpoint of overall performance, these initial views of data often lacked the detail required to perform specific comparative analysis and did not always reflect current trends in the industry. However, these early attempts at capturing, analyzing, and displaying industry data were instrumental in promoting software measurement and raising the level of awareness with regard to potential benefits of using this type of benchmark data.

Today, application development benchmarks are available from several credible sources. Although the integrity of data and the standards supporting the collecting of data are still issues, these benchmark values can be responsibly used to set standards of performance that reflect industry trends and best practices.

In this chapter we will examine how IT departments are using industry data to advance their competitive positions and improve performance. We will discuss benchmarking principles and the difference between internal benchmarking and external benchmarking, and we will introduce the idea of benchmarking partners.

Concerns about the consistency, accuracy, and integrity of industry data are still prevalent; however, as we learn more about the source of the data and how it was collected and analyzed, we become smarter shoppers of that data. Function points, which are used in a variety of industry benchmarks, help to standardize, in part, the definition of size.

Options for the types of data and the breadth and depth of data abound. We will provide you with a cross-sectional sampling of benchmark providers and describe the types of benchmark data and services they offer.

How IT Is Using Industry Data

Benchmarking operational hardware performance has been the norm in IT departments for many years. Within the past ten years, there has been an equal emphasis on benchmarking rates of productivity relative to the development and deployment of software systems. Companies such as Motorola, AT&T, and IBM have been collecting and analyzing their application development and maintenance benchmark data for purposes of measuring and monitoring IT performance.

The level of interest and the need for industry data within IT has increased dramatically over the past several years. This increased demand stems from the necessity of IT organizations to benchmark their progress and compare their rate of improvement to an industry standard. The focus on improved productivity and cost reduction has driven many companies to outsource their IT activities when faced with the realization that their performance levels are below par.

Certain experts, such as Howard Rubin and Capers Jones, are strong advocates for using benchmark data as a means to improve IT performance. These two men are noted for their articles and publications documenting research and results from analyzing industry performance data. As more and more benchmark data becomes available, IT professionals begin to realize the importance and value of having their own internal data points available. Companies want to evaluate their current productivity levels relative to industry performance benchmarks.

Two main forces are driving this increased appetite for information on IT performance: competitive positioning and outsourcing. IT has become a direct contributor to bottom-line business value. The need to build systems faster, better, and cheaper is ever present. Toward that end, IT is constantly seeking ways to improve as it manages the increasing scrutiny from senior executives with regard to how it is spending budget dollars.

Industry data offers IT organizations insights into the software development practices that can contribute to improved methods for designing, developing, and deploying software on time and within budget. Often defined as best practices, benchmark data provides quantitative assessments of tools and methods that yield the best return on the IT investment.

The goal is to improve and become more competitive. Improvements are possible whether an organization uses industry benchmark data or not; however, industry data can set reasonable expectations about the level of expected improvement, and it can provide valuable information with regard to decisions that must be made around technology strategies.

For IT groups that have chosen to outsource their application development and maintenance functions, industry benchmark data is invaluable. Industry data may be a contributing factor in the initial decision to outsource. On the basis of internal levels of performance as contrasted to external industry benchmarks, the company may decide that outsourcing is a reasonable strategy for realizing gains in productivity. As the outsourcing deal is being developed, external benchmark data can be used to properly set the service levels and define improvement goals. And as the outsourcing deal matures, periodic checks on industry trends can be of great value.

In summary, companies require accurate, detailed data to manage their software business. They need cost information that permits more informed decisions with regard to technology strategies, effective implementation of architectures, and cost-efficient resource management. They need to understand their capacity to deliver with regard to their utilization of methods and tools, effective deployment of training programs, and potential outsourcing opportunities. Simply stated, they require business measures based on facts, not fiction.

Benchmarking

The need for industry data is usually presented in the context of an organization benchmarking its current levels of performance and wanting to compare to an industry average or best-practice benchmark. Benchmarking efforts may require a significant amount of resources for an extended period of time. Benchmark data is collected over a predefined period of time ranging from several months to one year. The decision of what and when to benchmark is made on the basis of the needs of the organization.

At the heart of the issue is the need to obtain an accurate and representative view of current performance levels. This view may be based on recently completed projects and results, or it may require a year's worth of data collection and analysis to piece together an accurate assessment of internal levels of performance. When companies are establishing benchmark measures in support of outsourcing arrangements, they usually use a benchmarking strategy that takes a sample set of benchmark data and uses it to represent the whole.

A sample set of benchmark data can be obtained economically and can provide a reasonably accurate set of data values. For example, company XYZ may want to outsource its maintenance support activities and elements of its software development. The outsource provider could be providing these services to company XYZ over the next five years. The outsourcing contract promises cost reductions in maintenance support and improved performance in software development. Benchmark values are established that will enable the company and the provider to agree to a set of service levels that will monitor trends in cost reduction and performance improvement.

Continuing with our example for company XYZ, we realize that two benchmarks are required. One benchmark needs to be established to show current performance levels within the software development environment. We can obtain this benchmark by taking a select group of recently completed development projects and measuring performance relative to time to market, costs, duration, and so on.

The second benchmark will monitor the costs associated with maintenance of the application portfolio. As a result of maintenance fixes, small enhancements, regulatory changes, and new applications, the portfolio of maintained applications will grow. This rate of growth will be a factor in monitoring the costs of maintaining the portfolio. Therefore, a baseline measure of the entire portfolio must be obtained.

Concerns with Industry Data

Whenever an organization researches available sources of industry data, the overriding question has to be, How can we ensure that the data we obtain is valid? The organization needs to be comfortable with the integrity of the data it receives and subsequently uses in establishing benchmark points of comparison. Three major criteria should be used to assess industry data:

1. Is the data representative?
2. Has the data been collected in a consistent fashion?
3. Does the data meet standard definitions?

Representativeness

An increasing amount of industry data is available from a variety of reputable sources. However, a large portion of that data is not current and could even be considered outdated—for several obvious reasons. Most importantly, the availability of reliable data is always at issue. The lifecycle of collecting enough data to be statistically representative, scrubbing the data to ensure consistency and accuracy, and analyzing the data to produce valid benchmarks can take several years and result in data benchmarks that may have limited value. On the surface, it may seem impressive to find a vendor who has access to a database consisting of thousands of projects; however, it is neither impressive nor useful to have data that is "Jurassic" in nature.

We are witnessing an ever-changing technology landscape, making it all the more important to have data that is current. The most effective way to achieve currency is to develop the capacity to collect and present industry data as quickly as possible. To bring meaningful data to the industry, the collection of data must be clean (i.e., carried out consistently and accurately) and swift, and the data must be made accessible at a level of detail that permits the consumer to develop customized views of that data.

Consistency

Lack of consistency in the collection and display of industry data has long been an issue. Discrepancies in data definitions, lack of operational definitions, and a limited description of how the data is reported can frequently be found in two or more commercial sources of industry data. Unfortunately, this is not a situation that is likely to improve anytime soon. IT organizations using vendor-supplied benchmark data for comparison purposes must ensure that data being collected internally matches the definitions and descriptions of the data supplied by their benchmarking partners.

The variability in the numerous data collection methods contributes significantly to the issue of inconsistency. Benchmark service providers, academic research groups, and industry consortia all have different approaches to collecting and analyzing industry data. Collection devices such as interviews, self-administered surveys, and random samplings lack the control and rigor necessary to produce meaningful and statistically sound sets of industry data points. It is difficult to believe that data that has been collected through self-administered survey instruments represents an objective view of an organization's level of performance.

Standard Definitions

If you asked a roomful of IT professionals to define a person-month or the boundaries of a maintenance project, or to detail the cost elements in a calculation of cost per function point, what would you get? You would get as many different answers as there are people in the room. The reason is a lack of definition or standardization for the definitions and terms we use in software measurement and benchmarking.

To make reasonable comparisons (apples to apples), we need clear, concise, and repeatable definitions. If there is a lack of trust or understanding in what the data represents, then the use and the value of the data will be limited. Inconsistency among various data sources will not be rectified until there is a governing body that standardizes the use of software measurement terms and definitions.

What Role Do Function Points Play?

As stated already, a primary concern with industry benchmark data is the lack of standard definitions leading to the potential for inconsistency. Without standardized definitions, how we define a person-month or a defect or a line of code can be very subjective. When these values are being used to create measures such as lines of code per person-month, the results of any comparisons to industry data are sure to disappoint.

The use of function points eliminates some of the concerns about the lack of standard definitions. The function point methodology is well defined and has been proven to yield a consistent result when used by experienced practitioners. Coupled with other well-defined metrics, such as hours (instead of person-months), the resulting measure, such as hours per function point, can be used with greater assurance of an "apples to apples" comparison.

Function points are also an effective normalizing agent. A function point is a function point is a function point. It represents the size of the deliverable. A function point count is not influenced by the technology or the languages being used. These are certainly important factors that affect the outcome of the deliverable, but they do not influence the size. Using function points, you can compare any two applications, each written in a different language, and objectively measure the impact of language complexity on overall productivity.

Sources of Industry Data

Listed in this section are nine organizations that provide benchmark data on performance levels within the software industry. Most of these providers offer benchmarking services among a myriad of other related services. Their approaches to gathering benchmark data vary, and so does the content of deliverables they have to offer. We have been directly involved with most of these organizations; therefore, we are presenting them as credible sources of benchmark data. Obviously there are other suppliers and other sources of data, and we would encourage our readers to pursue all opportunities available to them.

For each vendor we have described its offerings and contact information. To guard against any inadvertent positive or negative commentary on our part, we have attempted simply to summarize the vendors' offerings on the basis of the information we have gathered from their Web sites or marketing materials.

As always, we would caution the consumer of these products and services to delve deeper and be sure they evaluate these industry views of data relative to the concerns discussed earlier in this chapter.

The Gartner Group (www.gartner.com)

The Gartner Group offers benchmarking opportunities within its Application Development Support services. The benchmarking service provides an assessment of software development and maintenance environments. The primary focus of the assessment is an in-depth analysis of cost and management practices based on business needs.

The results provide an organization with the ability to:

- Analyze the capability and functionality of applications relative to business needs
- Target areas of performance and analyze the possible underlying causes
- Compare performance measurements to a peer group of best-in-class companies

The deliverables include a comparison to peer organizations in the Gartner-Measurement database based on industry and business operations, geographic area, and IT complexity. This comparison allows you to answer the following questions: How do my costs and performance compare to those of my peers? and How can I best take advantage of new technologies?

META Group (www.metagroup.com)

META Group's benchmarking and strategic measurement of IT performance services are organized into major areas based on the stated needs of companies and experience. One of the major areas is infrastructure and application benchmarks. These benchmark assessments are designed to provide in-depth analysis and identify opportunities for improvement in four IT functional areas: data center, network (voice and data), help desk, and application development and maintenance.

META Group advertises that its Application Development and Maintenance Assessment is a one-time assessment best suited to situations requiring across-the-board analysis of IT operations in support of a major business decision, such as evaluating outsourcing alternatives or renegotiating an existing outsourcing contract. The assessment collects, analyzes, and compares relevant data encompassing the application portfolio, organization and staffing, cost, and technology in order to gauge the overall performance and effectiveness of application development and maintenance organizations. META consultants provide recommendations for long- and short-term goals. In addition, their assessment assists in the following tasks:

- Measuring productivity and performance
- Optimizing staffing levels
- Measuring return on application development technology investments
- Evaluating planned technology directions for hardware platforms, development technologies, and programming aids

Rubin Systems, Inc. (www.hrubin.com)

Howard Rubin is a leader in the software performance benchmarking arena. He has teamed up with META Group to offer the IT Performance Engineering and Measurement Strategies (PEMS). This service combines META Group's analytic expertise with the IT benchmarking data resources and worldwide database of Rubin Systems.

Rubin Systems conducts several surveys throughout the year, The Worldwide Benchmark Annual Survey among them. The results of this survey are offered on the Web site. The results offer a comprehensive worldwide view of software development performance across myriad easy-to-understand variables.

Software Productivity Research (www.spr.com)

Software Productivity Research (SPR) was founded by Caper Jones, the world-renowned expert on software measurement and benchmarking. SPR offers a free service of comprehensive software diagnostics capabilities. Users are asked to describe their software organization, technology, and process. In return, SPR benchmarks the data against a comprehensive knowledge base of 8,000 projects.

The eBenchmark process is a confidential, Web-based assessment intended to demonstrate the impact of software diagnostic services on software productivity and quality. Benchmark responses are compared with an extensive knowledge base. SPR e-mails a two-page benchmark analysis. The report assesses a client's software environment in four broad areas: personnel, technology, process, and environment. Responses are compared to industry average and best-in-class data that is resident in the SPR knowledge base.

ISBSG (www.isbsg.org.au)

The International Software Benchmarking Standards Group, Ltd. (ISBSG) is a joint initiative of several national software metrics organizations from around the world, including IFPUG. Its goal is the improvement of software engineering approaches and IT management through the establishment of a data repository of software projects.

ISBSG provides a standard template for recording and collecting software project data and offers free software to accomplish these tasks. It manages a software project repository and coordinates a research program. The results are made available to software industry practitioners through reports, books, and data diskettes. ISBSG regularly publishes an analysis of its database, to help its users keep abreast of development productivity trends. ISBSG can provide you with a diskette of repository data so that you can do your own analysis of the world's projects.

ISBSG can inform you of productivity levels in other organizations that have profiles similar to that of your organization. The group provides products and services to permit software developers to benchmark themselves against the world's best and to build an experience database of their organizations' productivity.

Compass America (www.compass-analysis.com)

Compass America provides benchmarking services in support of the application development and maintenance environment. It retains a database of projects that can be used to perform comparative analysis at a detailed level, depending on the needs of the client. It offers benchmarking services designed to determine factors that drive performance and to identify actions to improve performance.

Compass America's assessment positions the organization, enabling it to analyze a variety of measures, including development project cost and productivity; package acquisition and implementation cost; development project and package cycle time; project return on investment; delivery reliability; maintenance costs, productivity, and service levels; and user support cost and productivity.

The David Consulting Group (www.davidconsultinggroup.com)

The David Consulting Group (DCG) offers a selection of industry data and IT information on its Web site. It displays, for example, software delivery rates specific to the financial industry. Its delivery rates are available from the extensive David Consulting Group database of over 3,800 recently (1997–2000) completed new development and enhancement projects. In addition, it provides an online service that gives users the opportunity to input project data and receive in return an estimated industry delivery rate that matches their customized characteristics. Responses are sent via e-mail by a DCG analyst.

The authors of this book are principals in The David Consulting Group.

The Benchmarking Exchange (www.benchnet.com)

The Benchmarking Exchange (TBE) is a comprehensive electronic communication and information system designed specifically for use by organizations involved in benchmarking and process improvement. TBE's BenchNet provides users with a centralized and specialized forum for all phases of benchmarking, including networking with other organizations, consortium studies, and information exchange.

TBE offers an electronic survey (TBE Surveyor), which allows you to compare your data to that of other organizations. You can assess responses by type of industry, country, size of organization, and so on.

Hackett Benchmarking & Research (www.answerthink.com)

Hackett Benchmarking & Research is part of answer*think* consulting group. It maintains benchmarks in finance, human resources, information technology, performance measurement, and other areas. Hackett is known for its comprehensive ongoing knowledge-worker benchmarks of business best practices. Participants in its benchmarks include more than 1,400 leading companies representing a majority of Fortune 100 companies.

Hackett assists companies in developing improvement programs to move its organizations toward world-class performance. Benefits include supporting clients' needs to reduce costs and ready their business infrastructures to permit future growth while positioning them to contribute more value to the corporation.

Hope for the Future

The software industry is rapidly changing, and IT organizations require immediate access to information that is necessary to manage their changing environment. As companies seek to mature and become more productive, and as commercial software companies attempt to gain competitive advantage, the availability of valid industry benchmark data becomes critical. Decisions should always be based on the best available information. If that information is invalid, resulting decisions will not be well founded.

Many organizations are realizing the need to benchmark their performance to an industry standard, but sources of data are limited. Typically organizations are reluctant to share their data by placing it into the public domain. They fear a loss of control and exposure that will erode their competitive advantage. This reluctance severely limits the amount and quality of data that is available for comparison. If we are to advance as an industry, we must share our ideas and our data.

Fortunately, efforts are under way to collect accurate, consistent industry data. Organizations such as the International Software Benchmarking Standards Group (highlighted in the previous section) are dedicated to soliciting and anonymously displaying very detailed industry data values. The variety of data they have available enables a participating company to make comparisons on the basis of its own customized view of data elements.

For the future, the vision we like to promote is "all the data, all the time" (see Figure 5-1). A standardized and easy-to-use collection process should feed a well-defined set of collected data to a common repository. The data should be validated and secured. Automated tools should be linked to the repository to perform many of the collection, validation, and statistical analysis functions required. Public access to the data should be online and provided through the Internet.

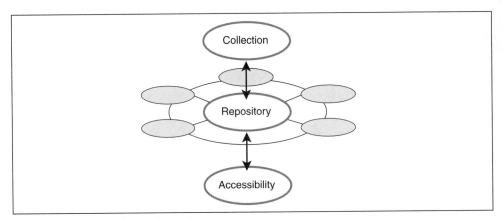

Figure 5-1 All the data, all the time

Summary

The level of interest and the need for industry data within IT has increased over the past several years. IT organizations need to benchmark their progress and compare their rate of improvement to an industry standard in order to stay competitive. The focus is on improved productivity and cost reduction. As a result of comparing benchmark results to internal measures, many IT organizations decide to outsource their IT activities when faced with the realization that their performance levels are below par.

Industry data offers IT organizations insights into the software development practices that can contribute to improved methods for designing, developing, and deploying software on time and within budget. Often defined as best practices, benchmark data provides quantitative assessments of tools and methods that yield the best return on the IT investment.

Whenever an organization researches available sources of industry data, the overriding question has to be, How can we ensure that the data we obtain is valid? The organization must be comfortable with the integrity of the data it receives and subsequently uses in establishing benchmark points of comparison. Three major criteria should be used to assess industry data:

1. Is the data representative?
2. Has the data been collected in a consistent fashion?
3. Does the data meet standard definitions?

The use of function points eliminates some of the concerns surrounding the lack of standard definitions. The function point methodology is well defined and has been proven to yield a consistent result when used by experienced practitioners. Coupled with other well-defined metrics, such as hours (instead of person-months), the resulting measure, such as hours per function point, can be used with greater assurance of an "apples to apples" comparison.

The software industry is rapidly changing, and IT organizations require immediate access to information necessary to manage their changing environment. As companies seek to mature and become more productive, and as commercial software companies attempt to gain competitive advantage, the availability of valid industry benchmark data becomes critical. Decisions should be based on the best available information. If that information is invalid, resulting decisions will not be well founded.

Many organizations are realizing the need to benchmark their performance to an industry standard, but sources of data are limited. Typically organizations are reluctant to share their data by placing it into the public domain. They fear a loss of control and exposure that will erode their competitive advantage. This reluctance severely limits the amount and quality of data that is available for comparison. If we are to advance as an industry, we must share our ideas and our data.

Perhaps most importantly, the industry needs to be committed to this task. It is not an individual exercise, but a movement that must begin at the national level.

CHAPTER SIX

Introduction to Function Point Analysis

Introduction

Function point analysis (FPA) is a proven, widely accepted methodology for determining the size of a software development project or of an installed software application. This and the function point counting rules have continued to be reviewed, clarified, and updated to coincide with the advancement of new technologies. These updates have resulted in significantly more consistent counts and improved correlation of size to project effort.

The Counting Practices Committee of the International Function Point Users Group (IFPUG) promulgates the Counting Practices Manual, which contains the current standards and guidelines for the counting process. This book is based on and reflects the rules contained within version 4.1, released in 1999, of that manual. This chapter will discuss the IFPUG process for counting function points, the types of counts, the application boundary, and the determination of the counting scope that identifies the functionality being sized.

Chapters 7 through 10 will describe the data functions, the transactional functions, the general system characteristics, and the calculations, respectively, involved in function point counting. So together, this chapter and the next four demonstrate concretely how to apply FPA to software and derive the measurements required to accurately size and estimate the cost of development, maintenance, or outsourcing decisions.

The Function Point Counting Process

Function point analysis is an accepted standard for the measurement of software size. FPA is nothing more than a normalizing factor for software comparison, much the same as other standard units of size—for example, cubic yards or cubic meters, gallons or liters, pounds or kilograms, miles or kilometers. Function point counts on their own reflect nothing about their value or cost; other factors must be considered in estimates of the cost, value, or resource requirements for the purchase, development, acquisition, or maintenance of software. This does not diminish the value of function point analysis; rather, it places it in perspective with other consistent standards of measurement. A cubic yard of gold is worth more than a cubic yard of dirt; a mile of beachfront property is worth significantly more than a frontage mile of inaccessible land; a gallon of gasoline is currently valued higher than a gallon of water; a pound of steak costs more than a pound of potatoes. Nevertheless, none of these measures are inappropriate.

The size of an application, in function points, can be used together with consideration of other application characteristics (e.g., performance requirements, security, algorithmic content) and project attributes (such as skill level of the developers, development languages to be used, the methodology and technology to be applied, and the tasks to be performed) to estimate cost and resource requirements. Consequently, function point analysis can be introduced early in the estimation process; counts should be reevaluated whenever the scope changes or a new phase of the development process begins.

Function points should represent the functionality that a business user requests (whether that user is a marketing specialist, business analyst, factory manager, banker, or buyer); therefore, it is never too early to perform a functional analysis. In fact, gathering the interested parties together early in the software project proposal phase to achieve a functional analysis ultimately makes the developers' job easier and ensures that the users clearly state what they want developed.

Function point analysis should be applied throughout the software development and maintenance process to quantify application functionality provided to the users of that software. The measurement is independent of the methodology and technology utilized for the development and/or maintenance work effort.

The Process Used to Size Function Points

The total process used to size function points can be summarized by the following seven steps:

1. Determine the type of function point count
2. Identify the counting scope and the application boundary
3. Identify all data functions (internal logical files and external interface files) and their complexity (see Chapter 7)
4. Identify all transactional functions (external inputs, external outputs, and external inquiries) and their complexity (see Chapter 8)
5. Determine the unadjusted function point count
6. Determine the value adjustment factor, which is based on the 14 general system characteristics presented in Chapter 9
7. Calculate the adjusted function point count (see Chapter 10)

To further facilitate your understanding of this process, we will begin with an example of an application that simply maintains and displays information about individuals at a location. In this discussion we will limit ourselves to the first four steps here and exclude any complexity assessment for the data and transactional functions, which will be covered in Chapters 7 and 8, respectively. In this example the **type of count** will be an application function point count; much more information on the different types of counts will be provided later. The **counting scope** reflects the functionality that we are currently sizing. The **application boundary** separates the application being measured from the user domain and/or other independent applications. The **data functions**—internal logical files (ILFs) and external interface files (EIFs)—relate to the logical data stored and available for update and/or retrieval. The **transactional functions**—external inputs (EIs), external outputs (EOs), and external inquiries (EQs)—perform the processes of data maintenance, retrieval, output, and so on (transactions you would normally expect to see in a process model).

The following high-level example (see Figure 6-1) illustrates a sample of the functional components included in a function point count of a Location Directory application:

Step 1 in the function point counting process is to determine the type of function point count. There are three possible types of function point counts:

1. Development project counts
2. Enhancement project counts
3. Application counts

We will describe each type in detail later in the chapter. In this example we are counting an existing application without regard to its history of development; therefore, the count is an application count.

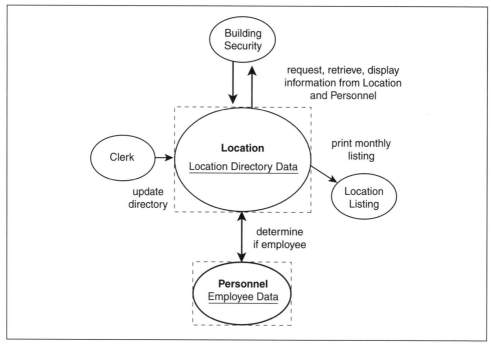

Figure 6-1 Sample functional components

Step 2 in the function point counting process is to identify the counting scope and the application boundary. Our counting scope for the application count includes all functionality currently present in the application. Our boundary separates the Clerk, Building Security, and Personnel application, as well as the produced Location Listing—that is, everything outside the actual software of the Location Directory application—from the Location Directory itself.

Step 3 in the function point counting process is to identify the data functions (ILFs and EIFs). The Location Directory data, an internal logical file (ILF), is maintained within the boundary of the application. The Employee data, an external interface file (EIF), is maintained within the boundary of the Personnel application and is used by the Location Directory application for retrieval of reference data. We will provide much more information in the following chapters to assist you in making these determinations, but for now you will have to take them on faith.

Step 4 in the function point counting process is to identify the transactional functions (EIs, EOs, and EQs). The clerk updates, as an external input (EI), Location Directory data. The Location Listing, which also includes totals, is generated as an external output (EO). Building Security personnel request the retrieval and display, an external inquiry (EQ), of information maintained in the Location Directory ILF, as well as Employee data from an EIF, currently maintained in the Personnel application. An EQ can retrieve data from one or more ILFs or EIFs.

These are examples of only the functional components within an application. If you can understand these concepts, you are well on your way to counting function points. We will provide much more extensive definitions and many more examples in the chapters that follow.

The timing of function point counts varies depending on the particular status of an application. Typically, less information is available early in development; significantly more information is available as an application is developed and delivered. Early in the process, the only information available might be verbal. During development, the information available to assist in counting increases to include some of the following potential documents, which are helpful in determining function point counts:

- Project proposals
- High-level system diagrams (showing relationships to other interacting applications)
- Entity relationship diagrams
- Logical data models
- Data flow diagrams
- Object models
- Process models
- Requirement documents
- Prototypes
- Functional specifications
- Use cases
- System specifications
- Detailed design specifications
- Physical design models
- Operational models
- Program and module specifications
- Feature cases
- File layouts
- Database layouts
- Screens and screen prints for on-line systems
- Copies of reports or report layouts
- Test cases (features)

- User manuals and technical documentation
- Training materials
- System help

Types of Counts

As already identified, the first step in the function point counting process is to determine the type of function point count to be conducted. The three possible types of function point counts we listed earlier are described here.

1. **Development project function point counts** measure the functionality provided to end users with the first installation of the application. They include the functionality that will be counted in the initial application function point count, as well as any functionality required for data conversion. If we were replacing the Location Directory application discussed in the previous section with a newly developed application, we would count the functionality provided by the new application. We should, as well, count any conversion functionality required by the users to convert data that resided in the old data files to the new data files. A development project function point count must often be updated as development proceeds. These subsequent counts would not start from scratch, but they would validate previously identified functionality and attempt to capture added functionality, commonly called scope creep. Counts could occur during the following phases, whether the means of development was a waterfall approach (see Figure 6-2) or an iterative process—for example, rapid application development (RAD).

2. **Enhancement project function point counts** measure modifications to existing applications and include the combined functionality provided to

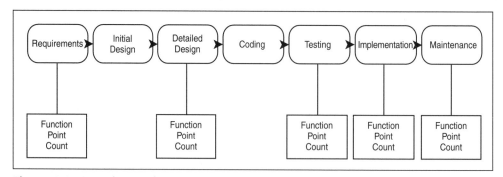

Figure 6-2 Counting during development

users by adding new functions, deleting old functions, and changing existing functions. Conversion functionality could also exist in an enhancement project. After an enhancement, the application function point count must be revised to reflect the appropriate changes in the application's functionality.

3. **Application function point counts** measure an installed application. They are also referred to as baseline or installed counts, and they evaluate the current functionality provided to end users by the application. An activity's total installed application function point count represents the sum of the application counts for all installed applications currently being utilized and maintained.

Identifying the Counting Scope and the Application Boundary

The counting scope is determined by the purpose of the count. It identifies the systems, applications, or subsets of an application that will be sized. It could include functions that will be satisfied by the purchase of a package; it could include all applications that will be outsourced; it could be restricted to functions within an application that perform a specific purpose—for example, reports. The application boundary is the border between the application being measured and either external applications or the user domain.

IFPUG has defined specific rules for identifying boundaries:

- **The boundary is based on the user's view.** The user should be able to define the scope of the application and the business functionality in the user's language.
- **The boundary between related applications is based on separate business functionality rather than on technical considerations.** Several examples are appropriate. Microsoft Office currently consists of Word, Excel, PowerPoint, and Access; each is a separate application within the Microsoft Office suite. System Alpha consists of an online data entry process that is followed by a nightly batch file update process; System Alpha is a single application that includes both the online and the batch processes.
- **The initial boundary already established for an application is not influenced by the counting scope.** The application boundary for an application being enhanced remains as it was, except, of course, that added functionality may expand the boundary and deleted functionality may reduce the boundary. An enhancement does not become its own application boundary, but is defined by the counting scope. Development projects and enhancement projects often include more than a single application. In these cases, the multiple

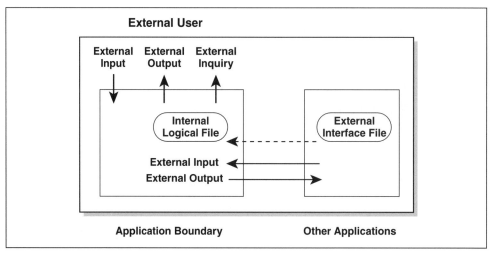

Figure 6-3 Functionality recognized in function point counting

application boundaries are identified within the counting scope, but they are counted separately. Function point counting is often depicted by a version of the graphic shown in Figure 6-3.

A great deal of confusion exists in the function point user world relating to the definition of boundaries used in the sizing of applications. It is extremely important that all facets of function point counting be accomplished consistently. However, function point counting has little benefit if the counting is consistent but incorrect—especially when application boundaries are being identified. Boundaries most definitely should not be established at the software program or software module level. Function points appear to be relevant only at a higher application level.

It is also possible to count at a level too high. For example, an accounting system might consist of several unique and separate applications (e.g., Accounts Receivable, General Ledger, and Accounts Payable), which may have internal relationships (see Figure 6-4). Each of these applications should be counted separately.

Likewise, a plant production system could consist of many subordinate but independent applications (e.g., Shop Planner, Material Inventory, Work Schedule) that are separately developed, maintained, and utilized and that may have internal relationships (see Figure 6-5).

IFPUG has published additional definitions and hints to be utilized in identifying boundaries. We will address the types of counts and boundaries in the following chapters, as well as in the case studies presented in Chapters 11, 13, and 14.

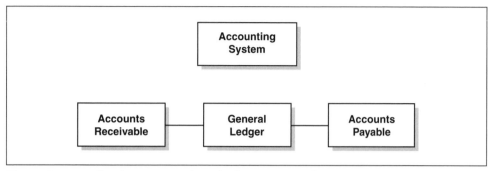

Figure 6-4 Application boundaries within an accounting system

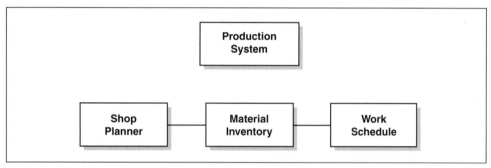

Figure 6-5 Application boundaries within a production system

Summary

Function point analysis provides a well-defined, internationally accepted process for sizing software. This chapter introduced

- The process for counting function points
- The three different types of function point counts (development project counts, enhancement project counts, and application counts)
- The application boundary (the border between the application being measured and either external applications or the user domain)
- The counting scope (the functionality being sized at a particular time for a specific purpose)

The next chapter will introduce the rules for counting data functions (ILFs and EIFs).

CHAPTER SEVEN

Sizing Data Functions

Introduction

Data functions relate to logical data stored and available for update, reference, and retrieval. Data functions are identified as either internal logical files (ILFs) or external interface files (EIFs). Both are user-identifiable groups of logically related data or control information. As such they are logical groupings and not physical representations of those groupings of data. It is possible, but very unlikely, that the logical will match the physical; consequently, ILFs and EIFs should be counted in an identical manner regardless of how the database is physically implemented.

An application should be identified with the same number of ILFs and EIFs whether the physical file structure is constructed with flat files, an IDMS database, an IMS database, a relational database, DB2 tables, or objects; however, the delivery and maintenance requirements and the productivity rates will be different. ILFs are maintained within the boundary of the application being counted, but EIFs can only be read and/or referenced within the boundary of the application being counted. EIFs are maintained within a different application boundary. When experienced function point counters size an application in function points, the most difficult task they encounter is identifying the data functions.

This chapter will describe the International Function Point Users Group (IFPUG) definitions, rules, and guidelines for identifying both ILFs and EIFs. More detailed guidance and examples are contained within the IFPUG Counting Practices Manual. The previous chapter discussed the IFPUG process for counting function points, the types of counts, the counting scope, and the application boundaries or the software process being measured. The next three chapters will describe the transactional functions, the general system characteristics, and the calculations involved, respectively.

Data Functions

The total process used to size function points was presented in Chapter 6 and is repeated here. It can be summarized by the following seven steps:

1. Determine the type of function point count
2. Identify the counting scope and the application boundary
3. Identify all data functions (internal logical files and external interface files) and their complexity
4. Identify all transactional functions (external inputs, external outputs, and external inquiries) and their complexity
5. Determine the unadjusted function point count
6. Determine the value adjustment factor, which is based on the 14 general system characteristics
7. Calculate the adjusted function point count

Remember that the application boundary separates the application being measured from the user domain and/or other independent applications. The data functions relate to the logical data stored and available for update, reference, and retrieval. The transactional functions—external inputs (EIs), external outputs (EOs), and external inquiries (EQs)—perform the processes of update, retrieval, output, and so on (transactions you would expect to see in a process model).

Experienced function point practitioners typically attempt to count data functions first, for two reasons:

1. We must know which ILFs and EIFs are maintained and/or referenced by each transactional function in order to assign each its own complexity rating. As you'll see when we discuss the complexity ratings for all functions, each data and transactional function will be assigned a weight of low, average, or high on the basis of standard matrices.
2. By identifying the database files first, we can validate their original designations as ILFs or EIFs as we proceed to identify the transactional functions.

Remember from Chapter 6 that the Location Directory data, an internal logical file (ILF), was maintained within the boundary of the application (see Figure 6-1). The Employee data, an external interface file (EIF), was maintained within the boundary of the Personnel application and was used by the Location Directory application solely for reference data. Consequently, to be counted as an ILF, the logical grouping of data must be updated or maintained by at least one of the external inputs (EIs) within the application.

In addition, the ILF must be read or referenced by an EO, EQ, or another EI, or that capability must be planned. The ILF is almost always read or referenced in the application being counted, but it could be read or referenced within another application. To be counted as an EIF, some of the data from that logical grouping, though maintained elsewhere, must be read or referenced by at least one EI, EO, or EQ within the application being counted. Data is read or referenced for a variety of reasons—for example, to edit the data, to retrieve the data for display, or to retrieve the data to perform a calculation or comparison.

Internal Logical Files

An internal logical file (ILF) is a *user-identifiable* group of *logically related data* or *control information maintained* within the boundary of the application. The primary intent of an ILF is to hold data maintained through one or more *elementary processes* of the application being counted.

Each of the italicized terms in this definition is described here:

- **User-identifiable** refers to defined requirements for processes and or groups of data that are agreed on, and understood by, both user(s) and software developer(s). As an example, a checking account record might be required in a financial application.
- **Logically related** refers to the requirement that each group should fit logically together within the descriptions provided. An ILF should not be dependent on or attributive to another ILF in order to maintain its existence. Groups should be merged as necessary, particularly those that were created for performance or implementation reasons. ILFs are typically represented by entity types in second or third normal form. The data analysis equivalent to such high-level logical groupings is a singular named data store on a data flow diagram. As an example, an address table would probably belong to a higher level, such as a client file, a billing file, an inventory location file, or an employee file.

- **Data** refers to the collection of facts and/or figures maintained within the application. For example, check number, amount, date, payee, memo entry, and account number might be maintained in the checking account record for each check written.
- **Control information** is data used by the application to influence an elementary process (see below) of the application being counted. It specifies what, when, or how data is to be processed. In the case of ILFs, these data, rules, or parameters are stored and maintained within the application. For example, control data is maintained in Print Manager; edit data is maintained in order to reject improper or inappropriate input data; dates and times are maintained by the users to establish the sequence or timing of events; or certain thresholds are established to control an event such as setting the temperature on a thermostat to control the timing of heating or air-conditioning.
- **Maintained** refers to the fact that the data is modified through an elementary process (see below) of the application. The data or control data could be maintained through such transactions as add, bill, change, delete, delegate, evaluate, fail, grant, hold, populate, revise, update, and so on. An ILF may be maintained by and counted as an ILF within more than one application; however, an ILF is counted only once per application.
- An **elementary process** is the smallest unit of activity that is meaningful to the user. For example, an issue of stock in a warehouse might be decomposed into various subprocesses, such as create, read, update, and display, so that the issue would create an amount due, read a file to validate whether the individual had credit, and update the quantity of stock on hand. The issue is the elementary process, and it may update more than one ILF through the same transaction.

For the data or control information to be counted as an ILF, both of the following IFPUG counting rules must apply:

- The group of data or control information is logical and user identifiable.
- The group of data *is maintained through an elementary process within* the application boundary being counted.

Once a group of data has been identified as an ILF within an application, it cannot also be counted as an EIF within the same application, even if it is used for reference by other transactions, nor can it be counted as an EIF during an enhancement project for that application.

Some additional examples of ILFs follow. These are examples only; any group of data or control information must conform to the stated definition and rules in order to be counted as an ILF:

- Application transaction data such as inventory issue records, employee training records, payroll records, credit card transactions, product sales, customer calls, or accounts payable
- Application security or password data maintained within the application
- Help data maintained within the application
- Edit data maintained within the application
- Parameter data maintained within the application
- Error files and their descriptions maintained within the application

The following examples of files have frequently been erroneously identified as ILFs. Be sure *not* to count them as ILFs:

- Temporary files or various iterations of the same file; these are not counted within function point analysis (FPA).
- Work files; these are not counted within FPA.
- Sort files; these are not counted within FPA.
- Extract files, or view files, which contain data extracted from other ILFs or EIFs prior to display or print; these are not counted within FPA, but they are recognized as part of the processing necessary to produce the EO or EQ.
- Files introduced because of technology; these are not counted within FPA.
- Copies of the same file; a file arranged or sorted differently or maintained in additional locations is not counted separately.
- Alternative indices, joins, relationships, or connections, unless they contain separately maintained non-key attributes.
- Audit or historical data; this should be counted together with the application transaction data.
- Files maintained by other applications and read or referenced only; these should be counted as EIFs.
- Backup data such as that used for corporate backup and recovery; this capability is recognized within the general system characteristics only.
- Suspense files containing incomplete transactions, unless they are separately maintained.

External Interface Files

> **An external interface file (EIF) is a *user-identifiable* group of *logically related data* or *control information* referenced by the application but *maintained* within the boundary of a different application. The primary intent of an EIF is to hold data referenced through one or more *elementary processes* within the boundary of the application counted. An EIF counted for an application must be in an ILF in another application.**

Each of the italicized terms in this definition is described here. The definitions are very similar to those provided in the previous section for ILFs:

- **User-identifiable** refers to defined requirements for processes and or groups of data that are agreed on, and understood by, both user(s) and software developer(s). As an example, a checking account record might be used for validation in an application, which reads the data only while validating an unrelated transaction.

- **Logically related** refers to the requirement that each group should fit logically together within the descriptions provided. An EIF should not be dependent on or attributive to another EIF in order to maintain its existence. Groups should be merged as necessary, particularly those that were created for performance or implementation reasons. EIFs are typically represented by entity types in second or third normal form. The data analysis equivalent to such high-level logical groupings is a singular named data store on a data flow diagram. As an example, an address table would probably belong to a higher level, such as a client file, a billing file, an inventory location file, or an employee file.

- **Data** refers to the collection of facts and/or figures maintained within another application. For example, check number, amount, date, payee, memo entry, and account number might be maintained in the checking account record for each check written.

- **Control information** is data used by the application to influence an elementary process (see below) of the application being counted. It specifies what, when, or how data is to be processed. In the case of EIFs, these data, rules, or parameters are stored and maintained within a different application. For example, control data is maintained in Print Manager and read by Power-Point; edit data is referenced from another application in order to reject improper or inappropriate input data; dates and times are maintained by the users in one application so that they can be read or referenced within many different applications to establish the sequence or timing of events; or certain thresholds are established to control an event in a different application, such as setting the temperature on a thermostat, which is then read by separate heating or air-conditioning systems.

- **Maintained** refers to the fact that the data is modified through an elementary process (see below) of another application.
- An **elementary process** is the smallest unit of activity that is meaningful to the user. For example, a screen display of stock in a warehouse might be decomposed into various subprocesses, so that one file would be read to determine the quantity of stock on hand and a separate file would be read to determine descriptions of the items. The issue is the elementary process, and it may read more than one EIF through the same transaction.

The data or control data could be maintained through such transactions as add, bill, change, delete, delegate, evaluate, fail, grant, hold, populate, revise, update, and so on. An EIF may be referenced by and counted as an EIF within more than one application; however, an EIF is counted only once per application.

For the data or control information to be counted as an EIF, all of the following IFPUG counting rules must apply:

- **The group of data or control information is logical and user identifiable.**
- **The group of data is referenced by, and external to, the application being counted.**
- **The group of data *is not maintained by* the application being counted.**
- **The group of data is maintained in an ILF of another application.**

Once a group of data has been identified as an EIF within an application, the EIF cannot be counted again within the same application, even if it is used for reference by other transactions or contains different data from the same file.

Some common examples of EIFs follow. These are examples only; any group of data or control information must meet the stated definition and rules in order to be counted as an EIF:

- Application data extracted and read from other applications
- Application security or password data maintained outside the application
- Help data maintained outside the application
- Edit data maintained outside the application
- Parameter data maintained outside the application
- Error files and their descriptions maintained outside the application

The following examples of files have frequently been erroneously identified as EIFs. Be sure *not* to count them as EIFs:

- Data received from another application that maintains one or more ILFs within the application being counted; this is considered transactional data and should be counted as an EI.
- Data that is maintained by the application being counted but accessed and used by a different application; it is counted as an EIF to the accessing application.
- Data formatted and sent by the application being counted to other applications; it should be counted as an EO or EQ.
- Temporary files or various iterations of the same file; these are not counted within FPA.
- Work files; these are not counted within FPA.
- Sort files; these are not counted within FPA.
- Extract files, or view files, that contain data extracted from previously counted EIFs prior to display or print; these are not counted within FPA, but they are recognized as part of the processing necessary to produce the external output or external inquiry.
- Files introduced because of technology; these are not counted within FPA.
- Alternative indices, joins, relationships, or connections, unless they contain separately maintained non-key attributes.
- Audit or historical data, which should be counted together with the application transaction data.

Complexity and Contribution: ILFs and EIFs

The physical count of ILFs and EIFs, together with the relative functional complexity for each, determines the contribution of the data function types to the unadjusted function point count. Each identified ILF and EIF must be assigned a *functional complexity* based on the number of *data element types (DETs)* and *record element types (RETs)* associated with the ILF or EIF.

Each of the italicized terms in this definition is described here:

- **Functional complexity** is the rating assigned to each data function. Possible scores of low, average, and high are assigned according to a complexity matrix, which considers the number of DETs and RETs.
- **Data element types (DETs)** are unique user-recognizable, nonrepeated fields or attributes.

- **Record element types (RETs)** are user-recognizable subgroups (optional or mandatory) of data elements contained within an ILF or EIF. Subgroups are typically represented in an entity relationship diagram as entity subtypes or attributive entities, commonly called parent-child relationships. (The user has the option of using one or none of the optional subgroups during an elementary process that adds or creates an instance of the data; the user must use at least one of the mandatory subgroups.)

The following IFPUG rules apply to the counting of data elements, fields, or attributes (termed DETs by IFPUG) for ILFs and EIFs:

- **Count a DET for each unique user-recognizable, nonrepeated field maintained in or retrieved from an ILF or EIF.** For example, check number, amount, date, payee, memo entry, and account number, maintained in the checking account record, would each count as one DET, regardless of the number of checks written with unique data for each and regardless of how the data is physically stored.
- **When two or more applications maintain and/or reference the same ILF or EIF but separate DETs, count only the DETs being used by each application to size the ILF or EIF.** For example, an ILF that is updated by two applications (A and B) and referenced by a third (C) would count the DETs uniquely, as shown in Table 7-1. Consequently, A would be counted with 8 DETs, B with 7 DETs, and C with 2 DETs.
- **Count a DET for each piece of data required by the user to establish a relationship with another ILF or EIF.** This type of DET is commonly referred to as a foreign key. For example, a relationship that exists to another ILF or EIF requires a key with the part number and manufacturer code; the part number and manufacturer code would be counted as two DETs unless, of course, either or both had been previously counted.

Fields that appear more than once in an ILF or EIF because of technology or implementation technique, such as the key just mentioned, are counted only once in that ILF or EIF. However, a field may be a DET to many ILFs and/or EIFs.

Repeating fields that are identical in format and exist to allow for multiple occurrences of a data value are counted only once in that ILF or EIF. For example, an ILF containing 12 monthly amount fields and an annual total would be credited with two DETs—one for the repetitive monthly amounts and one to identify the total; one additional DET would undoubtedly be provided to identify the month.

Table 7-1: Counting Example

DET	DET Usage	DETs Counted
Part number	Primary key to A, B, and C	DET to A, B, and C
Part name	Maintained by A Referenced by B and C	DET to A DET to B and C
Weekly usage	Maintained by B	DET to B
Department using	Maintained by B	DET to B
Purchase price	Maintained by A Referenced by B	DET to A DET to B
Supplier name	Maintained by A Referenced by B	DET to A DET to B
Supplier street address	Maintained by A	DET to A
Supplier city	Maintained by A	DET to A
Supplier state	Maintained by A	DET to A
Supplier postal code	Maintained by A	DET to A
Supplier total address, read as one block of data	Referenced by B	1 DET to B

Audit data, which includes before and after images of 15 distinct fields, is counted as two DETs—one for the before image and one for the after image.

Time stamps that record the time that an event (update) occurred as required by the user are counted as a DET.

Calculations that occur internally during the processing of an external input (EI) and are stored in the database are counted as a DET on the ILF.

The following IFPUG rules apply to the counting of record element types or subgroups of data elements (termed RETs by IFPUG) within an ILF or EIF:

• **Count a RET for each optional or mandatory subgroup of the ILF or EIF.**
Do not count any RETs that exist because of the technology or methodology

utilized—for example, headers, trailers, or separate text files. Two subgroups or more often belong to the same logical file (ILF or EIF). These RETs can also be identified by the existence of secondary keys used for storing data and for creating relationships between the logical files. The data in a logical file is typically data in the third normal form. Examples of RETs will be provided in the counting example that follows.

- **If there are no subgroups, count the ILF or EIF as one RET.**

An Example of Counting ILFs and EIFs

The following example of an employee application will be utilized in this chapter to count data functions and in the next chapter to count transactional functions. The user requirements for this example include the following:

- The ability to maintain, inquire on, and report employee information. The report will include location data for specific employees obtained from a file maintained by another application.
- The ability to maintain, inquire on, and report on information about jobs, including the job description.
- The ability to maintain, inquire on, and report on job assignments for employees.
- The ability to inquire and report on different locations within the company, including a list of employees at a particular location. The location data is read only and is maintained by another application.

A process model for this example might appear as follows:

EMPLOYEE-MAINTENANCE
    CREATE-EMPLOYEE
    EMPLOYEE-INQUIRY
    UPDATE-EMPLOYEE
    DELETE-EMPLOYEE
    EMPLOYEE-REPORT

JOB-MAINTENANCE
    CREATE-JOB
    JOB-INQUIRY
    UPDATE-JOB
    DELETE-JOB
    JOB-REPORT

JOB-ASSIGNMENT-MAINTENANCE
   ASSIGN-EMPLOYEE-TO-JOB
   JOB-ASSIGNMENT-INQUIRY
   TRANSFER-EMPLOYEE
   EVALUATE-EMPLOYEE
   DELETE-ASSIGNMENT
   JOB-ASSIGNMENT-REPORT

LOCATION-REPORTING
   LOCATION-INQUIRY
   LOCATION-REPORT

An entity relationship (ER) diagram might depict the requirements as in Figure 7-1.

Note that various database structures could be utilized. This is not a book on databases, so forgive any author interpretation or misinterpretation. Neither is it necessary to understand database methodology in order to count function points. A relational database structure is provided in Figure 7-2 as a tool to those who understand database methodologies.

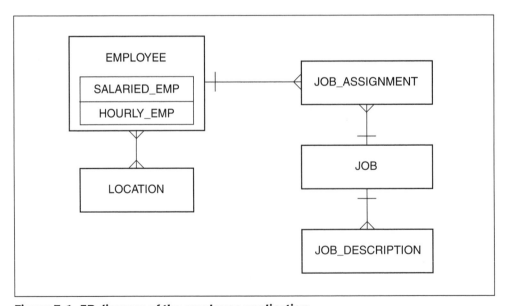

Figure 7-1 ER diagram of the employee application

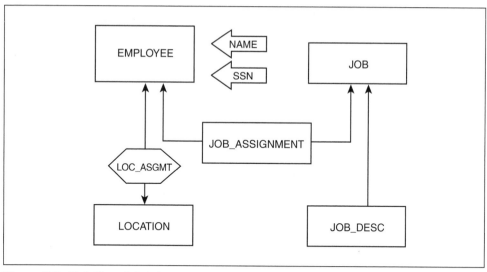

Figure 7-2 Relational database structure of the employee application

The fields contained in each of the entity types are as follows:

EMPLOYEE entity type
Employee_Name
Social_Security_Number
Nbr_Dependents
Type_Code (Salaried or Hourly)
Location_Name (Foreign Key)

SALARIED_EMPLOYEE entity subtype
Supervisory_Level

HOURLY_EMPLOYEE entity subtype
Standard_Hourly_Rate
Collective_Bargaining_Unit_Number

JOB entity type
Job_Name
Job_Number
Pay_Grade

JOB_DESCRIPTION entity type (entity type for implementation process
only, not a subgroup to users)

Job_Number (Foreign Key)
Line_Number (implementation process only; not significant to users)
Description_Line

JOB_ASSIGNMENT entity type
Effective_Date
Salary
Performance_Rating
Job_Number (Foreign Key)
Employee_SSN (Foreign Key)

LOCATION entity type
Location_Name
Address
Interoffice_Code

We will use the same model as we review the rules for transactional functions. We recommend that you review the list of fields and try to categorize the ILFs and EIFs with their DETs and RETs. The complexity matrix for ILFs and EIFs is presented in Figure 7-3.

Now let's look at the answer to the categorization problem posed in the preceding paragraph. If you followed all of the guidelines, you probably had more detail than you would ever have in counting one of your own applications. Maybe there was too much! In our view, however, you should have counted the following:

- EMPLOYEE as an ILF with 8 DETs and 2 RETs
- JOB as an ILF with 4 DETs and 1 RET

		Data Element Types		
		1–19	20–50	≥51
Record Element Types	1	Low	Low	Average
	2–5	Low	Average	High
	>5	Average	High	High

Figure 7-3 Complexity matrix for ILFs and EIFs

- JOB_ASSIGNMENT as an ILF with 5 DETs and 1 RET
- LOCATION as an EIF with 3 DETs and 1 RET

Let's review how we arrived at these answers:

EMPLOYEE entity type	A maintained ILF; not counted as a separate RET because there are subgroups
Employee_Name	DET 1
Social_Security_Number	DET 2
Nbr_Dependents	DET 3
Type_Code (Salaried or Hourly)	DET 4
Location_Name (Foreign Key)	DET 5
SALARIED_EMPLOYEE entity subtype	RET 1 under EMPLOYEE
Supervisory_Level	DET 6
HOURLY_EMPLOYEE entity subtype	RET 2 under EMPLOYEE
Standard_Hourly_Rate	DET 7
Collective_Bargaining_Unit_Number	DET 8
JOB entity type	A maintained ILF with 1 RET
Job_Name	DET 1
Job_Number	DET 2
Pay_Grade	DET 3
JOB_DESCRIPTION entity type	Exists for technological reasons only; part of JOB
Job_Number (Foreign Key)	Previously counted as DET 2
Line_Number	Exists for technological reasons only in our example
Description_Line	DET 4
JOB_ASSIGNMENT entity type	A maintained ILF with 1 RET; separately maintained with its own attributes
Effective_Date	DET 1
Salary	DET 2
Performance_Rating	DET 3
Job_Number (Foreign Key)	DET 4

Employee_SSN (Foreign Key)	DET 5
LOCATION entity type	A referenced EIF with 1 RET
Location_Name	DET 1
Address	DET 2
Interoffice_Code	DET 3

We end up with three low-complexity ILFs and one low-complexity EIF on the basis of the complexity matrix for ILFs and EIFs (see Figure 7-3). Most of our actual files will be much larger, and we will have some average- and high-complexity files as well. So what does all of this mean in terms of function points? Data transactions receive the highest weights or values when compared to transactional functions. Table 7-2 is the IFPUG unadjusted function point table. We count 7 unadjusted function points for each of the 3 low-complexity ILFs, for a total of 21, and 5 unadjusted function points for the low-complexity EIF.

Table 7-2: IFPUG's Unadjusted Function Point Table

	Function Levels		
Components	Low	Average	High
ILF	× 7	× 10	× 15
EIF	× 5	× 7	× 10
EI	× 3	× 4	× 6
EO	× 4	× 5	× 7
EQ	× 3	× 4	× 6

Note: Apply application characteristics adjustment (0.65 – 1.35) to calculate adjusted function points.

Summary

This chapter introduced the rules for recognizing internal logical files (ILFs) and external interface files (EIFs) from the database or memory requirements of our application. Examples of each were provided. An example in counting enabled the reader to distinguish ILFs and EIFs and assign unadjusted function point weights based on established IFPUG matrices, using data element types (DETs) and record element types (RETs).

The following chapter will cover transactional functions—that is, external inputs (EIs), external outputs (EOs), and external inquiries (EQs). Chapter 9 will describe the application characteristics adjustment (step 6 in the process of sizing function points).

We will provide many additional practical exercises later in the book to assist you in applying the IFPUG rules in counting data functions (ILFs and EIFs) as well as transactional functions (EIs, EOs, and EQs). The IFPUG Counting Practices Manual should also be consulted for the latest guidance on counting standards. In this book we use the rules contained in release 4.1 of that manual.

CHAPTER EIGHT

Sizing Transactional Functions

Introduction

Information systems are usually developed to mechanize manual tasks; these tasks are expected to be accomplished more economically and effectively if they are automated. The tasks that have been mechanized are identified as transactional functions, which represent the functionality provided to the user for the processing of data by an application.

Suppose we are running a home business selling business cards. We currently process everything on a manual basis. We keep a file folder of descriptions for each business card; we add cards to that file folder, change descriptions when appropriate, and delete items from the folder when they are no longer available. When a customer calls and asks for the description of a card, we retrieve it from the folder. Of course, we have other file folders as well; some may contain inventory data, others sales data, and still others customer data. We produce a report at the end of the month that totals our sales for the month. Using the data function terminology we learned in Chapter 7, we identify file folders that are available for update and retrieval as internal logical files (ILFs), and file folders maintained elsewhere, which might contain supplier addresses, as external interface files (EIFs).

This chapter will describe the International Function Point User Group (IFPUG) definitions, rules, and guidelines for identifying transactional functions. They include the functions described here of adding business cards to the internal logical file, changing descriptions, deleting items, retrieving and displaying the description of a card, and producing a report at the end of the month. These transactional functions are separated into three different types:

1. External inputs (EIs) process incoming data (to maintain ILFs) or control information (to alter the behavior of the system). Examples include adding, changing, and deleting descriptions in our hypothetical file folder.
2. External inquiries (EQs) send data outside the application through retrievals of data or control information from ILFs and/or EIFs. An example would be the retrieval and display of a current description from our file folder.
3. External outputs (EOs) send data outside the application with processing logic other than, or in addition to, retrieval of data or control information. An example would be the report of monthly sales with calculations by category.

More detailed guidance and examples are contained within the IFPUG Counting Practices Manual. In the book you have in hand, Chapters 9 and 10, respectively, will describe the general system characteristics and the calculations involved in finalizing an adjusted function point count.

Transactional Functions

The total process used to size function points was introduced in Chapter 6 and is repeated here. It can be summarized by the following seven steps:

1. Determine the type of function point count
2. Identify the counting scope and the application boundary
3. Identify all data functions (internal logical files and external interface files) and their complexity
4. Identify all transactional functions (external inputs, external outputs, and external inquiries) and their complexity
5. Determine the unadjusted function point count
6. Determine the value adjustment factor, which is based on the 14 general system characteristics
7. Calculate the adjusted function point count

Remember that the application boundary separates the application being measured from the user domain and/or other independent applications. The data functions relate to the logical data stored and available for update, reference, and retrieval. The transactional functions—external inputs (EIs), external outputs

(EOs), and external inquiries (EQs)—perform the processes of update, retrieval, output, and so on (transactions you would expect to see in a process model). Each has its own unadjusted function point weight based on its unique complexity matrix.

In the discussion that follows, external inputs will be the first transaction type covered, followed by external outputs and external inquiries, respectively.

External Inputs

An external input (EI) is an *elementary process* of the application that processes *data* or *control information* that enters from outside the boundary of the application. Processed data *maintains* one or more ILFs; processed control information may or may not maintain an ILF. The primary intent of an EI is to maintain one or more ILFs and/or to alter the behavior of the application through its *processing logic*.

Each of the italicized terms in this definition is described here:

- An **elementary process** is the smallest unit of activity that is meaningful to the user. This process must be self-contained and leave the business of the application being counted in a consistent state. For example, an input form for employee benefits could consist of three screens; if the form were incomplete until all three screens were completed, the elementary process would require the completion of all three screens. We would not question this decision if the form were to be completed manually; we would just hand it back to the individual and request that the entire form be completed. Completing some of the fields, even those on one screen, would neither be self-contained nor leave the business in a consistent state. If all information, recognizing that some of the fields may not be mandatory and could be left blank, were completed, this transaction would be complete and the business would be left in a consistent state.
- **Data** refers to the collection of facts and/or figures processed by the input transaction. For example, data would be the data fields included in the employee benefits transaction described above. We might expect to see employee name, selection of beneficiary, agreement (Y/N) to participate in 401K, percentage of contribution, and so on.
- **Control information** is data used by the application to influence an elementary process of the application being counted; in the case of EIs, these data,

rules, or parameters may be saved or stored, or they may be used solely to maintain or initiate a process without being saved or stored after the process is complete. For example, control data is used to maintain system defaults. Control information is used by the application to ensure compliance with business function requirements specified by the user. It could include other features, such as zoom in or out, and in real-time systems it could include incoming signals from an alarm, an instrument, a sensor, or another application.

- **Maintains** refers to the ability to modify data through an elementary process. Count one EI for each separate data maintenance activity—for example, add, change, delete, populate, revise, update, assign, save as, and create. There is practically no limit to the number of different verbs that might be chosen to maintain data. Remember, however, that a transaction must be an elementary process; be cautious not to count the changing, deleting, or saving of lines, terms, or screens, which do not constitute the total process.
- **Processing logic** includes those requirements specifically requested by a user to complete an elementary process. Usually a combination of processing logic is required to complete an elementary process. Processing logic on its own should not be used to determine unique EIs, EOs, or EQs. One external input's elementary process could include multiple validations, filters, re-sorts, and so on. Re-sorting, as an example, does not determine the uniqueness of a transaction; that is, the capability to re-sort does not equate to additional transactions.

Processing logic for an EI might include

- Validations
- Mathematical formulas or calculations
- Conversions of equivalent values
- Filtering and selecting of data by the use of specified criteria to compare multiple sets of data
- Analysis of conditions to determine which is applicable
- Update of ILFs (it is mandatory for an EI to maintain one or more ILFs or to alter the behavior of the system)
- Referencing of ILFs or EIFs
- Retrieval of data or control information
- Creation of derived data
- Alteration of the behavior of the system (it is mandatory for an EI to maintain one or more ILFs or to alter the behavior of the system)
- Preparation and presentation of information outside the boundary

- Capability to accept data or control information that enters the application boundary (mandatory for an EI)
- Re-sorting or rearranging of a set of data

Separate sets of IFPUG rules are applied to EI data transactions and EI control information.

For the *data* being processed to be counted as an EI, all of the following IFPUG counting rules must apply:

- The data must be received from outside the application boundary.
- The data in at least one ILF must be maintained through an elementary process of the application.
- The process must be the smallest unit of activity that is meaningful to the user (elementary process rule).
- The process must be self-contained and leave the business of the application being counted in a consistent state (elementary process rule).
- For the identified process, one of the three following rules must apply:

  1. Processing logic must be unique or different from the processing logic performed by other external inputs within the application.
  2. The set of data elements identified is different from the sets identified for other external inputs in the application.
  3. The ILFs or EIFs referenced are different from those referenced by other external inputs in the application.

For the *control information* being processed to be counted as an EI, all of the following IFPUG counting rules must apply:

- The control information must be received from outside the application boundary.
- The control information must be specified by the user to ensure compliance with the business function requirements of the application.
- The process must be the smallest unit of activity that is meaningful to the user (elementary process rule).
- The process must be self-contained and leave the business of the application being counted in a consistent state (elementary process rule).
- For the identified process, one of the three following rules must apply:

  1. Processing logic must be unique or different from the processing logic performed by other external inputs within the application.

2. **The set of data elements identified is different from the sets identified for other external inputs in the application.**
3. **The ILFs or EIFs referenced are different from those referenced by other external inputs in the application.**

The processed control information may or may not maintain an ILF.

Some additional examples of EIs follow. These are examples only; any data or control information listed here must conform to the stated definition and rules in order to be counted as an EI:

- Transactional data used to maintain an ILF, such as a sale, a lost item, a scheduled appointment, a transfer, a new hire, or an insurance form.
- Input that provides control information, such as an earthquake sensor reporting earth movement.
- Messages from other applications that require processing.
- Transaction files from other applications; these may include multiple transactions of a different type that require separate and unique processing—for example, cash sales and credit card transactions, in which case there would be multiple EIs.
- Inputs that maintain an ILF.
- User functions that either initiate control or enter data.
- File of data maintained in a prior application that must be processed through a conversion effort into a newly developed ILF when data is being migrated as part of a development or enhancement project; this would be included as part of the project count but not the application count.
- Physical data that initiates processing, such as the temperature.
- Maintenance of any ILF, including help, any message file, parameters, and so on.

The following examples have frequently been misidentified as EIs. Be sure *not* to count them as EIs:

- Reference data that is read by the application from data stored in another application but is not used to maintain an ILF in the counted application; this is typically recognized as an EIF.
- The input request side of either an inquiry or an output.
- Menu screens that are used for navigation or selection and that do not maintain an ILF.
- Log-on screens that facilitate user entry into an application.

- Multiple methods of invoking the same logic; for example, two action keys that perform the same function or the same transaction on multiple screens should be counted only once.
- Pointing and clicking of data on a screen in order to fill field(s) or to move data.
- Refreshing or canceling of screen data.
- Responses to messages that request a user to confirm a delete or any other transaction.
- Data passed between online and batch within the same application; it doesn't cross the application boundary.
- Data passed between client and server within the same application; it doesn't cross the application boundary.

Complexity and Contribution: EIs

The physical count of EIs, together with the relative functional complexity for each, determines the contribution of the external inputs to the unadjusted function point count. Each identified EI must be assigned a *functional complexity* **based on the number of** *data element types (DETs)* **and** *file types referenced (FTRs)* **associated with the EI.**

Each of the italicized terms in this definition is described here:

- **Functional complexity** is the rating assigned to each transactional function. Possible scores of low, average, and high are assigned according to a complexity matrix that considers the number of DETs and FTRs.
- **Data element types (DETs)** are usually unique user-recognizable, nonrepeated fields or attributes, including foreign key attributes, that cross the boundary of the application. Some other specific characteristics of a transaction's elementary process, to be discussed under rules below, are also counted as DETs.
- **File types referenced (FTRs),** or more simply files referenced, refers to the total number of ILFs maintained or read and of EIFs read by the EI transaction.

The following IFPUG rules apply to the counting of data elements, fields, or attributes (termed DETs by IFPUG) for EIs:

- **Count a DET for each unique user-recognizable, nonrepeated field or attribute, including foreign key attributes, that crosses (either enters or exits) the boundary of the application in order to complete the elementary**

process of the EI. Typically, such fields or attributes maintain an ILF. For example, item number, quantity sold, and date will each count as a DET on a sale transaction, regardless of how the data is physically stored.

- *Do not* **count a DET for a field that is not entered by the user (does not cross the boundary), but through an EI is retrieved or derived by the application and maintained on an ILF.** A system-generated date, a retrieved value, an account number, and a calculated value would be examples.
- **Count one DET for a logical field that is stored physically as multiple fields but is required by the user as a single piece of information, such as lines of an address.**
- **Count one DET for the capability to send a system response message outside the application boundary to indicate that an error occurred during processing, confirm that processing is complete, or verify that processing should continue.** Even though there are multiple message possibilities, count only one DET for the elementary process. That is, count only one DET total for messages, even though there are multiple error, verification, and confirmation messages.
- **Count one DET for the capability to specify the action to be taken by the EI even if there are multiple methods for invoking the same logical process.** Count as one DET command lines or function/action (PF) keys that provide the capability to specify the action to be taken by the EI. Count this as one DET per EI. Do not count a DET for each command line and function/action (PF) key.

The following IFPUG rules apply to the counting of file types referenced (termed FTRs by IFPUG) for EIs:

- **Count a file type referenced for each ILF maintained by the elementary process of the EI.**
- **Count a file type referenced for each internal logical file (ILF) or external interface file (EIF) read during the processing of the EI.**
- **Count only one FTR for each ILF that is both maintained and read by the EI.**

An Example of Counting EIs

The user requirements for the employee application discussed in Chapter 7 include the following:

- The ability to maintain, inquire on, and report employee information. The report will include location data for specific employees obtained from a file maintained by another application.
- The ability to maintain, inquire on, and report on information about jobs. The user considers job description to be a collection of 80-character lines that describe the job; this information is not maintained independently from the job.
- The ability to maintain, inquire on, and report on job assignments for employees.
- The ability to inquire and report on different locations within the company, including a list of employees at a particular location. The location data is read only and is maintained by another application.

A process model for this example might appear as follows:

EMPLOYEE-MAINTENANCE
   CREATE-EMPLOYEE
   EMPLOYEE-INQUIRY
   UPDATE-EMPLOYEE
   DELETE-EMPLOYEE
   EMPLOYEE-REPORT

JOB-MAINTENANCE
   CREATE-JOB
   JOB-INQUIRY
   UPDATE-JOB
   DELETE-JOB
   JOB-REPORT

JOB-ASSIGNMENT-MAINTENANCE
   ASSIGN-EMPLOYEE-TO-JOB
   JOB-ASSIGNMENT-INQUIRY
   TRANSFER-EMPLOYEE
   EVALUATE-EMPLOYEE
   DELETE-ASSIGNMENT
   JOB-ASSIGNMENT-REPORT

LOCATION-REPORTING
   LOCATION-INQUIRY
   LOCATION-REPORT

The ILFs and EIFs were counted as follows:

EMPLOYEE entity type	A maintained ILF; not counted as a separate RET because there are subgroups
Employee_Name	DET 1
Social_Security_Number	DET 2
Nbr_Dependents	DET 3
Type_Code (Salaried or Hourly)	DET 4
Location_Name (Foreign Key)	DET 5
SALARIED_EMPLOYEE entity subtype	RET 1 under EMPLOYEE
Supervisory_Level	DET 6
HOURLY_EMPLOYEE entity subtype	RET 2 under EMPLOYEE
Standard_Hourly_Rate	DET 7
Collective_Bargaining_Unit_Number	DET 8
JOB entity type	A maintained ILF with 1 RET
Job_Name	DET 1
Job_Number	DET 2
Pay_Grade	DET 3
JOB_DESCRIPTION entity type	Exists for technological reasons only; part of JOB
Job_Number (Foreign Key)	Previously counted as DET 2
Line_Number	Exists for technological reasons only in our example
Description_Line	DET 4
JOB_ASSIGNMENT entity type	A maintained ILF with 1 RET; separately maintained with its own attributes
Effective_Date	DET 1
Salary	DET 2
Performance_Rating	DET 3
Job_Number (Foreign Key)	DET 4
Employee_SSN (Foreign Key)	DET 5

LOCATION entity type	A referenced EIF with 1 RET
Location_Name	DET 1
Address	DET 2
Interoffice_Code	DET 3

We end up with three low-complexity ILFs and one low-complexity EIF on the basis of the complexity matrix for ILFs and EIFs (see Figure 7-3).

We recommend that you review what we've discussed here and try to identify the EIs with their DETs and FTRs. The complexity matrix for EIs is presented in Figure 8-1.

If you correctly identified only the EIs above, you would have come up with 10. We really don't have enough data to count the DETs and FTRs, but we can estimate if we make a few assumptions. Let's assume (even though doing so can get us into trouble) that each input transaction returns error messages (we count a DET for each EI for the error messages) and that each has at least one command key (we count another DET for each EI). Let's also assume that our create and update functions access all fields for the specific ILF that is being created or updated, but the delete functions touch only the primary key field(s) to that ILF. The assign and transfer functions should not touch the performance rating field, and the evaluate function should not touch the salary field. Remember the extra two DETs for each transaction.

For our FTRs, we must count the ILF being maintained and any other ILF or EIF, which we must reference for edit purposes. For example, we must reference LOCATION when we enter the LOCATION field upon creating an employee, so we have two FTRs when we create an employee: EMPLOYEE and LOCATION.

		Data Element Types		
		1–4	5–15	≥16
File Types Referenced	<2	Low	Low	Average
	2	Low	Average	High
	>2	Average	High	High

Figure 8-1 Complexity matrix for EIs

When we delete an employee, we maintain EMPLOYEE and reference or update JOB_ASSIGNMENT:

EMPLOYEE-MAINTENANCE
    CREATE-EMPLOYEE   10 DETs and 2 FTRs, EMPLOYEE and LOCATION

    UPDATE-EMPLOYEE   10 DETs and 2 FTRs, EMPLOYEE and LOCATION

    DELETE_EMPLOYEE   3 DETs and 2 FTRs, EMPLOYEE and JOB_ASSIGNMENT (don't delete an employee with a job)

JOB-MAINTENANCE
    CREATE-JOB   6 DETs and 1 FTR, JOB
    UPDATE-JOB   6 DETs and 1 FTR, JOB
    DELETE-JOB   3 DETs and 2 FTRs, JOB and JOB_ASSIGNMENT (don't delete a job with an assigned employee)

JOB-ASSIGNMENT-MAINTENANCE
    ASSIGN-EMPLOYEE-TO-JOB   6 DETs and 3 FTRs, EMPLOYEE, JOB, and JOB_ASSIGNMENT
    TRANSFER-EMPLOYEE   6 DETs and 3 FTRs, EMPLOYEE, JOB, and JOB_ASSIGNMENT
    EVALUATE-EMPLOYEE   6 DETs and 1 FTR, JOB_ASSIGNMENT
    DELETE-ASSIGNMENT   4 DETs and 1 FTR, JOB_ASSIGNMENT

Calculating the complexities with this information, we would have six low-complexity EIs, two average-complexity EIs (create and update employee), and two high-complexity EIs (assign and transfer employee). EIs are highlighted in the IFPUG unadjusted function point table presented as Table 8-1.

Altogether the external inputs contribute 38 unadjusted function points.

Table 8-1: IFPUG's Unadjusted Function Point Table

	Function Levels		
Components	Low	Average	High
ILF	× 7	× 10	× 15
EIF	× 5	× 7	× 10
EI	× 3	× 4	× 6
EO	× 4	× 5	× 7
EQ	× 3	× 4	× 6

Note: Apply application characteristics adjustment (0.65 – 1.35) to calculate adjusted function points.

External Outputs

An external output (EO) is an *elementary process* of the application that generates *data* or *control information* that exits the boundary of the application. The primary intent of an external output is to present information to a user through *processing logic* other than, or in addition to, the retrieval of data or control information. The processing logic must contain at least one mathematical formula or calculation, create *derived data, maintain* one or more ILFs, and/or alter the behavior of the system.

Each of the italicized terms in this definition is described here:

- An **elementary process** is the smallest unit of activity that is meaningful to the user. This process must be self-contained and leave the business of the application being counted in a consistent state. For example, a report may consist of numerous pages, but if the pages are not independently required and produced, the report counts as only one EO. Producing some of the fields, even one page, would neither be self-contained nor leave the business in a consistent state. If all information, recognizing that some of the fields may not be filled and could be left null or blank, were completed, this transaction would be complete and the business would be left in a consistent state.
- **Data** refers to the collection of facts and/or figures processed by the output transaction. For example, data would be the data fields included in the report

transaction described above. We might expect to see fields such as department name, department number, address, month, total monthly sales, total monthly purchases, and current running total for the year.

- **Control information** is data used by the application to influence an elementary process of the application being counted; in the case of EOs, these data, rules, or parameters may be sent by the application to a user or to another application. For example, control information could be sent by the application to ensure compliance with business function requirements specified by the user. It could include messages to the user advising that certain internal controls have been set, such as an alarm, as a result of an elementary process to send data to a user. In real-time systems, it may include outgoing signals such as an alarm, a message, or shutdown of a manufacturing line.

- **Processing logic** includes those requirements specifically requested by a user to complete an elementary process. Usually a combination of processing logic is required to complete an elementary process. Processing logic on its own should not be used to determine unique EIs, EOs, or EQs. One external output's elementary process could include multiple validations, filters, re-sorts, and so on. Rearranging, reformatting, or re-sorting a set of data is not considered to be unique processing logic; however, there may be other unique processing logic during any of these operations. As an example, a report could sort totals by month, product, and department. If the report fields were the same (even if displayed in a different format), the totals were by column, and the processing calculations were not unique, we would count one EO. Multiple EOs would be counted if the totals were summarized differently and the calculations were unique for each different sort. Perhaps internal totals would represent totals of a product by month within a department, monthly totals of a department by division, and product sales by days of the month.

Processing logic for an EO might include

- Validations
- Mathematical formulas or calculations (one of the forms of processing logic that qualify an elementary process of presenting information to a user as an EO)
- Conversions of equivalent values
- Filtering and selecting of data by the use of specified criteria to compare multiple sets of data
- Analysis of conditions to determine which is applicable

- Update of ILFs (one of the forms of processing logic that qualify an elementary process of presenting information to a user as an EO)
- Referencing of ILFs or EIFs
- Retrieval of data or control information
- Creation of derived data (one of the forms of processing logic that qualify an elementary process of presenting information to a user as an EO)
- Alteration of the behavior of the system (one of the forms of processing logic that qualify an elementary process of presenting information to a user as an EO)
- Preparation and presentation of information outside the boundary (mandatory for an EO)
- Capability to accept data or control information that enters the application boundary
- Re-sorting or rearranging of a set of data

- **Derived data** requires processing, other than direct retrieval, conversion, and editing of information, from one or more ILFs and/or EIFs. Derived data is created by the transformation of existing data to create additional data. EOs frequently contain derived data.
- **Maintain** refers to the ability to modify data through an elementary process. For example, we might automatically enter a check number in an ILF during the process of generating payroll checks.

For the data or control information being processed to be counted as an EO, all of the following IFPUG counting rules must apply:

- **The data or control information must exit the application boundary.**
- **The processing logic of the elementary process of an EO must perform one of the following:**

  1. **Contain at least one mathematical formula or calculation**
  2. **Create derived data**
  3. **Maintain at least one ILF**
  4. **Alter the behavior of the application**

- **The process must be the smallest unit of activity that is meaningful to the user (elementary process rule).**
- **The process must be self-contained and leave the business of the application being counted in a consistent state (elementary process rule).**

- **For the identified process, one of the three following rules must apply:**

  1. **Processing logic must be unique or different from the processing logic performed by other external outputs within the application.**
  2. **The set of data elements identified is different from the sets identified for other external outputs in the application.** Note that these are different data elements and not different data in the same fields. For example, account statements produced for individuals that have different data in the same fields are counted as one EO. Two separately produced reports at the detail and summary levels would be counted as two EOs because of the unique processing logic and calculations.
  3. **The ILFs or EIFs referenced are different from those referenced by other external outputs in the application.**

Some additional examples of EOs follow. These are examples only; any data or control information listed here must conform to the stated definition and rules in order to be counted as an EO:

- Reports that require the use of algorithms or calculations—for example, monthly checking account statements or weekly sales reports.
- Data transfers, files, and/or messages sent to other applications when data is calculated or derived or an update occurs as part of the elementary process—for example, a file of transactions sent from the accounts receivable application to the separately maintained general ledger application when some totals are calculated or a database entry occurs within the accounts receivable application to indicate which transactions were sent (an EO to the accounts receivable application and one or more EIs to the general ledger application).
- A check that, when created, simultaneously updates the check record with the check number (this is one elementary process).
- A conversion report that reports the totals of the conversion effort when data is being migrated as part of a development or enhancement project; this would be included as part of the project count but not the application count.
- Derived or calculated information displayed on a screen or passed in a file.
- Graphical displays such as bar charts and pie charts, when they require calculations.
- Calculated responses returned by telephone.

- A calculated firing solution for a weapon, returned to the user or sent to another application within the weapon system.
- Notification that a credit card has been reported missing, with the calculated totals of current charges.
- Calculation of a proposed premium on an insurance policy.

The following examples have frequently been misidentified as EOs. Be sure *not* to count them as EOs:

- Identical reports with different data values, such as department reports.
- Reports that have no formulas, calculations, or derived data and that do not maintain an ILF within the application sending the data (most likely counted as EQs).
- Summary fields contained on a detail report (the detail report is the EO).
- Files sent to other applications that have no formulas, calculations, or derived data and that do not maintain an ILF within the application sending the data (most likely counted as EQs).
- Multiple media when the processing logic is not different.
- Refreshing or canceling of screen data (not counted).
- Re-sorting or rearrangement of a set of data without other processing logic.
- Reference data that is read by another application from data stored in the application being counted (the data is not processed as an EO by the counted application).
- Help (most likely counted as EQs).
- Log-off system.
- Multiple methods of invoking the same output process.
- Error messages that result from an edit or validation of an EI or the request side of an EO or EQ.
- Confirmation messages acknowledging that the data has been processed.
- Messages that request a user to confirm a delete or any other transaction.
- Identical data sent to more than one application.
- Ad hoc reports that the user directs and controls through the use of a language such as SQL or FOCUS.
- Data passed between online and batch within the same application; it doesn't cross the application boundary.
- Data passed between client and server within the same application; it doesn't cross the application boundary.

Complexity and Contribution: EOs

> The physical count of EOs, together with the relative functional complexity for each, determines the contribution of the external outputs to the unadjusted function point count. Each identified EO must be assigned a *functional complexity* based on the number of *data element types (DETs)* and *file types referenced (FTRs)* associated with the EO.
>
> Each of the italicized terms in this definition is described here:

- **Functional complexity** is the rating assigned to each transactional function. Possible scores of low, average, and high are assigned according to a complexity matrix that considers the number of DETs and FTRs.
- **Data element types (DETs)** are usually unique user-recognizable, nonrepeated fields or attributes that cross the boundary of the application. Some other specific characteristics of a transaction's elementary process, to be discussed under rules below, are also counted as DETs.
- **File types referenced (FTRs),** or more simply files referenced, refers to the total number of ILFs read or maintained and of EIFs read by the EO transaction.

> **The following IFPUG rules apply to the counting of data elements, fields, or attributes (termed DETs by IFPUG) for EOs:**

- **Count a DET for each user-recognizable, nonrepeated field that enters the application boundary and is required to specify what, when, and/or how data is to be retrieved and/or generated by the elementary process.** Such fields are often considered to be control information, selection information, or processing parameters.
- **Count a DET for each unique user-recognizable, nonrepeated field or attribute that exits the application boundary.** Included are foreign key attributes and control information.
- **If a DET both enters and exits the boundary, count it only once for the elementary process.**
- **Count one DET for the capability to send a system response message outside the application boundary to indicate that an error has occurred during processing, confirm that processing is complete, or verify that processing should continue.** Even though there are multiple message possibilities, count only one DET for the elementary process. That is, count only one DET total for messages, even though there are multiple error, verification, and confirmation messages.

- Count one DET for the capability to specify an action to be taken by the EO even if there are multiple methods or multiple keys required for invoking the same logical process—for example, OK button, function key, action keys (A, C, D, and so on), or mouse click.
- Do not count paging-variable or system-generated stamps, including page numbers, positioning information (row *x* of *y*), paging commands (previous, next, arrows), or date/time fields. DETs counted do include date fields retrieved, but not system-generated dates, such as when a report is printed.
- Do not count literals, including report titles, screen IDs, column headings, and field titles.
- Do not count fields that are maintained on an ILF during the elementary process of the external output if the fields do not cross the boundary.
- Count one DET for a logical field that is stored physically as multiple fields but is required by the user as a single piece of information. For example, a date or name stored as three fields but used as one field is counted as one DET. An address (street, city, and zip code) may be counted as one DET on an address label if it is considered to represent one group of data.
- Count one DET for each type of label and each type of numerical equivalent in a graphical display. For example, a pie chart might have two DETs, one for the category and one for the applicable percentage, even if the percentage is not labeled as such.
- Count one DET for text information that may consist of a single word, a sentence, a paragraph, or many paragraphs.

The following IFPUG rules apply to the counting of file types referenced (termed FTRs by IFPUG) for EOs:

- Count a file type referenced for each internal logical file (ILF) or external interface file (EIF) read during the processing of the EO.
- Count one FTR for each ILF maintained by the elementary process of the EO.
- Count only one FTR for an ILF that is both read and maintained by the EO.

An Example of Counting EOs

The user requirements for the employee application discussed in Chapter 7 include the following:

- The ability to maintain, inquire on, and report employee information. The report will include location data for specific employees obtained from a file maintained by another application.

- The ability to maintain, inquire on, and report on information about jobs. The user considers job description to be a collection of 80-character lines that describe the job; this information is not maintained independently from the job.
- The ability to maintain, inquire on, and report on job assignments for employees.
- The ability to inquire and report on different locations within the company, including a list of employees at a particular location. The location data is read only and is maintained by another application.

A process model for this example might appear as follows:

```
EMPLOYEE-MAINTENANCE
    CREATE-EMPLOYEE
    EMPLOYEE-INQUIRY
    UPDATE-EMPLOYEE
    DELETE-EMPLOYEE
    EMPLOYEE-REPORT

JOB-MAINTENANCE
    CREATE-JOB
    JOB-INQUIRY
    UPDATE-JOB
    DELETE-JOB
    JOB-REPORT

JOB-ASSIGNMENT-MAINTENANCE
    ASSIGN-EMPLOYEE-TO-JOB
    JOB-ASSIGNMENT-INQUIRY
    TRANSFER-EMPLOYEE
    EVALUATE-EMPLOYEE
    DELETE-ASSIGNMENT
    JOB-ASSIGNMENT-REPORT

LOCATION-REPORTING
    LOCATION-INQUIRY
    LOCATION-REPORT
```

The ILFs and EIFs were counted as follows:

EMPLOYEE entity type	A maintained ILF; not counted as a separate RET because there are subgroups
Employee_Name	DET 1
Social_Security_Number	DET 2
Nbr_Dependents	DET 3
Type_Code (Salaried or Hourly)	DET 4
Location_Name (Foreign Key)	DET 5
SALARIED_EMPLOYEE entity subtype	RET 1 under EMPLOYEE
Supervisory_Level	DET 6
HOURLY_EMPLOYEE entity subtype	RET 2 under EMPLOYEE
Standard_Hourly_Rate	DET 7
Collective_Bargaining_Unit_Number	DET 8
JOB entity type	A maintained ILF with 1 RET
Job_Name	DET 1
Job_Number	DET 2
Pay_Grade	DET 3
JOB_DESCRIPTION entity type	Exists for technological reasons only; part of JOB
Job_Number (Foreign Key)	Previously counted as DET 2
Line_Number	Exists for technological reasons only in our example
Description_Line	DET 4
JOB_ASSIGNMENT entity type	A maintained ILF with 1 RET; separately maintained with its own attributes
Effective_Date	DET 1
Salary	DET 2
Performance_Rating	DET 3
Job_Number (Foreign Key)	DET 4
Employee_SSN (Foreign Key)	DET 5

LOCATION entity type	A referenced EIF with 1 RET
Location_Name	DET 1
Address	DET 2
Interoffice_Code	DET 3

We end up with three low-complexity ILFs and one low-complexity EIF based on the complexity matrix for ILFs and EIFs (see Figure 7-3).

We recommend that you review what we've discussed here and try to identify the EOs with their FTRs. There is not enough information to count the DETs. In fact, there really isn't enough information to distinguish the EOs from the EQs. Let's assume that each report contains derived or calculated data and that all inquiries will be counted as EQs. Let's also assume that each of the reports, except the job report, has between 6 and 19 DETs that cross the boundary. In fact, when we determine the complexities of any transaction, we need to know only DETs within a particular range based on the complexity matrix for that particular transaction. Note that the applicable ranges for DETs on EOs equate to fewer than 6, 6 to 19, and more than 19. We can usually make a good estimate of the range of DETs before we reach the design phase. Finally, let's assume that the job report has five DETs. The complexity matrix for EOs is presented in Figure 8-2.

In this relatively simply counting example, you should have counted four EOs. Counting EOs is usually not terribly difficult, particularly when you have knowledge of the system to be counted. The EOs in this case are as follows:

EMPLOYEE-MAINTENANCE
  EMPLOYEE-REPORT

JOB-MAINTENANCE
  JOB-REPORT

		Data Element Types		
		1–5	6–19	≥20
File Types Referenced	<2	Low	Low	Average
	2–3	Low	Average	High
	>3	Average	High	High

Figure 8-2 Complexity matrix for EOs

JOB-ASSIGNMENT-MAINTENANCE
JOB-ASSIGNMENT-REPORT

LOCATION-REPORTING
LOCATION-REPORT

Then how many FTRs are there? Counting FTRs is a more difficult task. If we had a user or developer, we could ask. If we had a copy of the reports, we could search our ILFs for the fields contained. But because we haven't told you anything, you might just have to guess.

The employee report would reference the employee file and might also reference the location file, because there is a relationship between the two files. With two FTRs and 6 to 19 DETs, the EO would be average. The job report contains five DETs (that number was given) and probably only one FTR, the job file. Consequently, the EO for the report would be low. The job assignment report, with 6 to 19 DETs, could have three FTRs: JOB_ASSIGNMENT, EMPLOYEE, and JOB. Even with three FTRs, this report is an average EO. Finally, the location report must reference two FTRs; how else could it contain at least six DETs? Let's guess the EO to be average.

The result is three average-complexity EOs and one low-complexity EO. EOs are highlighted in the IFPUG unadjusted function point table presented as Table 8-2.

Altogether the external outputs contribute 19 unadjusted function points.

Table 8-2: IFPUG's Unadjusted Function Point Table

	Function Levels		
Components	Low	Average	High
ILF	× 7	× 10	× 15
EIF	× 5	× 7	× 10
EI	× 3	× 4	× 6
EO	× 4	× 5	× 7
EQ	× 3	× 4	× 6

Note: Apply application characteristics adjustment (0.65 – 1.35) to calculate adjusted function points.

External Inquiries

An external inquiry (EQ) is an *elementary process* of the application that results in retrieval of *data* or *control information* that is sent outside the application boundary. The primary intent is to present information to a user through the retrieval of data or control information from an ILF or EIF. The *processing logic* contains no mathematical formulas or calculations and creates no *derived data*. No ILF is *maintained* during processing, and the behavior of the application is not altered.

Each of the italicized terms in this definition is described here:

- An **elementary process** is the smallest unit of activity that is meaningful to the user. This process must be self-contained and leave the business of the application being counted in a consistent state. For example, to perform a particular retrieval, the users have requested that they be able to enter up to five different fields of control information—for example, model, color, style, year manufactured, and warranty. Any number of combinations would be possible, but each of the five can be selected as an "and/or" selection. Entering one of the fields would not be an elementary process; neither would entering all five. Possible candidates fulfilling the criteria of the control information entered must be extracted and presented to the requester before the transaction is considered an elementary process. An EQ involves a request for information (generated either internally within the application from a process or externally to the application from a process, person, thing, or other application), an extract from one or more ILFs or EIFs, and the delivery of information to a user; without all three subactivities, the transaction is not complete.

- **Data** refers to the fields of information processed by the inquiry transaction. An example would be the data fields retrieved and displayed as a result of the request described above—that is, model, color, style, year manufactured, and warranty.

- **Control information** is data that influences an elementary process of the application being counted; in the case of EQs, these data, rules, or parameters specify what, when, or how the data is to be processed. The control information is not an elementary process on its own.

- **Processing logic** includes those requirements specifically requested by a user to complete an elementary process. Usually a combination of processing logic is required to complete an elementary process. Processing logic on its own should not be used to determine unique EIs, EOs, or EQs. One external inquiry's elementary process could include multiple validations, filters, re-sorts, and so on. Rearranging, reformatting, or re-sorting a set of data is not considered to be unique processing logic; however, there may be other unique processing logic during any of these operations.

- **Derived data** requires processing, other than direct retrieval, conversion, and editing of information, from one or more ILFs and/or EIFs. Derived data is created by the transformation of existing data to create additional data. EQs do not contain derived data.
- **Maintained** refers to the ability to modify data through an elementary process. An EQ does not maintain data; an EI or an EO maintains data.

For the data or control information being processed to be counted as an EQ, all of the following IFPUG counting rules must apply:

- **The data or control information must exit the application boundary.**
- **The data or control information must be retrieved from one or more ILFs or EIFs.**
- **The processing logic of the elementary process must not create derived data.**
- **The processing logic of the elementary process must not contain a mathematical formula or calculation.**
- **The processing logic of the elementary process must not alter the behavior of the application.**
- **The process must not maintain an ILF.**
- **The process must be the smallest unit of activity that is meaningful to the user (elementary process rule).**
- **The process must be self-contained and leave the business of the application being counted in a consistent state (elementary process rule).**
- **For the identified process, one of the three following rules must apply:**

  1. **Processing logic must be unique or different from the processing logic performed by other external inquiries within the application.**
  2. **The set of data elements identified is different from the sets identified for other external inquiries in the application.**
  3. **The ILFs or EIFs referenced are different from those referenced by other external inquiries in the application.**

Some additional examples of EQs follow. These are examples only; any data or control information listed here must conform to the stated definition and rules in order to be counted as an EQ:

- Transactional data that is retrieved from one or more ILFs and/or EIFs and displayed—for example, an appointment, an item description, employee data, or payment data.
- User functions such as view, lookup, display, browse, print (remember a print and a view with the same processing logic are counted as one EQ rather than two).
- Implied inquiries (retrievals of data prior to a change or delete function), provided that the inquiry can be used as a stand-alone process and is not a duplication of another previously counted EQ.
- Reports generated on a periodic basis that do not contain formulas, calculations, or derived data and do not maintain an ILF.
- Return of maintained system data, parameters, and setup, unless computed.
- Log-on screens that provide application-specific security.
- Each level of help—for example, field or screen when retrieved from an ILF or EIF.
- Retrievals of maintained data via electronic data interface or phone (using tones).
- Files sent to other applications that do not have formulas, calculations, or derived data and do not maintain an ILF within the application sending the data (the transaction may be an EI to the receiving application).
- Retrieval of mail from mailbox.
- List boxes or pointing and clicking of data on a screen in order to return maintained data from an ILF or EIF.

The following examples have frequently been misidentified as EQs. Be sure *not* to count them as EQs:

- Multiple methods of invoking the same logic—for example, two action keys that perform the same function or the same transaction on multiple screens (counted only once).
- Multiple media when the processing logic is not different.
- Inquiries that can be accessed from multiple areas or screens of an application (counted once).
- Menu screens that are used for navigation or selection and do not retrieve maintained data (not counted).
- Log-on screens that facilitate user entry into an application but do invoke security (not counted).
- Derived or calculated data versus retrieval of data (counted as an EO).
- Re-sorting or rearrangement of a set of data without other processing logic.

- Responses to messages that request a user to confirm data.
- Error and/or confirmation messages.
- Online system documentation.
- Data passed between online and batch within the same application; it doesn't cross the application boundary.
- Data passed between client and server within the same application; it doesn't cross the application boundary.
- Data that is not retrieved from maintained data—for example, hard-coded data (not counted).

Complexity and Contribution: EQs

The physical count of EQs, together with the relative functional complexity for each, determines the contribution of the external inquiries to the unadjusted function point count. Each identified EQ must be assigned a *functional complexity* based on the number of *data element types (DETs)* and *file types referenced (FTRs)* associated with the EQ.

Each of the italicized terms in this definition is described here:

- **Functional complexity** is the rating assigned to each transactional function. Possible scores of low, average, and high are assigned according to a complexity matrix that considers the number of DETs and FTRs.
- **Data element types** (**DETs**) are unique user-recognizable, nonrepeated fields or attributes that cross the boundary of the application. Some other specific characteristics of a transaction's elementary process, to be discussed under rules below, are also counted as DETs.
- **File types referenced** (**FTRs**), or more simply files referenced, refers to the total number of ILFs and EIFs read by the EQ transaction.

The following IFPUG rules apply to the counting of data elements, fields, or attributes (termed DETs by IFPUG) for EQs:

- **Count a DET for each user-recognizable, nonrepeated field that enters the application boundary and is required to specify what, when, and/or how data is to be retrieved and/or generated by the elementary process.** Such fields are often considered to be control information, selection information, or processing parameters.
- **Count a DET for each unique user-recognizable, nonrepeated field or attribute that exits the application boundary.** Included are foreign key attributes and control information.

- If a DET both enters and exits the boundary, count it only once for the elementary process.
- Count one DET for the capability to send a system response message outside the application boundary to indicate that an error has occurred during processing, confirm that processing is complete, or verify that processing should continue. Even though there are multiple message possibilities, count only one DET for the elementary process. That is, count only one DET total for messages, even though there are multiple error, verification, and confirmation messages.
- Count one DET for the capability to specify an action to be taken by the EQ even if there are multiple methods or multiple keys required for invoking the same logical process—for example, OK button, function key, action keys (A, C, D, and so on), or mouse click.
- Do not count paging-variable or system-generated stamps, including page numbers, positioning information (row x of y), paging commands (previous, next, arrows), or date/time fields. DETs counted do include date fields retrieved, but not system-generated dates, such as when a report is printed.
- Do not count literals, including report titles, screen IDs, column headings, and field titles.
- Count one DET for a logical field that is stored physically as multiple fields but is required by the user as a single piece of information. For example, a date or name stored as three fields but used as one field is counted as one DET. An address (street, city, and zip code) may be counted as one DET on an address label if it is considered to represent one group of data.
- Count one DET for each type of label and each type of numerical equivalent in a graphical display. For example, a pie chart might have two DETs, one for the category and one for the applicable percentage, even if the percentage is not labeled as such. A graph can be an EQ if there is no calculation when the graph is generated; that is, the percentage is read from stored data.
- Count one DET for text information that may consist of a single word, a sentence, a paragraph, or many paragraphs.

The following IFPUG rules apply to the counting of file types referenced (termed FTRs by IFPUG) for EQs:

- Count a file type referenced for each internal logical file (ILF) or external interface file (EIF) read during the processing of the EQ.

An Example of Counting EQs

The user requirements for the employee application discussed in Chapter 7 include the following:

- The ability to maintain, inquire on, and report employee information. The report will include location data for specific employees obtained from a file maintained by another application.
- The ability to maintain, inquire on, and report on information about jobs. The user considers job description to be a collection of 80-character lines that describe the job; this information is not maintained independently from the job.
- The ability to maintain, inquire on, and report on job assignments for employees.
- The ability to inquire and report on different locations within the company, including a list of employees at a particular location. The location data is read only and is maintained by another application.

A process model for this example might appear as follows:

EMPLOYEE-MAINTENANCE
    CREATE-EMPLOYEE
    EMPLOYEE-INQUIRY
    UPDATE-EMPLOYEE
    DELETE-EMPLOYEE
    EMPLOYEE-REPORT

JOB-MAINTENANCE
    CREATE-JOB
    JOB-INQUIRY
    UPDATE-JOB
    DELETE-JOB
    JOB-REPORT

JOB-ASSIGNMENT-MAINTENANCE
    ASSIGN-EMPLOYEE-TO-JOB
    JOB-ASSIGNMENT-INQUIRY
    TRANSFER-EMPLOYEE
    EVALUATE-EMPLOYEE
    DELETE-ASSIGNMENT
    JOB-ASSIGNMENT-REPORT

LOCATION-REPORTING
　　LOCATION-INQUIRY
　　LOCATION-REPORT

The ILFs and EIFs were counted as follows:

EMPLOYEE entity type	A maintained ILF; not counted as a separate RET because there are subgroups
Employee_Name	DET 1
Social_Security_Number	DET 2
Nbr_Dependents	DET 3
Type_Code (Salaried or Hourly)	DET 4
Location_Name (Foreign Key)	DET 5
SALARIED_EMPLOYEE entity subtype	RET 1 under EMPLOYEE
Supervisory_Level	DET 6
HOURLY_EMPLOYEE entity subtype	RET 2 under EMPLOYEE
Standard_Hourly_Rate	DET 7
Collective_Bargaining_Unit_Number	DET 8
JOB entity type	A maintained ILF with 1 RET
Job_Name	DET 1
Job_Number	DET 2
Pay_Grade	DET 3
JOB_DESCRIPTION entity type	Exists for technological reasons only; part of JOB
Job_Number (Foreign Key)	Previously counted as DET 2
Line_Number	Exists for technological reasons only in our example
Description_Line	DET 4
JOB_ASSIGNMENT entity type	A maintained ILF with 1 RET; separately maintained with its own attributes
Effective_Date	DET 1
Salary	DET 2
Performance_Rating	DET 3

Job_Number (Foreign Key)	DET 4
Employee_SSN (Foreign Key)	DET 5
LOCATION entity type	A referenced EIF with 1 RET
Location_Name	DET 1
Address	DET 2
Interoffice_Code	DET 3

We end up with three low-complexity ILFs and one low-complexity EIF based on the complexity matrix for ILFs and EIFs (see Figure 7-3).

We recommend that you review what we've discussed here. We have already identified the EIs and EOs; therefore only the EQs remain. Their DETs and FTRs are not obvious, so the following logic is suggested:

An EQ as well as an EO may have fields and control information that enter the application boundary to accomplish the retrieval of the data. Let's assume for this exercise that the control information for each is also displayed on the output side. In addition, we might expect error, verification, or confirmation messages (we count a DET for each EQ or EO for error, verification, or confirmation messages) and might have at least one command key (we count another DET for each EQ or EO for command keys when applicable).

The FTRs and the DETs that cross the boundary for each of the EQs could be as follows:

- **EMPLOYEE-INQUIRY:** 1 FTR and 10 DETs, counting one DET each for messages and command keys
- **JOB-INQUIRY:** 1 FTR and 6 DETs, counting one DET each for messages and command keys
- **JOB-ASSIGNMENT-INQUIRY:** 1 FTR and 7 DETs, counting one DET each for messages and command keys
- **LOCATION-INQUIRY:** 1 FTR and 5 DETs, counting one DET each for messages and command keys

You might ask why there is only one file referenced on these EQs. We do not need to reference other files for validation, and none of the fields were retrieved from files other than the primary file in this contrived example.

The complexity matrix for EQs (Figure 8-3) considers the FTRs and the total of the incoming and outgoing DETs that cross the application boundary.

	Data Element Types		
	1–5	**6–19**	**≥20**
File Types Referenced 1	Low	Low	Average
2–3	Low	Average	High
>3	Average	High	High

Figure 8-3 Complexity matrix for EQs

Calculating the complexities with this information, we would end up with four low-complexity EQs. EQs are highlighted in the IFPUG unadjusted function point table presented as Table 8-3.

Altogether the external inquiries contribute 12 unadjusted function points.

Table 8-3: IFPUG's Unadjusted Function Point Table

	Function Levels		
Components	Low	Average	High
ILF	× 7	× 10	× 15
EIF	× 5	× 7	× 10
EI	× 3	× 4	× 6
EO	× 4	× 5	× 7
EQ	× 3	× 4	× 6

Note: Apply application characteristics adjustment (0.65 – 1.35) to calculate adjusted function points.

Summary

This chapter introduced the rules for recognizing the three transactional functions—external inputs (EIs), external outputs (EOs), and external inquiries (EQs)—of our application. Examples of each were provided. Our example of counting used in Chapter 7 to distinguish ILFs and EIFs was continued in this chapter to count EIs, EOs, and EQs and to assign unadjusted function point weights based on established IFPUG matrices, using data element types (DETs) and file types referenced (FTRs). Remember that DETs and RETs were used in Chapter 7 to weight data functions, but DETs and FTRs were used in this chapter to assign unadjusted function point weights to the transactional functions.

Chapter 9 will describe general system characteristics, upon which the application characteristics adjustment (step 6 of the process used to size function points) is based.

As we mentioned in Chapter 7, we will provide many additional practical exercises later in the book to assist you in applying the IFPUG rules in counting data functions (ILFs and EIFs) as well as transactional functions (EIs, EOs, and EQs). The IFPUG Counting Practices Manual should also be consulted for the latest guidance on counting standards. In this book we use the rules contained in release 4.1 of that manual.

General System Characteristics

Introduction

Functionality delivered by information systems includes pervasive general factors that are not sufficiently represented by the previously discussed transactional and data functions. This chapter will describe the International Function Point User Group (IFPUG) definitions, rules, and guidelines for identifying the value adjustment factor (VAF), which is used as a multiplier of the unadjusted function point count in order to calculate the adjusted function point count of an application. Although the guidelines for deriving and utilizing the unadjusted function point count have strong support throughout the world, recent IFPUG surveys have indicated that the VAF does not.

Many users, though still a minority, of the function point methodology have chosen to ignore the general system characteristics altogether and to utilize the unadjusted function point count as the adjusted function point count. As we write this book, the International Organization for Standardization (ISO) is proceeding to exclude the general system characteristics from the standards for functional size measurement for software. Although we use the VAF, we recognize that the general system characteristics relate better to the mainframe environment then to current environments—for example, PC, client-server, and Web. Consequently, we have provided in this chapter *Authors' notes* to assist you in utilizing these factors.

The VAF is calculated on the basis of the identification of 14 general system characteristics (GSCs):

1.   Data communications
2.   Distributed data processing
3.   Performance
4.   Heavily used configuration
5.   Transaction rate
6.   Online data entry
7.   End user efficiency
8.   Online update
9.   Complex processing
10.   Reusability
11.   Installation ease
12.   Operational ease
13.   Multiple sites
14.   Facilitate change

Detailed guidance is contained within the IFPUG Counting Practices Manual. Chapter 10 in this book will utilize the results of the identification of data and transactional function types, as well as the values obtained from identifying the GSCs, to calculate an adjusted function point count.

The Process

The total process used to size function points was introduced in Chapter 6 and is repeated here. It can be summarized by the following seven steps:

1. Determine the type of function point count
2. Identify the counting scope and the application boundary
3. Identify all data functions (internal logical files and external interface files) and their complexity
4. Identify all transactional functions (external inputs, external outputs, and external inquiries) and their complexity
5. Determine the unadjusted function point count
6. Determine the value adjustment factor, which is based on the 14 general system characteristics (discussed in this chapter)
7. Calculate the adjusted function point count

Remember that the application boundary separates the application being measured from the user domain and/or other independent applications. The data functions relate to the logical data stored and available for update, reference, and retrieval. The transactional functions—external inputs (EIs), external outputs (EOs), and external inquiries (EQs)—perform the processes of update, retrieval, output, and so on (transactions you would expect to see in a process model). Each has its own unadjusted function point weight based on its unique complexity matrix.

The 14 general system characteristics (GSCs) will each be evaluated independently and assigned a unique value: **degree of influence (DI)**. Each characteristic has associated descriptions that help determine the DI of that characteristic. The DI for each characteristic ranges on a scale of 0 (no influence) to 5 (strong influence).

The 14 GSCs are totaled to calculate a **total degree of influence (TDI)**. A **value adjustment factor (VAF)** is calculated as follows: VAF = (TDI × 0.01) + 0.65. Note that the values 0.01 and 0.65 are constants in this equation.

When applied, the VAF adjusts the unadjusted function point count by ±35 percent to produce the adjusted function point count.

General System Characteristics

Each GSC must be evaluated in terms of its degree of influence (DI) on a scale of 0 to 5:

0 Not present, or no influence
1 Incidental influence
2 Moderate influence
3 Average influence
4 Significant influence
5 Strong influence throughout

IFPUG has guidelines for assigning the DIs. The remainder of this chapter will provide those IFPUG guidelines for DIs to each of the GSCs. In addition, the *Authors' notes* will assist you in assigning these values to different types of applications. If none of the IFPUG guideline descriptions fit the application exactly, a judgment must be made about which DI (0–5) most closely applies to the application.

1. Data Communications

Data communications describes the degree to which the application communicates directly with the processor.

The data and control information used in the application are sent or received over communication facilities. Terminals connected locally to the control unit are considered to use communication facilities. Protocol is a set of conventions, which permit the transfer or exchange of information between two systems or devices. All data communication links require some type of protocol.

Score as follows:

0 **The application is pure batch processing or a stand-alone PC.**
1 **The application is batch but has remote data entry or remote printing.**
2 **The application is batch but has remote data entry and remote printing.**
3 **The application includes online data collection or a teleprocessing (TP) front end to a batch process or query system.**
4 **The application is more than a front end, but the application supports only one type of TP communications protocol.**
5 **The application is more than a front end, but the application supports more than one type of TP communications protocol.**

Authors' notes: We would expect only batch applications with no interactivity to be valued at 0. Most applications, stand-alone PC as well as batch, have remote data entry as well as printing capability. Applications that have front-end data entry screens, but that update internal logical files through a batch process, should be scored at 3. If update occurs interactively, score 4. In order to score 5, there must be multiple types of telecommunication protocol. Typically, batch applications receive a score of 0 to 3; online applications a score of 3 to 4; and real-time, telecommunication, or process control systems receive a score of 4 or 5.

2. Distributed Data Processing

Distributed data processing describes the degree to which the application transfers data among components of the application. Distributed data or processing functions are a characteristic of the application within the application boundary.

Score as follows:

0 **The application does not aid the transfer of data or processing functions between components of the system.**

1   The application prepares data for user processing on another component of the system, such as PC spreadsheets and PC DBMS.
2   Data is prepared for transfer, then is transferred and processed on another component of the system (not for end user processing).
3   Distributed processing and data transfer are online and in one direction only.
4   Distributed processing and data transfer are online and in both directions.
5   Processing functions are dynamically performed on the most appropriate component of the system.

Authors' notes: Only distributed or real-time applications would be assigned a value within this category. Most applications score 0; primitive distributed applications could score 1 or 2; client-server or Web applications score 2 through 4; and real-time, telecommunication, or process control systems could score 0 through 5. In order to score a 5, there must be multiple servers or processors, each of which would be selected dynamically on the basis of its real-time availability.

3. Performance

Performance describes the degree to which response time and throughput performance considerations influenced the application development. Application performance objectives, stated or approved by the user, in *either* response *or* throughput, influence (or will influence) the design, development, installation, and support of the application.

Score as follows:

0   No special performance requirements were stated by the user.
1   Performance and design requirements were stated and reviewed, but no special actions were required.
2   Response time or throughput is critical during peak hours. No special design for CPU utilization was required. Processing deadline is for the next business day.
3   Response time or throughput is critical during all business hours. No special design for CPU utilization was required. Processing deadline requirements with interfacing systems are constraining.
4   In addition, stated user performance requirements are stringent enough to require performance analysis tasks in the design phase.

5   In addition, performance analysis tools were used in the design, development, and/or implementation phases to meet the stated user performance requirements.

Authors' notes: This characteristic is very similar in nature to transaction rate (GSC 5); both require consideration of performance during the design, development, and installation phases of development. Response time typically relates to interactive processing; throughput relates to batch processing. Consider the significance of performance to the particular application. A score of 4 requires performance analysis tasks during the design phase. A score of 5 requires the use of performance analysis tools. Typically, batch applications receive a score of 0 to 4; online applications a score of 0 to 4; and real-time, telecommunication, or process control systems a score of 0 to 5.

4. Heavily Used Configuration

Heavily used configuration describes the degree to which computer resource restrictions influenced the development of the application. A heavily used operational configuration, requiring special design considerations, is a characteristic of the application. For example, the user wants to run the application on existing or committed equipment that will be heavily used.

Score as follows:

0   No explicit or implicit operational restrictions are included.
1   Operational restrictions do exist, but are less restrictive than a typical application. No special effort is needed to meet the restrictions.
2   Some security or timing considerations are included.
3   Specific processor requirements for a specific piece of the application are included.
4   Stated operation restrictions require special constraints on the application in the central processor or a dedicated processor.
5   In addition, there are special constraints on the application in the distributed components of the system.

Authors' notes: We would expect most applications to be valued at 2. In order to score 3 to 5, the application would be expected to be a client-server, real-time, telecommunication, or process control system. Even then, you would need either a dedicated processor or multiple processors processing the same transactions and searching for the most expeditious means of processing.

5. Transaction Rate

Transaction rate describes the degree to which the rate of business transactions influenced the development of the application. The transaction rate is high, and it influences the design, development, installation, and support of the application.

Score as follows:

0 **No peak transaction period is anticipated.**
1 **A peak transaction period (e.g., monthly, quarterly, seasonally, annually) is anticipated.**
2 **A weekly peak transaction period is anticipated.**
3 **A daily peak transaction period is anticipated.**
4 **High transaction rate(s) stated by the user in the application requirements or service-level agreements are high enough to require performance analysis tasks in the design phase.**
5 **High transaction rate(s) stated by the used in the application requirements or service-level agreements are high enough to require performance analysis tasks and, in addition, require the use of performance analysis tools in the design, development, and/or installation phases.**

Authors' notes: This characteristic is very similar in nature to performance (GSC 3); both require consideration of performance during the design, development, and installation phases of development. Consider the significance of transaction rates to the particular application. A score of 4 requires performance analysis tasks during the design phase. A score of 5 requires the use of performance analysis tools. Typically, batch applications receive a score of 0 to 3; online applications a score of 0 to 4; and real-time, telecommunication, or process control systems a score of 0 to 5.

6. Online Data Entry

Online data entry describes the degree to which data is entered through interactive transactions. Online data entry and control functions are provided in the application.

Score as follows:

0 **All transactions are processed in batch mode.**
1 **1 to 7 percent of transactions are interactive data entry.**
2 **8 to 15 percent of transactions are interactive data entry.**
3 **16 to 23 percent of transactions are interactive data entry.**

4 24 to 30 percent of transactions are interactive data entry.

5 More than 30 percent of transactions are interactive data entry.

Authors' notes: Transactions refer to EIs, EOs, and EQs, each of which is an elementary process (see Chapter 8). One of the major problems with the scoring for GSCs is that the guidelines have not been updated in years. Consequently, these scores are not realistic. Nevertheless, industry data has been calculated using these guidelines. Typically, batch applications receive a score of 0 to 1; and online, real-time, telecommunication, or process control systems a score of 5.

7. End User Efficiency

End user efficiency describes the degree of consideration for human factors and ease of use for the user of the application measured. The online functions provided emphasize a design for end user efficiency.

The design includes:

- Navigational aids (e.g., function keys, jumps, dynamically generated menus)
- Menus
- Online help and documents
- Automated cursor movement
- Scrolling
- Remote printing (via online transactions)
- Preassigned function keys
- Batch jobs submitted from online transactions
- Cursor selection of screen data
- Heavy use of reverse video, highlighting, colors, underlining, and other indicators
- Hard-copy user documentation of online transactions
- Mouse interface
- Pop-up windows
- As few screens as possible to accomplish a business function
- Bilingual support (supporting two languages; counted as four items)
- Multilingual support (supporting more than two languages; counted as six items)

Score as follows:

0 None of the above.

1 One to three of the above.

2 Four to five of the above.

3 Six or more of the above, but there are no specific user requirements related to efficiency.

4 Six or more of the above, and stated requirements for end user efficiency are strong enough to require design tasks for human factors to be included (for example, minimize key strokes, maximize defaults, use of templates).

5 Six or more of the above, and stated requirements for end user efficiency are strong enough to require use of special tools and processes in order to demonstrate that the objectives have been achieved.

Authors' notes: We would expect batch applications with no interactivity to be valued at 0. Most interactive applications have front-end data entry screens, but unless they have templates and/or defaults built into the application, they should be scored at 3. If defaults, templates, and/or significant navigational tools are present, score 4. In order to score 5, there must be user labs to test the usability of the application rather than the functionality. Real-time, telecommunication, or process control systems may not score anything for this GSC.

8. Online Update

Online update describes the degree to which internal logical files are updated online. The application provides online update for the internal logical files.

Score as follows:

0 None.

1 Online update of one to three control files is included. Volume of updating is low, and recovery is easy.

2 Online update of four or more control files is included. Volume of updating is low, and recovery is easy.

3 Online update of major internal logical files is included.

4 In addition, protection against data loss is essential and has been specially designed and programmed in the system.

5 In addition, high volumes bring cost considerations into the recovery process. Highly automated recovery procedures with minimum of operator intervention.

Authors' notes: We would expect batch applications with no interactive update of internal logical files to be valued at 0 to 2. Most online applications update internal logical files and should be scored at 3 or higher. If protection of data loss has been programmed into the system (not just through backups), score 4. In order to score 5, there must be a highly automated recovery capability built within the application. Real-time, telecommunication, or process control systems often receive a score of 4 or 5.

9. Complex Processing

Complex processing describes the degree to which processing logic influenced the development of the application.

The following five components are present:

1. **Sensitive control (e.g., special audit processing) and/or application-specific security processing**
2. **Extensive logical processing**
3. **Extensive mathematical processing**
4. **Much exception processing, resulting in incomplete transactions that must be processed again (e.g., incomplete ATM transactions caused by TP interruption, missing data values, or failed validations)**
5. **Complex processing to handle multiple input/output possibilities (e.g., multimedia or device independence)**

Score as follows:

0 **None of the above**
1 **Any one of the above**
2 **Any two of the above**
3 **Any three of the above**
4 **Any four of the above**
5 **Any five of the above**

Authors' notes: With the prior GSCs, each guideline provided a little more than the previous score; this GSC credits five separate and individual characteristics. First, does the application provide security such that certain individuals see or enter data that others cannot? Second, is there a significant amount of logical (if/then/else) processing? Third, is there extensive mathematical processing (more than addition and subtraction—i.e., simple math)? Fourth, is there complex editing or validation? Fifth, are multiple media (e.g., voice and screen input) included in the application?

10. Reusability

Reusability describes the degree to which the application and the code in the application have been specifically designed, developed, and supported to be usable in *other* applications.

Score as follows:

0 **No reusable code.**
1 **Reusable code is used within the application.**
2 **Less than 10 percent of the application considered more than one user's needs.**
3 **Ten percent or more of the application considered more than one user's needs.**
4 **The application was specifically packaged and/or documented to ease reuse, and the application is customized by the user at source code level.**
5 **The application was specifically packaged and/or documented to ease reuse, and the application is customized for use by means of user parameter maintenance.**

Authors' notes: Function point counting gives credit here with a score of 1 to those who use reuse code. Standardized reusable software provides increased user/owner functionality through increased reliability and consistency. Scores of 2 through 5 are assigned on the basis of the resulting functionality and the extra effort dedicated to the development, documentation, and testing of code that is expected to be utilized in other applications.

11. Installation Ease

Installation ease describes the degree to which conversion from previous environments influenced the development of the application. Conversion and installation ease are characteristics of the application. A conversion and installation plan and/or conversion tools were provided and tested during the system test phase.

Score as follows:

0 **No special considerations were stated by the user, and no special setup is required for installation.**
1 **No special considerations were stated by the user, *but* special setup is required for installation.**

2 Conversion and installation requirements were stated by the user, and conversion and installation guides were provided and tested. The impact of conversion on the project is not considered to be important.

3 Conversion and installation requirements were stated by the user, and conversion and installation guides were provided and tested. The impact of conversion on the project is considered to be important.

4 In addition to 2 above, automated conversion and installation tools were provided and tested.

5 In addition to 3 above, automated conversion and installation tools were provided and tested.

Authors' notes: Developers are often required to devote significant effort to converting preexisting data into new data files, to populating the files with actual data, or to developing installation software, such as porting. Improved schedules and increased consistency offer functional advantages to the users. Consider the difficulty, or ease, of conversion and installation requirements, and assign the score in relationship to their significance.

12. Operational Ease

Operational ease describes the degree to which the application attends to operational aspects, such as start-up, backup, and recovery processes. Operational ease is a characteristic of the application. The application minimizes the need for manual activities, such as tape mounts, paper handling, and direct on-location manual intervention.

Score as follows:

0 No special operational considerations, other than the normal backup procedures, were stated by the user.

1–4 Select which of the following items apply to the application. Each item has a point value of 1, except as noted otherwise.
   · Effective start-up, backup, and recovery processes were provided, but operator intervention is required.
   · Effective start-up, backup, and recovery processes were provided, but no operator intervention is required (count as two items).
   · The application minimizes the need for tape mounts.
   · The application minimizes the need for paper handling.

5 The application is designed for unattended operation. Unattended operation means *no operator intervention* is required to operate the

system other than to start up or shut down the application. Automatic error recovery is a feature of the application.

Authors' notes: Unless we are counting a legacy system, we should score 1 each for the lack of tape mounts and the lack of paper (punched cards, punched paper tapes). We should count 3 if operator intervention is required for start-up, backup, and recovery. A score of 4 is assigned if no operator intervention is required; and 5 is assigned to an application that runs, and recovers automatically from errors, on its own—a lights-out operation. We usually expect to see a score of 3 for online applications; and a higher score for plant-processing, telecommunication, or real-time systems, which operate unencumbered by human interfaces.

13. Multiple Sites

Multiple sites describes the degree to which the application has been developed for multiple locations and user organizations. The application has been specifically designed, developed, and supported to be installed at multiple sites for multiple organizations.

Score as follows:

0 User requirements do not require the consideration of needs of more than one user or installation site.

1 Needs of multiple sites were considered in the design, and the application is designed to operate only under *identical* hardware and software environments.

2 Needs of multiple sites were considered in the design, and the application is designed to operate only under *similar* hardware and/or software environments.

3 Needs of multiple sites were considered in the design, and the application is designed to operate under *different* hardware and/or software environments.

4 Documentation and support plan are provided and tested to support the application at multiple sites, and the application is as described by 1 or 2 above.

5 Documentation and support plan are provided and tested to support the application at multiple sites, and the application is as described by 3 above.

Authors' notes: We consider within this characteristic the resulting user functionality and the effort required to deliver an application that will include software and/or hardware at multiple sites; this DI could reflect just the input devices, such as terminals or PCs. Are the software and/or hardware identical, similar (e.g., Windows 95, NT), or different (e.g., Windows, Mac, Unix)? Are documentation support plans to be provided and tested?

14. Facilitate Change

Facilitate change describes the degree to which the application has been developed for easy modification of processing logic or data structure.

Its characteristics are as follows:

- **Flexible query and report facility is provided.**
- **Business control data is grouped in tables maintainable by the user.**

Score as follows:

0   **No special user requirement to design the application to minimize or facilitate change.**

1–5   **Select which of the following items apply to the application:**
  - **Flexible query and report facility is provided that can handle simple requests—for example, *and/or* logic applied to only one internal logical file (count as one item).**
  - **Flexible query and report facility is provided that can handle requests of average complexity—for example, *and/or* logic applied to more than one internal logical file (count as two items).**
  - **Flexible query and report facility is provided that can handle complex requests—for example, *and/or* logic combinations on one or more internal logical files (count as three items).**
  - **Business control data is kept in tables that are maintained by the user with online interactive processes, but changes take effect only on the next business day (count as one item).**
  - **Business control data is kept in tables that are maintained by the user with online interactive processes, and the changes take effect immediately (count as two items).**

Authors' notes: We address two separate categories for this GSC, much the same as complex processing (GSC 9) had five separate categories. The first area deals with the query and/or report writer capability often provided by languages such as SQL or FOCUS or by some of the more dynamic reporting tools (e.g., Crystal Reports); scores of 0 to 3 are assigned to this particular characteristic, which is becoming more popular among computer-literate users. The second area and the last two questions relate to the interactivity in which data and/or control information is maintained within and/or by the application; interactive, real-time, telecommunication, and process control systems would typically be counted with the last two points.

Value Adjustment Factor

The 14 general system characteristics (GSCs) are summarized into the value adjustment factor (VAF). When applied, the VAF adjusts the unadjusted function point count by ±35 percent to determine the adjusted function point count.

As a general rule, we would expect a simple batch application to have a total score (total degree of influence, TDI) of less than 15, a front-end batch application to have a total score between 15 and 30, an interactive application between 30 and 45, and a real-time, telecommunication, or process control system between 30 and 60.

The following steps provide the procedure to calculate the VAF:

1. Evaluate the 14 GSCs on a scale from 0 to 5 to determine the degree of influence (DI) for each of the GSC descriptions.
2. Add the DIs for all 14 GSCs to produce the total degree of influence (TDI).
3. Use the application's TDI in the following equation to compute the VAF: $VAF = (TDI \times 0.01) + 0.65$.

Summary

This chapter introduced the definitions, rules, and guidelines for identifying the value adjustment factor (VAF), which is used as a multiplier of the unadjusted function point count in order to calculate the adjusted function point count of an application. The VAF is calculated on the basis of the identification of 14 general system characteristics (GSCs): data communications, distributed data processing, performance, heavily used configuration, transaction rate, online data entry, end user efficiency, online update, complex processing, reusability, installation ease, operational ease, multiple sites, and facilitate change. Each characteristic has associated descriptions that help determine the degree of influence (DI) of that characteristic. The degree of influence for each characteristic ranges on a scale of 0 (no influence) to 5 (strong influence). The 14 GSCs are totaled to calculate a total degree of influence (TDI). A VAF is calculated from the formula VAF = (TDI × 0.01) + 0.65.

When applied, the VAF adjusts the unadjusted function point count by ±35 percent to produce the adjusted function point count.

Detailed guidance is contained within the IFPUG Counting Practices Manual. Chapter 10 will utilize the results of the identification of data and transactional function types, as well as the values obtained from identifying the GSCs and the VAF, to calculate an adjusted function point count.

CHAPTER TEN

Calculating and Applying Function Points

Introduction

This chapter will use a catalog business as a quick and easy example of how to complete a function point count. The previous chapter described the definitions, rules, and guidelines for identifying the value adjustment factor (VAF), which is calculated on the basis of the identification of the 14 general system characteristics (GSCs). This chapter will utilize the rules for the identification of data functions (see Chapter 7) and transactional functions (see Chapter 8), together with the value adjustment factor, to calculate an adjusted function point count for this particular catalog business. Detailed guidance on all calculations is contained within the IFPUG Counting Practices Manual.

Final Adjusted Function Point Count

The total process used to size function points was introduced in Chapter 6 and is repeated here. It can be summarized by the following seven steps:

1. Determine the type of function point count
2. Identify the counting scope and the application boundary
3. Identify all data functions (internal logical files and external interface files) and their complexity
4. Identify all transactional functions (external inputs, external outputs, and external inquiries) and their complexity
5. Determine the unadjusted function point count

6. Determine the value adjustment factor, which is based on the 14 general system characteristics

7. Calculate the adjusted function point count (discussed in this chapter)

Remember that the application boundary separates the application being measured from the user domain and/or other independent applications. The data functions relate to the logical data stored and available for update, reference, and retrieval. The transactional functions—external inputs (EIs), external outputs (EOs), and external inquiries (EQs)—perform the processes of update, retrieval, output, and so on (transactions you would expect to see in a process model). Each has its own unadjusted function point weight based on its unique complexity matrix.

The general system characteristics (GSCs) are each evaluated independently and assigned a unique value between 0 and 5. These scores are summed to calculate a total degree of influence (TDI). Then the TDI is used in a separate calculation to determine the value adjustment factor (VAF). Finally, the total value of the unadjusted function points is multiplied by the VAF to obtain a final adjusted function point count.

Counting a Catalog Business: An Example

Use Figure 10-1 to assist you in determining the functionality contained in this example of a catalog business. A file folder containing prices, source data, and descriptive information for each item is counted as an internal logical file (ILF). If we determine that the only key (and record element type, RET) is the item number and that there are 30 separate and distinct fields, we count one low ILF for that descriptions file. When we add new items to the descriptions file, assuming that there are more than 15 fields or data element types (DETs) but only one file type referenced (FTR), which is the descriptions file, we count one average external input (EI).

When we change item information, assuming again that there are more than 15 DETs but only one FTR, we count another average EI.

When we delete an item from the descriptions file because it is no longer available, we have fewer than five DETs (only those fields that cross the boundary of the application; see the rules for EIs in Chapter 8 if this is confusing) and the same FTR, the descriptions file. Consequently, we have a low-complexity EI.

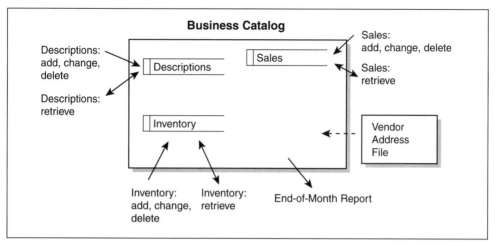

Figure 10-1 Context diagram of catalog business

When we retrieve the item information from the descriptions file and display more than 19 DETs from one file (FTR), we count the transaction as an average external inquiry (EQ).

Two other file folders are updated within the application that contain inventory data and sales data. Let's assume that the data and transactional function types are weighted the same as the descriptions file and its transactions. We count two more low-complexity ILFs, four more average-complexity EIs, two more low-complexity EIs, and two more average-complexity EQs.

A report at the end of the month, which totals our sales for the month, is counted as an external output (EO). If that report contains more than 19 DETs and retrieves data from two or more FTRs, we count a high-complexity EO.

A file maintained within another application, which contains vendor addresses, is used when we produce that report and consequently is counted as an FTR for the EO, but it is also counted as an external interface file (EIF). Let's make the assumption that it is a low-complexity EIF.

We can assign these functions appropriate point values on the basis of their complexity (the functions together with their respective values are included in Figure 10-3):

- Three low EIs are valued at 3 points each, for a total of 9.
- Six average EIs are valued at 4 points each, for a total of 24.

- One high EO is valued at 7 points, for a total of 7.
- Three average EQs are valued at 4 points each, for a total of 12.
- Three low ILFs are valued at 7 points each, for a total of 21.
- One low EIF is valued at 5 points, for a total of 5.
- The unadjusted function point count is 78.

Using the previous chapter, we can assign degrees of influence (DIs) to the general system characteristics (GSCs) of this catalog business. The authors have selected the following values from their view of this interactive Windows example:

1.	Data communications	4
2.	Distributed data processing	0
3.	Performance	3
4.	Heavily used configuration	2
5.	Transaction rate	3
6.	Online data entry	5
7.	End user efficiency	4
8.	Online update	3
9.	Complex processing	1
10.	Reusability	0
11.	Installation ease	0
12.	Operational ease	3
13.	Multiple sites	1
14.	Facilitate change	2
	Total degree of influence (TDI)	31

Using the formula for the value adjustment factor from Chapter 9—that is, VAF = (TDI $\times$ 0.01) + 0.65—we calculate that the VAF in this example is equal to 0.96, or 96/100.

The application function point count or the project function point count for this first install, with no conversion functionality, is equal to the unadjusted function point count multiplied by the VAF—for this example 78 $\times$ 0.96. Thus the adjusted function point count is 74.88, which we would round to 75.

We would actually use a function point count summary (Figure 10-2) and a function point calculation worksheet (Figure 10-3) to collect this information.

Function Point Count Summary

Project Number							
Date of Count			**Counter's Name**				

Project Name appears at top right.

Instructions: Enter all function types included. For development and initial function point counts there will not be entries in the "Before" columns. Annotate all function types added by the conversion. You may wish to use different sheets for files and transactions.

Description	Type[a]	DETs After	RETs/FTRs After	Complexity[b] After	DETs Before	RETs/FTRs Before	Complexity[b] Before
Descriptions	ILF	30	1	L			
Descriptions: add	EI	>15	1	A			
Descriptions: change	EI	>15	1	A			
Descriptions: delete	EI	<5	1	L			
Descriptions: retrieve	EQ	>19	1	A			
Inventory	ILF	30	1	L			
Inventory: add	EI	>15	1	A			
Inventory: change	EI	>15	1	A			
Inventory: delete	EI	<5	1	L			
Inventory: retrieve	EQ	>19	1	A			
Sales	ILF	30	1	L			
Sales: add	EI	>15	1	A			
Sales: change	EI	>15	1	A			
Sales: delete	EI	<5	1	L			
Sales: retrieve	EQ	>19	1	A			
End-of-month report	EO	>19	>1	H			
Vendor address file	EIF			L			

[a]ILF, EIF, EI, EO, or EQ.
[b]L = low; A = average; H = high.

Figure 10-2 Function point count summary

Function Point Calculation Worksheet

Project Number		Project Name	
Type of Count: Development Project/Application Counting (circle one)			
Phase of Count: Proposal/Requirements/Design/Code/Test/Delivery (circle one)			
Date of Count		Counter's Name	

IFPUG's Unadjusted Function Point Table*

	Function Levels			
Components	**Low**	**Average**	**High**	**Total**
External inputs	3×3	6×4	$\times 6$	33
External outputs	$\times 4$	$\times 5$	1×7	7
External inquiries	$\times 3$	3×4	$\times 6$	12
Internal logical files	3×7	$\times 10$	$\times 15$	21
External interface files	1×5	$\times 7$	$\times 10$	5

Total unadjusted function Points (UFP) = 78

*The development function point count includes function types added by the conversion. The application function point count does not include conversion requirements. An application count after an enhancement must include all existing function types, including those unchanged. If information on all existing function types is not available, the application adjusted function point count can be computed by the formula given in the text.

General System Characteristics

Characteristic	Degree of Influence	Characteristic	Degree of Influence
1. Data communications	4	8. Online update	3
2. Distributed data processing	0	9. Complex processing	1
3. Performance	3	10. Reusability	0
4. Heavily used configuration	2	11. Installation ease	0
5. Transaction rate	3	12. Operational ease	3
6. Online data entry	5	13. Multiple sites	1
7. End user efficiency	4	14. Facilitate change	2

Total degree of influence (TDI) = 31

VAF	Value adjustment factor	$= (TDI \times 0.01) + 0.65$	$= 0.96$
FP	Adjusted functionpoint count	$= UFP \times VAF$	$= 75$

Figure 10-3 Function point calculation worksheet

Function Point Calculations and Formulas

The following guidelines are provided for calculating function point counts.

Development Project Function Point Count

A development project function point count consists of three components of functionality:

1. Application unadjusted function point count, consisting of the EIs, EOs, EQs, ILFs, and EIFs
2. Conversion functionality to transfer previous data into the new ILFs through software (this component often consists of the input of the old data files [counted as EIs or input data into the already counted new ILFs] and possibly an EO for a conversion report)
3. Application value adjustment factor

The business catalog count could be considered a development project function point count or an application function point count, which will be discussed a little later in this chapter. These types of counts will also be included in the case studies presented in Chapters 11, 13, and 14.

Development Project Function Point Calculation

The following formula is used to calculate the development project function point count:

$$DFP = (UFP + CFP) \times VAF$$

where

- DFP is the development project function point count.
- UFP is the unadjusted function point count.
- CFP is the number of function points included by a conversion of data.
- VAF is the value adjustment factor.

Enhancement Project Function Point Count

An enhancement project function point count also consists of three components of functionality, but they are somewhat different:

1. Application unadjusted function point count, consisting of the EIs, EOs, EQs, ILFs, and EIFs that are:

- Added by the enhancement project (functions that did not previously exist—e.g., a new EQ, three new EIs, a new ILF, a new EQ, and a new EO)
- Changed by the enhancement project (functions that previously existed but now have different fields, FTRs, or require different processing)
- Deleted by the enhancement project (functions that have been deleted from the application—e.g., a deleted report)

2. Conversion functionality to transfer previous data into the new ILFs through software (this component often consists of the input of the old data files [counted as EIs or input data into the already counted ILFs] and possibly an EO for a conversion report)

3. Two application value adjustment factors (the VAFs could change as a part of the project; in which case, there would be a prior VAF and a new VAF)

An example of an enhancement is included in one of the case studies presented in Chapter 11 and in the practice Certified Function Point Specialist (CFPS) exam in Chapter 16. Remember that an enhancement project most likely will result in a change to the installed or application function point count. The change will not necessarily be additive to the previous application function point count.

Enhancement Project Function Point Calculation

The following formula is used to calculate the enhancement project function point count:

$$EFP = [(ADD + CHGA + CFP) \times VAFA] + (DEL \times VAFB)$$

where

- EFP is the enhancement project function point count.
- ADD is the unadjusted function point count of those functions added by the enhancement project.
- CHGA is the unadjusted function point count of those functions modified by the enhancement project (this component reflects the value of the functions after the modifications have occurred, not just the fields added by the modification; a typical error is to count only DETs and FTRs or RETs changed, but everything about the function should be counted to consider effort involved with the testing of existing functionality as well as that changed).
- CFP is the number of function points included by a conversion of data.

- VAFA is the value adjustment factor of the application after the enhancement project.
- DEL is the unadjusted function point count of those functions that were deleted by the enhancement project.
- VAFB is the value adjustment factor of the application before the enhancement project.

Application Function Point Count

An application function point count consists of two components of functionality (conversion effort functionality is not included in the application count because it is part of the development effort and not the application once established):

1. Application unadjusted function point count, consisting of the EIs, EOs, EQs, ILFs, and EIFs
2. Application value adjustment factor

There are two different times when we should perform an application function point count:

1. When the application is initially delivered
2. When an enhancement project has changed the value of the application's functionality (when the enhancement project is installed, the previous application function point count must be updated to recognize modifications to the application). The enhancement project could have modified the application by
   - Adding (new) functionality, increasing the function point size of the application
   - Changing functionality by increasing, decreasing, or having no effect on the function point size of the application
   - Deleting functionality, decreasing the function point size of the application
   - Changing the value adjustment factor, by adding, decreasing, or having no effect on the function point size of the application

These variations are reflected in two different counting formulas:

Initial Application Function Point Calculation

The following formula is used to calculate the initial application function point count:

$$AFP = ADD \times VAF$$

where

- AFP is the initial application function point count.
- ADD is the unadjusted function point count of those functions installed by the development project.
- VAF is the value adjustment factor.

Application Function Point Calculation after an Enhancement

The following formula is used to calculate the application function point count after an enhancement:

$$AFP = [(UFPB + ADD + CHGA) - (CHGB + DEL)] \times VAFA$$

where

- AFP is the application adjusted function point count.
- UFPB is the application unadjusted function point count before the enhancement project.
- ADD is the unadjusted function point count of those functions added by the enhancement project.
- CHGA is the unadjusted function point count of those functions changed by the enhancement project (this component reflects the function point value after the change).
- CHGB is the unadjusted function point count of those functions changed by the enhancement before the change (this component reflects the function point value before the enhancement project).
- DEL is the unadjusted function point count of those functions deleted by the enhancement project.
- VAFA is the value adjustment factor of the application after the enhancement project.

Summary

This chapter provided our first example of counting data functions (ILFs and EIFs) and transactional functions (EIs, EOs, and EQs) to determine the unadjusted function point count, calculate the value adjustment factor (VAF), and apply the VAF to produce the adjusted function point count of an application.

Formulas were presented for the calculation of a development project function point count, an enhancement project function point count, and two variations of an application function point count.

Detailed guidance is contained within the IFPUG Counting Practices Manual. We will provide several case studies in Chapter 11 to assist you in applying the IFPUG rules in counting data functions and transactional functions, as well as in calculating adjusted function point counts.

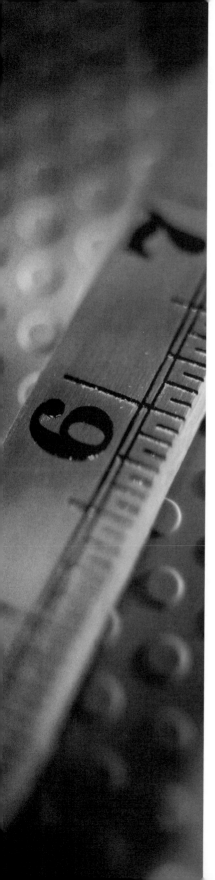

CHAPTER ELEVEN

Case Studies in Counting

Introduction

This chapter contains case studies to enable practice in the application of function point counting rules. The first example is a series of three problems, each one building on the previous problem. These are followed by a case study on counting a project management system. The final case study requires function point counting early in the lifecycle of a project. Although accurate and exact counts are not usually possible, if we have enough data to commence requirements definition, we have enough data to commence function point counting. Additional case studies will be presented in Chapters 13, 14, and 16.

Three Case Studies

Three problems (A, B, and C) follow. Complete the appropriate answer sheets for each problem.

Problem A

A corporation plans to build a simple locator application to maintain information about companies interested in its function point courses.

The logical grouping of *company contact data* to be maintained will include the following data fields:

- Company
- Name of contact
- Job title

- Date of initial contact
- Street address
- City
- State
- Zip code
- Phone number
- Fax number

This data initially will be created when an individual indicates an interest in any course. Employees will have the capability of creating, changing, and deleting any of this information, via an online screen, using the following commands: create, update, and delete. The create and update functions will maintain all ten fields indicated. The delete function requires only the company and name of contact to be entered.

Additional fields to be included in the *company contact data* but updated with separate transactions are as follows:

- Date packet sent
- Date of phone contact
- Notes

These fields are to be maintained by two separate elementary processes as follows: (1) When an information packet is sent, the individual mailing the package will use a separate screen to enter company, name of contact, and date the packet was sent, using a function key. (2) A follow-up phone call should be made within two weeks of the mailing to ensure receipt and respond to questions. When this contract has been completed, the caller will use a separate screen to enter company, name of contact, date of phone contact, and notes, using a function key. The date of phone contact will be used as a secondary key (a second record type) to save the multiple occurrences of information and to update the *company contact data.*

A menu-driven system will be required to navigate through the system. The six functions, offering selections, will be as follows:

- Create company contact
- Retrieve company contact
- Update company contact
- Delete company contact
- Packet sent
- Phone contact completed

All of these functions, except retrieve company contact, were already discussed. The retrieval, prompted by the entering of company, name of contact, and a function key, will display all fields maintained in the *company contact data*.

Errors could be returned, for any of the transactions, from an externally maintained Error file, which has four fields. One of these fields contains the error messages.

Identify the functions included here and their complexities, using the answer sheet for Problem A. (Figure 11-1). See Figure 11-4 (page 179) for the answers.

Problem B

For the preceding exercise, complete the corresponding function point calculation worksheet (Figure 11-2) using your functions from Problem A and the general system characteristics (already entered on the worksheet) to compute an adjusted function point count. See Figure 11-5 (page 180) for the answers.

Problem C

Shortly after the locator application was delivered, Caren Garmus stated that she wanted to utilize the help subsystem already being maintained by an external application to provide both field- and screen-level help. These two levels of help will be available on each screen and will access help text from a separately maintained external help file. Help, in all cases, has less than five fields.

Mary Herron said she wanted a weekly *overdue contact report* (Table 11-1) that would indicate those contacts who had not received packets and those contacts who had not been called within two weeks of the mailing. The report would

Table 11-1: Overdue Contact Report

Date Printed:	Page Number:
Retrieval as of:	
Company	
Name of contact	
Initial contact date	
Packet sent[a]	
Phone contact scheduled date[b]	
Totals overdue	

[a]Blank if not sent; date if sent.

[b]Blank if no packet sent, or 14 days after packet sent. This date is calculated when the packet is sent.

Function Point Count Summary

Project Number Problem A			Project Name	
Date of Count			Counter's Name	

Instructions: Enter all function types included. Annotate all function types added by the conversion. You may wish to use different sheets for files and transactions.

Description	Type[a]	DETs	RETs/FTRs	Complexity[b]

[a] ILF, EIF, EI, EO, or EQ
[b] Low (L), Average (A), High (H)

Figure 11-1 Function point counting summary for Problem A

Function Point Calculation Worksheet

Project Number Problem B	**Project Name** Locator Application

Type of Count ~~Development Project~~/Application Counting (circle one)
Phase of Count ~~Proposal~~/Requirements/Design/Code/Test/Delivery (circle one)
Date of Count   **Counter's Name**

IFPUG's Unadjusted Function Point Table*

	Function Levels			
Components	**Low**	**Average**	**High**	**Total**
External inputs	× 3	× 4	× 6	
External outputs	× 4	× 5	× 7	
External inquiries	× 3	× 4	× 6	
Internal logical files	× 7	× 10	× 15	
External interface files	× 5	× 7	× 10	

Total unadjusted function points (UFP) =

* The development function point count includes function types added by the conversion. The application function point count does not include conversion requirements. An application count after an enhancement must include all existing function types, including those unchanged. If information on all existing function types is not available, the application adjusted function point count can be computed by the formula given in the text.

General System Characteristics

Characteristic	Degree of Influence	Characteristic	Degree of Influence
1. Data communications	4	8. Online update	3
2. Distributed data processing	0	9. Complex processing	1
3. Performance	0	10. Reusability	3
4. Heavily used configuration	0	11. Installation ease	1
5. Transaction rate	0	12. Operational ease	3
6. Online data entry	5	13. Multiple sites	1
7. End user efficiency	3	14. Facilitate change	2

Total degree of influence (TDI) =

VAF	Value adjustment factor	$= (\text{TDI} \times 0.01) + 0.65 =$	
FP	Adjusted function point count	$= \text{UFP} \times \text{VAF}$	=

Figure 11-2 Function point calculation worksheet for Problem B

retrieve the data from the *company contact data file* on a weekly basis. No changes are required to the *company contact data file*.

Identify the functions and their complexities for the help and overdue contact report functions. Additionally, for the report, identify the number of DETs

Function Point Count Summary

Project Number Problem C	Project Name
Date of Count	Counter's Name

Instructions: Enter all function types included. Annotate all function types added by the conversion. You may wish to use different sheets for files and transactions.

Description	Type[a]	DETs	RETs/FTRs	Complexity[b]

[a] ILF, EIF, EI, EO, or EQ
[b] Low (L), Average (A), High (H)

Figure 11-3 Function point count summary for Problem C

and FTRs. It is not necessary to enter the number of DETs, RETs, and FTRs for the help functions. **Use the answer sheet for Problem C (Figure 11-3).** See Figure 11-6 (page 181) for the answers.

Answers to the Three Case Studies

Function Point Count Summary

Project Number Answers to Problem A   **Project Name**
Date of Count   **Counter's Name**
Instructions: Enter all function types included. Annotate all function types added by the conversion. You may wish to use different sheets for files and transactions.

Description	Type[a]	DETs	RETs/FTRs	Complexity[b]
Company contact data	ILF	13	2	L
Error file	EIF	4	1	L
Create company contact	EI	12	2	A
Retrieve company contact	EQ	15	2	A
Update company contact	EI	12	2	A
Delete company contact	EI	4	2	L
Packet sent	EI	5	2	A
Phone contact completed	EI	6	2	A

[a] ILF, EIF, EI, EO, or EQ
[b] Low (L), Average (A), High (H)

Figure 11-4 Problem A answers

Function Point Calculation Worksheet

Project Number Answers to Problem B	**Project Name** Locator Application
Type of Count ⟨Development Project⟩/Application Counting (circle one)	
Phase of Count ⟨Proposal⟩/Requirements/Design/Code/Test/Delivery (circle one)	
Date of Count	**Counter's Name**

IFPUG's Unadjusted Function Point Table*

	Function Levels			
Components	Low	Average	High	Total
External inputs	1×3	4×4	$\times 6$	19
External outputs	$\times 4$	$\times 5$	$\times 7$	0
External inquiries	$\times 3$	1×4	$\times 6$	4
Internal logical files	1×7	$\times 10$	$\times 15$	7
External interface files	1×5	$\times 7$	$\times 10$	5

Total unadjusted function points (UFP) = 35

* The development function point count includes function types added by the conversion. The application function point count does not include conversion requirements. An application count after an enhancement must include all existing function types, including those unchanged. If information on all existing function types is not available, the application adjusted function point count can be computed by the formula given in the text.

General System Characteristics

Characteristic	Degree of Influence	Characteristic	Degree of Influence
1. Data communications	4	8. Online update	3
2. Distributed data processing	0	9. Complex processing	1
3. Performance	0	10. Reusability	3
4. Heavily used configuration	0	11. Installation ease	1
5. Transaction rate	0	12. Operational ease	3
6. Online data entry	5	13. Multiple sites	1
7. End user efficiency	3	14. Facilitate change	2

Total degree of influence (TDI) = 26

VAF	Value adjustment factor	$= (TDI \times 0.01) + 0.65 =$	0.91
FP	Adjusted function point count	$= UFP \times VAF$	$= 31.85$

Figure 11-5 Problem B answers

Function Point Count Summary

Project Number Answers to Problem C		**Project Name**
Date of Count		**Counter's Name**
Instructions: Enter all function types included. Annotate all function types added by the conversion. You may wish to use different sheets for files and transactions.		

Description	Type[a]	DETs	RETs/FTRs	Complexity[b]
Field help	EQ	<5	1	L
Screen help	EQ	<5	1	L
Help file	EIF	<5	1	L
Overdue contact report	EO	7	1	L

[a] ILF, EIF, EI, EO, or EQ
[b] Low (L), Average (A), High (H)

Figure 11-6 Problem C answers

A Short Case Study in Project Management

The following case study describes an application that permits users to define skill sets, to designate personnel with those skill sets, to enter tasks to be performed, and to assign personnel to those tasks. The case study will define some characteristics of the system, the transactional functionality required, and the database (file) layouts.

The Problem

Transactional Functions

1. Users will log on to the application by validating a password against an externally maintained Security file (defined below).
2. Field-level help will be available for each field on each screen from an externally maintained Help file (defined below).
3. Error and confirmation messages will be provided for all screen transactions; the messages will be hard-coded and not user maintained.
4. Command keys will be required to initiate all screen transactions.
5. A Skill Sets file (defined below) will be maintained with add, update, and view transactions. There will be no delete functionality. All fields in the Skill Sets file will be available through a screen for the add, update, and view transactions.
6. Task coordinators will enter tasks to be performed on a screen. All fields in Tasks to Be Performed file (defined below) must be completed, and any appropriate fields will also be validated against the Location file (defined below) and the Skill Sets file. Each task to be performed will have a unique ID.
7. A drop-down list box will display task priority, which will be urgent, important, average, or low, from a hard-coded table.
8. A view will be available that contains all information from the Tasks to Be Performed file.
9. Tasks to be performed may be modified or deleted if they have not yet been assigned. The Assignment file (defined below) must be referenced in order to determine if the task has been assigned. In order to modify, change to any appropriate fields will also be validated against the Location file and the Skill Sets file.
10. Assignment clerks will make assignments to available personnel who possess the proper skill sets on the basis of the priority of the tasks. The Assignment file will be created with validation against the Personnel file (an externally maintained file defined below) and the Tasks to Be Performed file.

11. Assignment clerks will retrieve and display unassigned tasks with all fields from the Tasks to Be Performed file. The display may be sorted by task priority, skill set ID, task location ID, and/or requested start date. A list may also be printed with the same fields; the printed list will also include a total of tasks by priority (urgent, important, average, or low).

12. Assignment clerks will search for persons with specified skill sets, specific office locations, and their appropriate available date (the next assignment date available). The return screen display will include a person's name, skill sets, office location, and next assignment date available.

13. An assignment can be deleted if the job has not commenced. Assignment data cannot be modified or updated.

14. Employees have access to the system to enter assignment completion dates together with their name and the task ID. Only the Assignment file will be validated and updated.

15. A separate report will be generated daily that includes all currently assigned tasks (not reported as complete). It will include all fields from the Tasks to Be Performed file, as well as person's name, date assignment is to commence, and date assignment is expected to be complete from the Assignment file.

16. An e-mail message will be generated internally to the office supervisor and all task coordinators advising that a task (task ID) has been assigned to a person (person's name), the task location, and the date the assignment is to commence. The e-mail addresses will be retrieved from the Location file.

17. An e-mail will be sent to the person assigned a task, stating the person's name, e-mail address, task ID, duration of task in days, task location ID, and all location information, skill set IDs required, and skill set descriptions.

Data Functions

All files and their relevant fields and primary keys (PKs) are identified below:

1. Tasks to Be Performed file
- Task ID (unique, nonrepeating ID); PK
- Task priority (urgent, important, average, or low)
- Task location ID
- Skill set IDs required (up to two; no special priority or sequence)
- Requested start date
- Duration of task in days

2. Assignment file
- Person's name; PK
- Task ID; PK
- Date assignment is to commence
- Date assignment is expected to be complete (calculated and maintained internally)
- Next assignment date expected to be available (calculated and maintained internally)
- Assignment completion date (entered by employee)

3. Skill Sets file
- Skill set ID; PK
- Skill set description
- Licensing requirement
- Educational requirement
- Local training requirement
- Suggested corollary skill set IDs (up to three)

4. Personnel file (externally maintained)
- Person's name; PK
- Skill sets IDs (up to five skills possible)
- Office location
- E-mail address

5. Help file (externally maintained)
- Screen ID; PK
- Field ID; PK
- Help text (up to six lines possible)

6. Security file (externally maintained)
- Log-on user ID; PK
- Password
- Application authorization

7. Location file (externally maintained)
- Location ID; PK
- Street address (three lines)
- City
- State

- Zip code
- Office phone number
- Office supervisor's name
- Office supervisor's e-mail address
- Task coordinator's name
- Task coordinator's e-mail address

On the basis of the information provided, identify the data and transactional functions with their complexities.

Answers

Data Functions

1. Tasks to Be Performed	Low ILF	1 RET	6 DETs
2. Assignment	Low ILF	1 RET	6 DETs
3. Skill Sets	Low ILF	1 RET	6 DETs
4. Personnel	Low EIF	1 RET	4 DETs
5. Help	Low EIF	1 RET	3 DETs
6. Security	Low EIF	1 RET	3 DETs
7. Location	Low EIF	1 RET	10 DETs

Transactional Functions

1. User log-on	Low EQ	1 FTR	4 DETs
2. Field help	Low EQ	1 FTR	5 DETs
3. Error and confirmation messages	1 added DET for each screen transaction		
4. Command keys	1 added DET for each screen transaction		
5. Add skill sets	Low EI	1 FTR	8 DETs
Update skill sets	Low EI	1 FTR	8 DETs
View skill sets	Low EQ	1 FTR	8 DETs
6. Create tasks	High EI	3 FTRs	8 DETs
7. Task priority	Not counted; hard-coded		
8. View tasks to be performed	Low EQ	1 FTR	8 DETs
9. Modify tasks to be performed	High EI	4 FTRs	8 DETs
Delete tasks to be performed	Low EI	2 FTRs	3 DETs
10. Make assignments	High EI	3 FTRs	8 DETs
11. View unassigned tasks	Average EQ	2 FTRs	8 DETs
Print unassigned tasks	Average EO	2 FTRs	9 DETs
12. Search for persons	Average EQ	2 FTRs	6 DETs

13. Delete assignments	Low EI	1 FTR	4 DETs
14. Enter completion dates	Low EI	1 FTR	5 DETs
15. Generate daily report	Average EQ	2 FTRs	9 DETs
16. E-mail to supervisor and task coordinators	Average EQ	3 FTRs	8 DETs
17. E-mail to employee	High EQ	5 FTRs	16 DETs

A Function Point Counting Exercise in Early Definition

For this exercise we will assume that a company has decided to build an application to assign, maintain, and report on parking space assignments for both employees and visitors. A joint application design (JAD) session has resulted in agreement that a new application (the Parking Assignment application) will be developed and that some reference data will be retrieved from the Personnel file, which is maintained in the Building Personnel application. It was agreed that the following transactions would be required:

The Problem

Transactional Functions

1. View all unassigned parking spaces.
2. Look up an employee to be visited by first, middle, and last name from the Personnel file.
3. Assign a visitor parking space; validate the employee to be visited against the Personnel file.
4. Terminate an assigned visitor parking space.
5. View current visitors who are assigned parking spaces, together with employee information from the Personnel file.
6. Produce a visitor report at the end of day, with information from both the Parking Assignment file and the Personnel file and totals for the number of visitors.
7. Assign an employee permanent parking space; validate against Personnel file.
8. Transfer an employee permanent parking space; validate against the Personnel file.
9. Terminate an assigned employee permanent parking space.
10. Produce a weekly report on permanent parking space assignments, with information from the Parking Assignment file and the Personnel file and totals.

11. Mark a parking space closed for maintenance.
12. View parking spaces closed for maintenance.
13. Reopen a parking space closed for maintenance.
14. Produce a weekly report on parking maintenance, with totals.

A rough data model of the Parking Assignment file is developed with two mandatory subgroups of data, which will be based on whether the space is assigned to a visitor or an employee. In total there are 12 visitor parking spaces and 144 employee permanent parking spaces. As mentioned previously, it was decided that data would be retrieved and referenced from the Personnel file, which is maintained in the Building Personnel application. The data expected to be required is as follows:

Data Functions

PERSONNEL FILE
  • First name (considered to be one field)
  • Middle name (considered to be one field)
  • Last name (considered to be one field)
  • Employee ID
  • Office phone number
  • Office location

PARKING ASSIGNMENT FILE
Subgroup 1: Visitor space number (V1–V12)
  • Date
  • Time assigned
  • Time out
  • Visitor's name
  • ID of employee being visited
  • Space closed for maintenance (Y/N)
  • Date closed for maintenance
  • Date reopened

Subgroup 2: Employee space number (P1–P144)
  • Date effective
  • Name: first, middle, and last (entire name considered to be one field)
  • Employee ID
  • Date space released
  • Space closed for maintenance (Y/N)

- Date closed for maintenance
- Date reopened

Identify the data and transactional functions and estimate their complexities.

Answers

Data Functions

PERSONNEL FILE (Low EIF with 1 RET and 6 DETs)
- First name (considered to be one field)
- Middle name (considered to be one field)
- Last name (considered to be one field)
- Employee ID
- Office phone number
- Office location

PARKING ASSIGNMENT FILE (Low ILF with 2 RETs and 13 DETs)
Subgroup 1: Visitor space number (V1–V12) (RET 1)
- Date
- Time assigned
- Time out
- Visitor's name
- ID of employee being visited
- Space closed for maintenance (Y/N)
- Date closed for maintenance
- Date reopened

Subgroup 2: Employee space number (P1–P144) (RET 2; field already counted)
- Date effective
- Name: first, middle, and last (entire name considered to be one field)
- Employee ID
- Date space released
- Space closed for maintenance (Y/N); field already counted
- Date closed for maintenance; field already counted
- Date reopened; field already counted

Transactional Functions

1. View all unassigned parking spaces	Low EQ	1 FTR	<20 DETs
2. Look up employee to be visited	Low EQ	1 FTR	<20 DETs

3. Assign visitor parking space	Average EI	2 FTRs	5–15 DETs
4. Terminate assigned visitor parking space	Low EI	1 FTR	<16 DETs
5. View current visitors	Average EQ	2 FTRs	6–19 DETs
6. Produce visitor report	Average EO	2 FTRs	6–19 DETs
7. Assign employee parking space	Average EI	2 FTRs	5–15 DETs
8. Transfer employee parking space	Average EI	2 FTRs	5–15 DETs
9. Terminate assigned employee parking space	Low EI	1 FTR	<16 DETs
10. Produce weekly report on assignments	Average EO	2 FTRs	6–19 DETs
11. Mark a space closed for maintenance	Low EI	1 FTR	<16 DETs
12. View spaces closed for maintenance	Low EQ	1 FTR	<20 DETs
13. Reopen a space closed for maintenance	Low EI	1 FTR	<16 DETs
14. Produce weekly report on maintenance	Low EO	1 FTR	6–19 DETs

CHAPTER TWELVE

Counting Advanced Technologies

Introduction

Function point analysis (FPA) permits you to size software requirements independently of technology. Applications developed with advanced development methodologies (e.g., object-oriented analysis and design), in new environments (e.g., client-server, Web-based, or data warehouse applications), or using commercial off-the-shelf (COTS) tools (e.g., query/report generators) can easily be sized through FPA. Only after developing an understanding of the concepts of these methodologies, environments, or tools can the FPA practitioner map the concepts to the FPA methodology.

Object-Oriented Analysis

Object-oriented (OO) analysis and design is a methodology used to analyze the business problem and solution in unique components called **objects**. All data necessary to describe both the business problem and the solution are depicted in objects. Details and descriptions of the objects are defined as **attributes**. **Behaviors** of the objects are identified by values and revisions of the data. Once an object has been thoroughly analyzed, a set of rules must be defined that establish the policies of the object—that is, how the data can be used and changed. These rules become the basis for function point analysis.

An object is an abstraction of something in a problem domain that is relevant to the application. All like objects share the same characteristics. An object is made up of two parts: data (called attributes) and processing (called behavior). Because the major part of an OO project is the definition of objects, these components will be described in detail to clarify the applicability of IFPUG counting rules.

Objects are described by properties and can often be mapped in tabular form (see Table 12-1). An OO software system is composed of objects sending messages to each other. Objects communicate with each other by sending messages to predefined interfaces through various means. A **message** is a signal between objects. An **operation** is a process that can be requested as a unit. A **method** is a procedural specification of an operation, an implementation of an operation, often called **services**.

Objects are instances of classes. An **instance** is a unique object created by a **class**. These are often represented in an object model or class diagram. The term "object" is often used interchangeably with the term "class." An example of a class is aircraft. There are many types of aircraft, and all share common attributes. We can depict this relationship by capturing all of the common attributes at the highest level of the class diagram. Aircraft can be defined as flying machines with wings, wheels, and an engine. This relationship implies both an ancestor-descendent concept and the inheritance of the common attributes to the lower classes. A jet airplane inherits the attributes of wings, wheels, and an engine, but it is further defined by number of passenger seats and other specifics unique to that particular object.

Another feature of OO analysis and design is the concept of polymorphism, which means literally "many forms." This is one of the great selling points of reuse

Table 12-1: Properties of an Object

Component	Definition	Example
Name	Identifies the object	EMPLOYEE
Attribute	Describes common features or characteristics	NAME DATE OF BIRTH HIRE DATE DEPARTMENT NAME
Behavior	Describes processing performed (methods, operations, services) on or by the object	Change name Add employee Change departments
State	Defines life history of the object	Assigned On leave

in OO. In an OO application, an object can send a message to another object without knowing the instance's class. For example, to send a message from an object CD player to the object Audio, it is not necessary to know the model of the CD player; the behavior of a CD player is to play, start, and stop.

This overall flexibility permits the definition of an application, problem domain, and solution by the use of models. **Object models** capture the structures of objects in a system and include their identities and relationships to other objects, attributes, and operations. Dynamic models describe the timing and sequencing of operations in a system and capture events that cause changes in state. Functional models describe the transformation of values in a system and include functions, mappings, constraints, and dependencies.

From a function point analysis perspective, the object model is the most important. Included in the object models are the various links and associations. For example, a truck "is" a type of transportation vehicle. Company "has" an employee. It is this type of linkage that provides further insight into the application boundary and uses of the data (objects).

To count an application, review the business requirements and the object model:

- Identify the main functions of the application, as specified in the business requirements.
- Identify the main objects that support those requirements, as depicted in the object model.
- Draw a boundary around objects in the application. Often an object model includes all objects in the problem domain, and it could include multiple applications. The objects in the application are the first step in identifying the ILFs from a function point analysis perspective.
- Identify those objects used by the application to satisfy the business requirements. These objects become EIFs from a function point analysis perspective.

Table 12-2 matches OO components to function point counting rules. This mapping should aid you in counting the application independently of technology and implementation techniques. Keep in mind that we should be sizing the software on the basis of business requirements and reviewing the application from a logical perspective.

By carefully "translating" OO components into logical FPA components, we can count function points with relative ease. The simplified object model shown in Figure 12-1 will be the basis of the case study presented in Chapter 14.

Table 12-2: Mapping of OO Components to Function Point Counting Rules

FPA Concepts	OO Mapping
Data components	
ILF	Objects maintained by the application.
EIF	Objects referenced by the application.
RET	Inheritance; count optional or mandatory classes as RETs of the ILF.
	Polymorphism; may result in additional RETs.
	Specialization; may not be a RET; some classes may not map to a user requirement but may exist solely for technology or implementation.
DETs	Attributes; count as DETs.
Elementary process	Be careful in mapping all methods and services within objects; not all calls between objects are stand-alone elementary processes.
	OO projects often include use cases to further define the functionality of the application as it relates to users (actors); the use cases often depict elementary processes.
Function point components	If an object has communication with objects in another boundary and processing is required at both ends, there could be an EI and an EO or EQ.
	Service; look at the action verb or procedure relating to the user requirement; some examples of specific behavior of functional processing include create, calculate, access, and so on; however, calls and extracts are internal processing and are not counted.

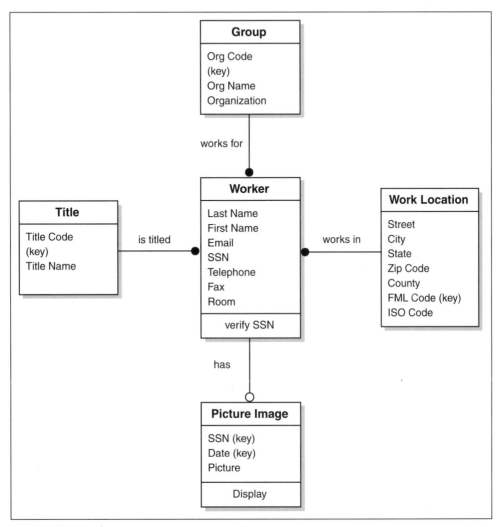

Figure 12-1 Object model of the database server

Client-Server Applications

Client-server applications introduce a technical architecture in which an application includes processing on multiple platforms that communicate directly with each other to support the business problem. For example, one platform could be responsible for requesting information (often called the **client**) and the other platform could be responsible for supplying the information (often called the

server). These platforms could reside in various physical environments, such as PC (desktop)–UNIX (server) or PC (desktop)–Web (server). In all cases, it is the combined architecture of both the client and the server that provides the solution to the application.

Often the client-server application is constructed in various layers:

- A graphical user interface (GUI) layer, often a presentation layer
- A data layer, which stores and retrieves data according to business rules (could be embedded in DBMS software such as Oracle or SQL)
- An application layer, which communicates with the GUI and the data layers, and often with other external applications as well

Client-server architectures typically contain distributed data; that is, data resides both on the client and on the server. Occasionally, data resides solely on the server. It is a misnomer, therefore, when counting FPA for a client-server application to claim that it is distributed data. The FPA practitioner must determine if data actually resides on the client as well as on the server in order to classify the application with distributed data processing, which is reflected in the second general system characteristic (see Chapter 9).

Application Boundary

The application boundary, as defined by the Counting Practices Manual, indicates the border between the software being measured and the user, defines what is external to the application, is the conceptual interface between the internal application and the external user world, and acts as a membrane through which data processes as transactions pass into and out of the application.

A client-server application includes the functionality of both the client and the server (see Figure 12-2). A function point count of the application should be conducted from the perspective of the business solution versus the technical solution. The client-server environment and the various layers of the application are part of the physical environment and are not part of the functional requirements.

All components need not reside on the same hardware platform. From a business perspective, the application boundary of a client-server application consists of all components that collectively meet the business requirements, regardless of physical implementation or platform.

Data Functions

Count data functions following the IFPUG counting rules, which state that data functions are groups of logically related data that are user identifiable. The

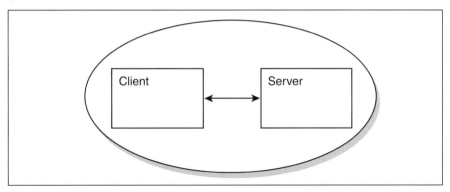

Figure 12-2 An application includes the functions that reside on both client and server platforms

presence of a table or file in an application does not make that group of data an ILF or EIF. Be sure that the data is maintained through an elementary process and that it satisfies business requirements.

Technical Features

On a server there could be a table called server-client cross-reference. This table might ensure consistency between the data layer and the presentation layer. Should this be counted?

On a client there could be a table containing presentation rules. It might contain a bit map, a color schema, screen coordinates, and metrics used by the presentation layer to properly display information in the window. Should this be counted?

In these examples the tables are not maintained through an elementary process. They don't fulfill business requirements of the application; they provide technical solutions. They should not be counted as functionality within the application.

Transactional Functions

Always look for an elementary process. Consider only the data that crosses the application boundary. Do not count messages or data transfers between the client and the server as transactional functions (see Figure 12-3).

Count transactional functions on the basis of IFPUG counting rules. An external input is defined as data that is received from *outside the boundary* whose primary intent is to maintain an ILF or alter the behavior of a system.

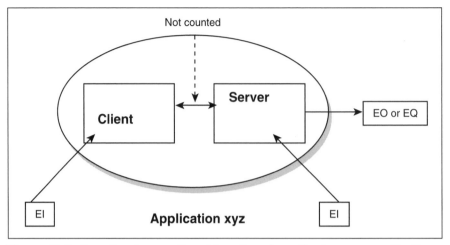

Figure 12-3 Counting transactional functions in a client-server application

Component A in the application represented in Figure 12-4 provides an online screen with the ability to add and/or change course information. External inputs are counted.

Component B provides a feed that is processed by the server, which includes a list of students enrolled in satellite courses; it is processed weekly. An external input is counted.

Component C reflects course information updated by data presentation, bundled and passed every two hours to the server. No data crosses the boundary; nothing is counted.

A transactional function that sends data or control information external to the boundary, whose primary intent is to present information through the retrieval of data or control information, is counted as an external inquiry.

Component D in Figure 12-5 provides a display of students enrolled in Advanced Function Point Analysis. Component D is counted as an external inquiry.

Component E provides a report on the percentage of enrolled students by instructor. It is produced, printed, and calculated on the server. Because calculations are performed, component E is counted as an external output.

Other FPA considerations include the general system characteristics (see Chapter 9). GSCs 1 (data communications), 2 (distributed data processing), 3 (performance), 4 (heavily used configuration), 5 (transaction rate), 6 (online data entry), and 9 (complex processing) are particularly important. Remember to be sure that the degrees of influence reflect the characteristics of the entire application, not just a few components.

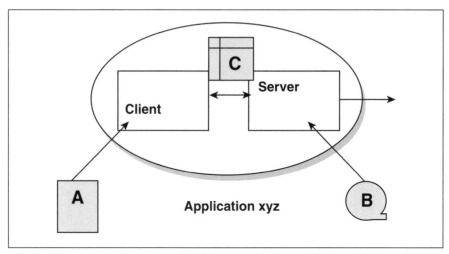

Figure 12-4 Counting example: Components A, B, and C

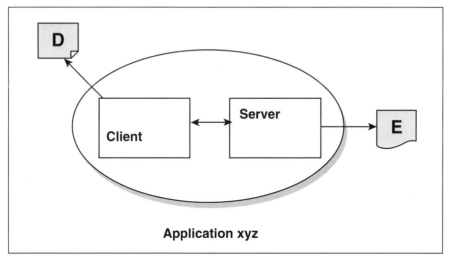

Figure 12-5 Counting example: Components D and E

Web-Based Applications

Web-based applications interface in part or in whole with the Internet or an intranet. The Internet is an international web of interconnected government, education, and business computer networks. Businesses have created their own intranets on private networks by using Internet technology. Companies now link traditional directory, e-mail, and other network software applications. The

Internet easily connects manufacturing sites, transportation channels, wholesale warehouses, retail outlets, and customers. The ease of use has contributed to the immense popularity of the Internet.

The Internet or an intranet provides a repository of information and enables data sharing for groups with specialized interests. Businesses advertise, market, and transact business on the Internet. Online catalogs and advertising are interspersed with directory-type information. Protection of copyrighted material or sensitive data presents a problem because a user can download an electronic copy. Many companies encrypt data that is available on the Internet, providing decoding keys only to buyers of the data.

The World Wide Web (WWW) enables a collection of independently owned Web servers to be linked worldwide. Using software browsers (e.g., Netscape Communicator or Microsoft's Internet Explorer), individuals can enter the WWW through local providers or through online services (e.g., AT&T, AOL, CompuServe, or MSN) and browse or "surf" the Internet through a system of hypertext links (e.g., www.davidconsultinggroup.com).

Because of the significant growth in e-business and the development of Web applications (over 500 percent growth during 1998 and 1999, according to the *Wall Street Journal*), there is an ever increasing requirement to correctly size Web-based applications by the use of function points.

Application Boundary

A Web application is a group of logically related stand-alone functions that fulfill specific business requirements as defined by users of the Internet or intranet. A Web site could be utilized by multiple applications. Users can access a Web application from different Web sites or other applications.

Several types of applications should be considered for function point sizing.

Functionality of Web-Based Applications

Traditional directory services permit lookup of individuals (e.g., employees or customers) or documents (Word documents, Excel spreadsheets, promotional literature, lists, and so on). These directory services typically include a master file of information and several online queries (with sophisticated search selection criteria) as their main functionality.

E-mail services are frequently stand-alone applications built using a Web interface. These applications and other networked software applications often include the ability to create mail messages, send messages, receive messages, retrieve messages, display or print messages, save messages, delete messages, create or modify an address book, and create groups for mass mailings. Each of these functions can be sized by function point analysis when each elementary process is identified.

As is often the case with new technology, the software development process falls behind the technology, so the function point counter is often confronted with a Web-based application that was built as the dialog with business users was occurring. Because the development of the application was accelerated without written requirements, it could be difficult for a function point counter to correctly identify the logical groups of data, elementary processes, and transactional components.

Some common components of Web-based applications include text (e.g., HTML, PostScript, or PDF), image (e.g., GIF or JPEG), sound (e.g., WAV), video (e.g., MPEG), and animation (e.g., ShockWave). These components represent the physical implementation of the functionality that must be explored in order to perform a correct function point count. One of the dangers in counting applications solely on the basis of their physical presentation (i.e., by logging onto the Web site to count the functionality) is the strong possibility of incorrectly identifying the "logical" view of the application independent of technology or implementation. A counter must always consider the functionality being provided, independently of the platform and implementation technology.

The guidelines shown in Table 12-3 have been established to ensure that you are following the counting rules contained in the Counting Practices Manual.

Table 12-3: Guidelines for Applying IFPUG's Counting Rules to Web-Based Applications

Function Point Component	Guidelines
Application boundary	• Look at ownership of the Web site in establishing the application boundary. • Look for user views of "business" functional areas to aid in the determination of different application boundaries. • The boundary does not include capabilities provided by individual Internet browsers (e.g., Netscape Communicator, Microsoft's Internet Explorer). • Search engines not developed by the Web site are not part of the application. *(continued)*

Table 12-3: (*cont.*)

Function Point Component	Guidelines
	• Consider the scope of the home page with its business functions within the same application. • Some Web sites could represent links to many different applications. • Establish application boundaries and be consistent.
User and user view	• Web application users include more than traditional operators. • Users could include an application administrator and/or the Webmaster.
Data functionality	• Consider all data that is maintained by the Web application. • Be sure that the data is maintained; often the data components are retrieved from another application and should be counted as EIFs.
Transaction functionality	• Follow the elementary process rules to correctly identify the transactions; don't count retrievals of like documents as separate transactions. • Don't be confused by multiple implementation examples of one user view. • Always come back to the logical view of the application; for example, multiple links are on the same page. Links to other applications may provide navigation only and not be recognized by function points. • Be sure that all functionality is correctly identified. • If the transaction allows the user to save data (e.g., post to a bulletin board that is maintained by the application), count it as an EI; however, if the data is being sent as an e-mail (and not maintained within the Web application), count it as an EQ. • Remember always to count elementary processes; if several physical pages are required to fulfill requirements, all of the pages together should be counted as a single component.

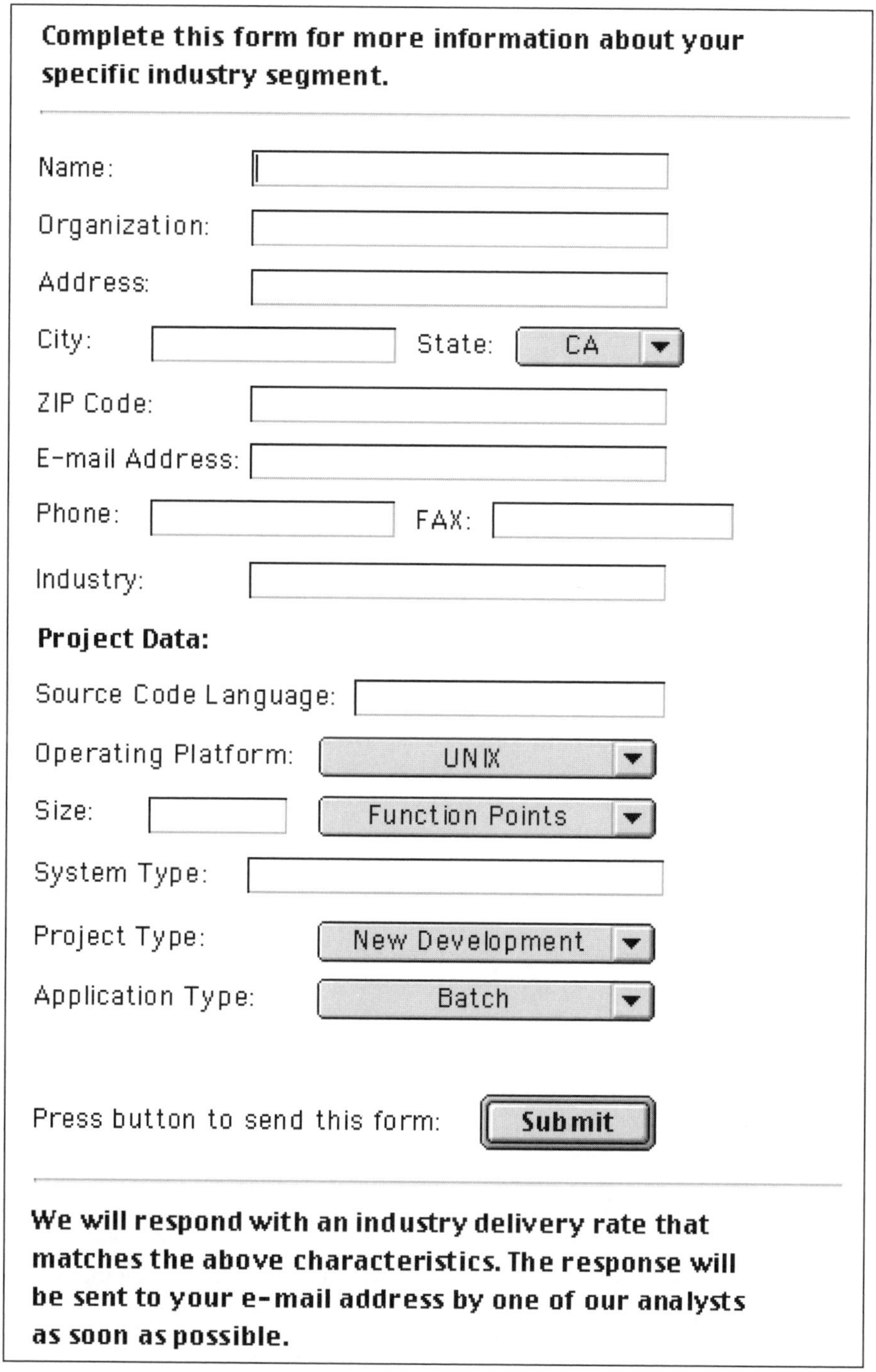

Complete this form for more information about your specific industry segment.

Name: [   ]

Organization: [   ]

Address: [   ]

City: [   ]   State: [CA ▼]

ZIP Code: [   ]

E-mail Address: [   ]

Phone: [   ]   FAX: [   ]

Industry: [   ]

Project Data:

Source Code Language: [   ]

Operating Platform: [UNIX ▼]

Size: [   ] [Function Points ▼]

System Type: [   ]

Project Type: [New Development ▼]

Application Type: [Batch ▼]

Press button to send this form: [**Submit**]

We will respond with an industry delivery rate that matches the above characteristics. The response will be sent to your e-mail address by one of our analysts as soon as possible.

Figure 12-6 Example of a user request for data initiated on a Web site

The David Consulting Group Web site permits the user to enter key information in order to request project estimation information (see Figure 12-6). The data is not stored by the Web application; the data is sent directly to an e-mail address outside the application. This transaction should be counted as an EQ.

Data Warehouse Applications

Data warehouses are functionally unique software applications that store large amounts of data in a central data repository. This data is used within a common industry, organization, or business function. Typically, data-warehousing productivity rates, based on functional sizing, are significantly lower than those of traditional IS applications.

A data warehouse application (see Figure 12-7) typically has the following common attributes:

- Repository of data supporting multiple users, providing centralized access
- Repository of data that has been normalized on the basis of an enterprise data model
- Processing and consolidation of large volumes and differing sources of data
- Multiple feeds of the same logical group of information from many sources
- Consolidated data objects often maintained by a central group
- Specialized views of related data that permit other systems to access the common data

Benchmarking studies by The David Consulting Group, Software Productivity Research, the International Software Benchmarking Standards Group (ISBSG), and others have indicated that certain trends and common attributes exist for the counted number of data and transaction components relative to the types of applications examined. Through the historical data available, certain component characteristics and delivery rates related to industry-specific applications (e.g., insurance or telecommunications) and application types (e.g., client-server, Web-based, batch processing, or interactive) were observed. Some data warehouse applications exhibited a larger number of external outputs and/or external inquiries compared to the total functionality provided (especially insurance applications and financial applications). Other data warehouse applications contained fewer external outputs and/or external inquiries, but more external inputs. These same benchmarking studies indicate similarities in the general system characteristics based on application types and often on industry types.

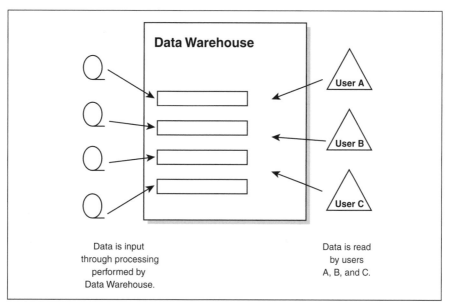

Figure 12-7 Example of a data warehouse

Functionality of Data Warehouse Applications

According to IFPUG counting rules, when other applications access data warehouse applications, the data stores that reside within the data warehouse are counted as EIFs by the other applications. No credit is given to the data warehouse for making this data available to the other applications.

When a software development organization develops an enterprise data model to minimize redundant data and to decrease the processing and overhead of many applications by embedding the processing in a single data warehouse application, the "feeder" applications recognize many functionality gains: improved ease of data access and of application design, and increased individual application productivity.

Concerns about Productivity Rates for Data Warehouse Applications

The overhead of maintaining the integrated data model by the data warehouse is not directly recognized. Often a development team's "invisible" efforts in delivering the support architecture of a data warehouse are compared unfavorably with more traditional, and highly visible, user functionality. Teams are often penalized by management-perceived lower delivery rates (in function points per staff-month) for the functionality provided. Software application development projects should be evaluated on the basis of the cost versus the value or payback. For data warehouse applications, the future payback in data retrieval is often significant in comparison to the cost of the project.

Query/Report Generators

A query/report generator could function within the boundary of the application being sized, or it could function as a separate, stand-alone application. Do not make a report/query generator a separate application if it is supporting one application; it is probably within the same boundary, much the same as both the client and the server are in a client-server application.

A query/report generator does not use a group of selection alternatives (parameters) to display data in predefined reports. These predefined reports are simply external outputs and/or external inquiries provided through a standardized process of the application.

A query/report generator provides the user the flexibility to design, build, and display data fields chosen by the user from data files chosen by the user in a format chosen by the user. The query/report generator provides access to the fields in the files, together with a group of parameters that enable the user to design and retrieve multiple reports in multiple formats.

Data Functionality

The file that holds user-generated and -saved query/report generator parameters is counted as one logically related group of data or control information (i.e., an internal logical file) that fulfills a specific user requirement. Count an additional ILF for the ability to save actual queries or reports with their actual data for later retrieval, separate from the generator parameters.

Consider the source of the data that can be accessed to populate the query or report. If the data components are retrieved from other applications, count them as external interface files (EIFs). If they are retrieved from the application being counted, they should have already been counted. Don't count the same ILF or EIF twice within the same application, which is defined by the query/report generator application boundary.

Transactional Functionality

Count independent, stand-alone functions that serve as separate elementary processes. Possible stand-alone elementary processes that could be counted as

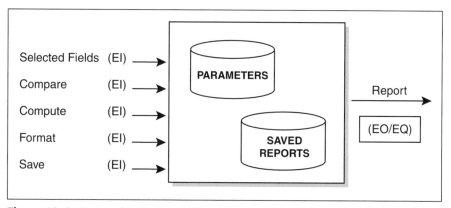

Figure 12-8 Example of a query/report generator

separate external inputs (EIs) include the selection of the fields and files to be used in creating a query or report, comparisons between fields selected and other fields or named values, formatting and sorting sequences, calculations to be performed, and so on (see Figure 12-8).

One external output or external inquiry is counted for the generated reports, despite the capability to create a factorial number of different and unique outputs. If there is a potential for calculated data, the transaction is counted as an EO.

Summary

All software requirements can be sized regardless of the type of software (e.g., real-time or simple management information systems). They must be sized independently of the technology, methodology, or tools. Obviously, all of these will have an impact on productivity.

In this chapter we have discussed some of the idiosyncrasies of counting applications developed by object-oriented analysis and design; client-server, Web-based, and data warehouse applications; and query/report generators. Chapters 11, 13, and 14 present a series of case studies that should enable you to determine whether you are ready to count your own applications or to take the practice Certified Function Point Specialist exam in Chapter 16.

CHAPTER THIRTEEN

Counting a GUI Application

Introduction

In Chapters 6 through 12 we discussed new development counts, enhancement counts, and application counts. This chapter will describe the same types of counts, again using the International Function Point User Group (IFPUG) definitions, rules, and guidelines, to evaluate a GUI application.

Counting GUI Functionality

Graphical user interfaces (GUIs) have become very common because they are easy to use for both professional and casual users. Although first introduced by Xerox, they became popular in the Apple line of computer, especially the Macintosh. They are now available in many environments—Windows, Presentation Manager, OPEN LOOK, NeXT, and Motif, to name several. GUIs typically consist of such user functionality as

- Primary and secondary windows
- Icons
- Pull-down and pop-up menus and selection lists
- Action bars
- Dialog boxes
- Selection lists permitting point-and-click capability
- Scroll bars
- Push buttons
- Sliders

- Spin buttons
- Radio buttons
- Many other user controls

A Microsoft GUI screen is shown in Figure 13-1 for discussion purposes only.

GUI Counting Guidelines

Remember that the application boundary separates the application being measured from the user domain and/or other independent applications. The data function types relate to the logical data stored and available for update, reference, and retrieval. The transactional function types—external inputs (EIs), external outputs (EOs), and external inquiries (EQs)—perform the processes of update, retrieval, output, and so on (transactions you would expect to see in a process model). Each has its own unadjusted function point weight based on its unique complexity matrix.

Elementary processes that create, update, or delete data should be counted as external inputs; be sure that the data itself—and not just a screen view—is being

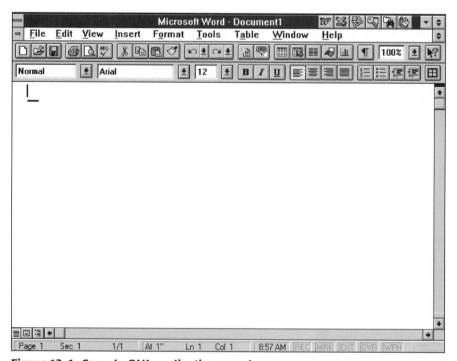

Figure 13-1 Sample GUI application panel

maintained. Often the selections Save and Save As in the File menu provide the command key functions for add and change functionality. Don't count the same function twice only because of the existence of multiple keys to accomplish the function. Also, be careful not to count the capability to add or delete individual fields on a screen as stand-alone EIs because they are not stand-alone elementary processes.

Selection of an item from a pick list is usually a DET on an EI, EO, or EQ and not a separate EI.

User functions that retrieve or extract data from one or more ILFs or EIFs and display that data should be counted as EQs. Such functions could include a simple list box or typically a File Open command without calculated data.

User functions that include calculations in order to display data, or that update an ILF in conjunction with the display, should be counted as EOs. Such functions could include a File Open command in qualified instances.

Print functions that create printed copies of a display should be counted as additional EQs (without calculated data) or EOs (with calculated data) only if they include separate and distinct unique processing, different DETs, or different FTRs. Simply sending to a different medium is not unique processing. Print format instructions are part of the elementary process to generate an EQ or EO (control data) and are counted on those transactions as DETs rather than as separate EIs.

Functions that are automatically provided by Windows or another operating system and not by the application being sized should not be counted—for example, minimize, maximize—unless you are counting the operating system itself.

Menus, icons, scroll bars, and other navigation devices are not counted unless they return retrieved user data.

Exit instructions are purely navigational, returning control to the system or calling program, and thus are not counted.

Individual selections from a menu (action bar, pull-down, pop-up, or iconic) or a push button may serve as the input side of an EQ or EO or the command key to perform an EI.

Selection lists, spin buttons, and list boxes are counted as EQs when they retrieve and display data from one or more ILFs or EIFs. The selection of one of the items displayed by point-and-click or a similar method is not usually a stand-alone function, but a DET within the applicable elementary process.

Functions that permit one choice from a selection of choices, available from a slider or radio buttons, count as one DET on the EI or on the input side of the

EQ or EO and not as a DET for each choice. However, if multiple selections can be accepted, as in check boxes, then each independent selection that is not a repeated field counts as a DET. Remember that repeated fields are not counted more than once.

Status, informational, and warning messages, other than error or confirmation messages that are not part of another elementary process, are usually EQs or EOs.

Control EIs should be counted for user-required stand-alone elementary processes that ensure compliance with business-related functionality.

Help is counted normally, with one EI per level of help per application.

Exercise in Counting a GUI System

Now let's conduct an independent exercise with an example of a GUI system. As you read through this exercise, review the screens and windows and the functionality counted. The Microsoft Windows Calendar application has been selected as our example for sizing. This is an existing application.

Remember that to conduct a function point analysis you must

1. Determine the type of function point count
2. Identify the counting scope and the application boundary
3. Identify all data functions (ILFs and EIFs) and their complexity (see Chapter 7)
4. Identify all transactional functions (EIs, EOs, and EQs) and their complexity (see Chapter 8)
5. Determine the unadjusted function point count
6. Determine the value adjustment factor, which is based on the 14 general system characteristics (see Chapter 9)
7. Calculate the adjusted function point count (see Chapter 10)

In the discussion that follows we will address each of these steps in turn.

1. Determine the Type of Function Point Count

This is an existing application.

2. Identify the Counting Scope and the Application Boundary

We are counting only the functionality included within Windows Calendar.

3 and 4. Identify All Data and Transactional Functions and Their Complexity

We will count the different functions as they are revealed during our functional walk-through of the application. Windows Calendar contains a monthly calendar

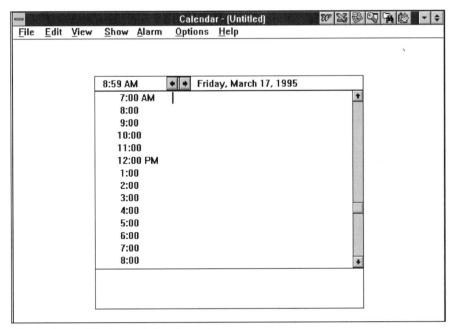

Figure 13-2 Windows Calendar primary window

and a daily appointment book. The untitled calendar (primary window) appears after being selected via an icon (see Figure 13-2).

Hidden Functions

FUNCTIONALITY OF TIME AND DAY/DATE: EQ

The calendar displays the current time and date (as shown in Figure 13-2), which are continuously updated from the Windows Clock application. Users of the Calendar application consider this to be a separate and distinct stand-alone elementary process. Time and day/date are considered to be two fields, and there is one FTR, Windows Clock. The resulting count for this EQ would be two DETs and one FTR. If we look at the matrices for applying the weights, we see that a value of low, or three function points, applies.

FUNCTIONALITY OF CLOCK: EIF

Two DETs are retrieved from the Windows Clock application. The resulting count for this EIF would be two DETs and one RET. If we look at the matrices for applying the weights, we see that a value of low, or five function points, applies.

In the sections that follow, we will discuss each action bar choice in turn.

Action Bar Selection: File

Selecting File on the action bar offers the following choices: New, Open, Save, Save As, Print, Page Setup, Print Setup, and Exit (see Figure 13-3).

FILE MENU SELECTION: NEW

Selecting New on the File menu returns an untitled calendar with no data, a blank formatted screen. Appointments will be entered later with the Save As function. No function points are counted for this New capability.

FILE MENU SELECTION: OPEN

Choosing Open on the File menu returns the selected record in the primary window for the current date. Data can be edited and saved with the Save function on the File menu or deleted with the Edit function on the action bar. Although a command key is required, there are no error or confirmation messages.

FUNCTIONALITY OF OPEN CALENDAR: EQ

We can open the calendar for the current date. The currently saved calendar date, appointment time, appointment information (next to the times), notes for the

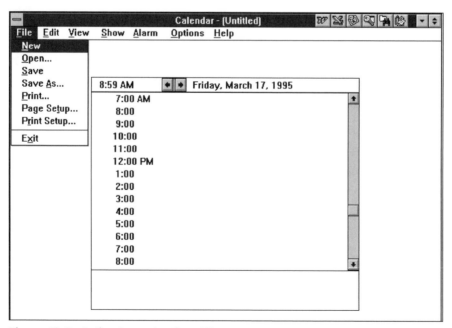

Figure 13-3 Action bar selection: File

day (bottom of the screen), and alarm indicator (discussed later) will be displayed. We also count one DET for the command key. The resulting count for this EQ would be six DETs and one FTR. If we look at the matrices for applying the weights, we see that a value of low, or three function points, applies.

FUNCTIONALITY OF ENTER CALENDAR DATA (SAVE AS): EI

We can enter data for a new calendar date, including the calendar date itself, selection of appointment time, appointment information, and notes for the day. We also count one DET for the command key. The resulting count for this EI would be five DETs and one FTR. If we look at the matrices for applying the weights, we see that a value of low, or three function points, applies.

FUNCTIONALITY OF UPDATE CALENDAR DATA (SAVE): EI

We can update data for an existing calendar date, including the calendar date itself, selection of appointment time, appointment information, and notes for the day. We also count one DET for the command key. The resulting count for this EI would be five DETs and one FTR. If we look at the matrices for applying the weights, we see that a value of low, or three function points, applies.

FUNCTIONALITY OF CALENDAR: ILF

We are saving information to a calendar file. The resulting count for this ILF would be fewer than 20 DETs (we don't have all of the information yet, but we know that calendar date, appointment time, appointment information, and notes are included, as well as the alarm indicator that was mentioned earlier, under Menu Selection: Open) and one RET. If we look at the matrices for applying the weights, we see that a value of low, or seven function points, applies.

FILE MENU SELECTION: PRINT

Selecting Print on the File menu permits appointments to be printed. A print dialog box (Figure 13-4) appears, permitting the selection of "from" and "to" dates. We can select a printed version of the calendar for specified days, but not months. Because we can select the "from" and "to" dates, and not because the medium is different, this functionality differs from the functionality of Open Calendar.

FUNCTIONALITY OF PRINT CALENDAR: EQ

We can select a printed version of the calendar for specified days. There is no derived data. There is a user request, a date retrieval from an ILF (Calendar), and a printed display. The transaction is counted as an additional EQ (to the Open

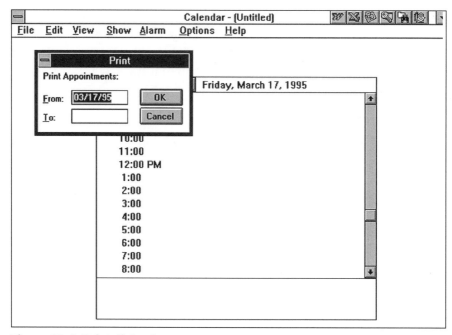

Figure 13-4 Print dialog box

Calendar function) because of the "from" and "to" dates, which would bring our total DET count to eight. Under release 4.1 of the Counting Practices Manual, we would also count the eight DETs necessary to accomplish the elementary process to print the calendar, which are described in Figures 13-4 and 13-5. The resulting count for this EQ would be 16 DETs and one FTR. If we look at the matrices for applying the weights, we see that a value of low, or three function points, applies.

FILE MENU SELECTION: PAGE SETUP

Choosing Page Setup on the File menu permits the selection of headers and footers, as well as setting of the margins (see Figure 13-5).

FUNCTIONALITY OF PAGE SETUP

Page Setup adds 4 DETs to the Print Calendar function for headers, footers, designation of a margin, and the margin amounts. Margins are a repeated field and are counted much the same as appointment information for an appointment time (a DET for the time and a DET for the information saved). Here we count a DET for the designation of the margin (left, right, top, bottom) and a DET for the entries of applicable numbers.

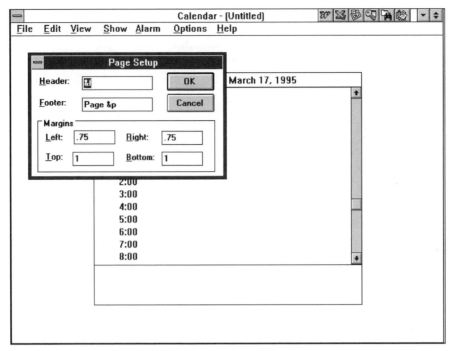

Figure 13-5 Page Setup dialog box

FILE MENU SELECTION: PRINT SETUP

Selecting Print Setup on the File menu permits the selection of the printer, paper size, paper source, and orientation (see Figure 13-6).

FUNCTIONALITY OF PRINT SETUP

Print Setup adds four DETs to the Print Calendar function for the selection of the printer, paper size, paper source, and orientation (portrait or landscape).

FILE MENU SELECTION: EXIT

Selecting Exit on the File menu closes the application.

FUNCTIONALITY OF EXIT

This command provides navigation capability only; it is not counted.

Action Bar Selection: Edit

Selecting Edit on the action bar offers the following choices: Cut, Copy, Paste, and Remove (see Figure 13-7).

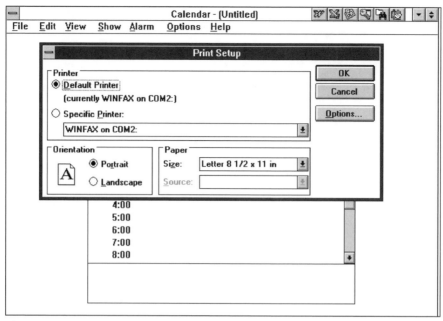

Figure 13-6 Print Setup dialog box

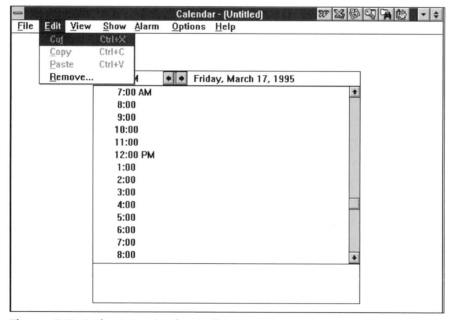

Figure 13-7 Action bar selection: Edit

EDIT MENU SELECTIONS: CUT, COPY, AND PASTE

Cut, Copy, and Paste are Windows tools.

FUNCTIONALITY OF CUT, COPY, AND PASTE

These functions are not considered to be additional functionality provided within Calendar. Thus they are not counted.

EDIT MENU SELECTION: REMOVE

Selecting Remove on the Edit menu permits the deletion of calendars for one or more dates (see Figure 13-8).

FUNCTIONALITY OF REMOVE (DELETE): EI

This function permits the deletion of all appointment information for one or more calendar dates. We have DETs for both the "from" and "to" dates and the command key, so the resulting count for this EI would be three DETs and one FTR. If we look at the matrices for applying the weights, we see that a value of low, or three Function Points, applies.

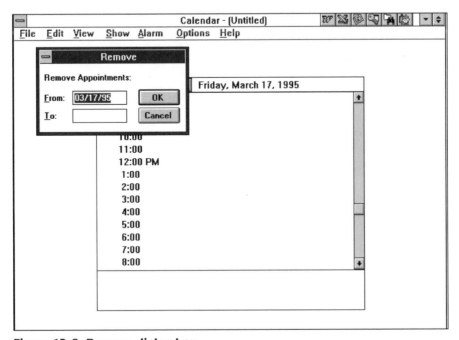

Figure 13-8 Remove dialog box

Action Bar Selection: View

Selecting View on the action bar permits the retrieval of daily or monthly views of the calendar (see Figure 13-9).

VIEW MENU SELECTION: DAY
Selecting Day on the View menu permits the retrieval of a daily view.

FUNCTIONALITY OF VIEW DAY

This function permits the display of a day's calendar. It was already counted along with the Open Calendar functionality, and there is no additional processing—just a different command key—so it is not counted here.

VIEW MENU SELECTION: MONTH
Selecting Month on the View menu permits the retrieval of a monthly view (see Figure 13-10).

FUNCTIONALITY OF VIEW MONTH: EQ

This function permits the display of a month's calendar. The currently saved monthly calendar month and year, days (repeated), and marks for a day (discussed

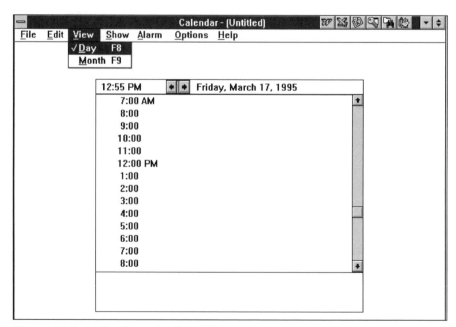

Figure 13-9 Action bar selection: View

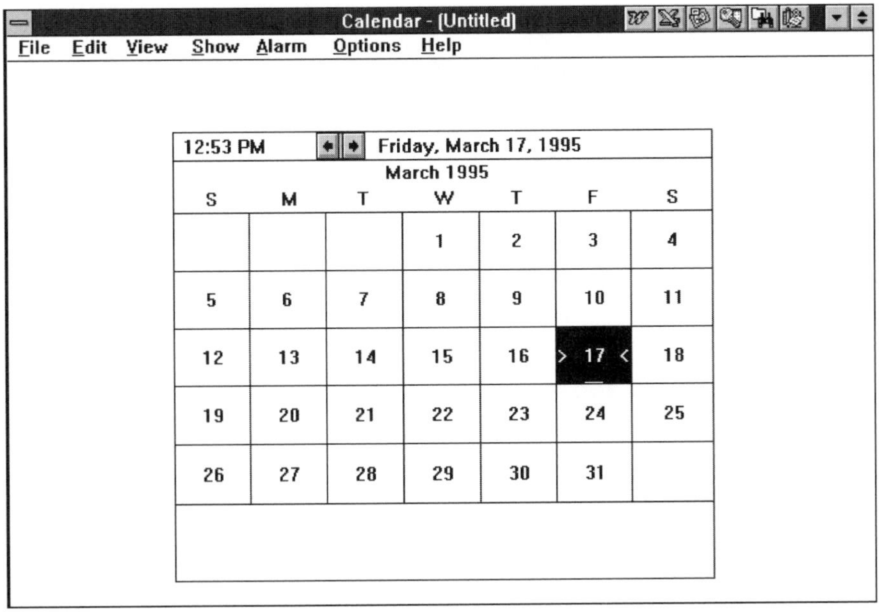

Figure 13-10 Monthly calendar view

later) will be displayed. The resulting count for this EQ would be four DETs and one FTR, counting one DET for the command key. If we look at the matrices for applying the weights, we see that a value of low, or three function points, applies.

Action Bar Selection: Show

Selecting Show on the action bar (see Figure 13-11) provides the control aspects of the View selection.

SHOW MENU SELECTIONS: TODAY, PREVIOUS, NEXT, AND DATE
Users can select Today, Previous, or Next to define the day or month selected on the View menu, or they can choose a specific Date (see Figure 13-12).

FUNCTIONALITY OF SHOW TODAY, PREVIOUS, OR NEXT

This functionality duplicates the two EQs for day and month that we already counted. They have the same elementary processes with some navigation included, similar to going backward or forward. This functionality is not separate, because it does not have different processing, different DETs, or different FTRs. It does have navigation, but that feature is not recognized with unadjusted function points.

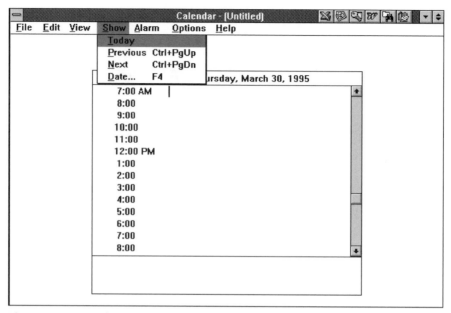

Figure 13-11 Action bar selection: Show

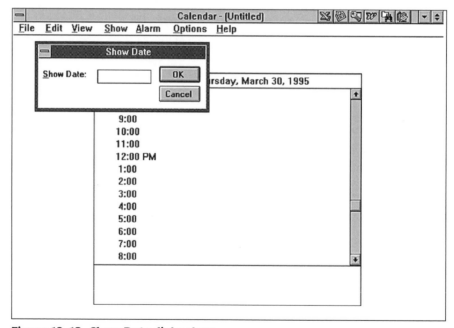

Figure 13-12 Show Date dialog box

FUNCTIONALITY OF SHOW DATE: EQ

This is an additional logical function of selecting a particular date and may be counted as a separate EQ. It works on its own, as opposed to being related to the Open Calendar function. We have an additional field on the request side. The currently saved calendar date, appointment time, appointment information (next to the times), notes for the day (bottom of screen), and alarm indicator (discussed later) will be displayed. The resulting count for this EQ would be six DETs and one FTR, counting one DET for the command key. If we look at the matrices for applying the weights, we see that a value of low, or three function points, applies.

Action Bar Selection: Alarm

Selecting Alarm on the action bar offers the following choices: Set and Controls (see Figure 13-13).

ALARM MENU SELECTION: SET

We can set or unset (remove) the alarm by selecting a particular time. The alarm displays and must be turned off when the alarm time is reached.

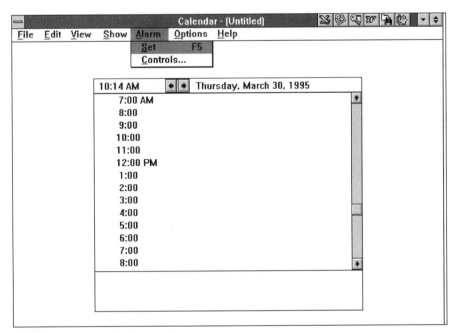

Figure 13-13 Action bar selection: Alarm

FUNCTIONALITY OF SET/REMOVE ALARM: EI

The capability of setting or removing an alarm for a particular time and date should be counted as an EI; this is simply a toggle, and not two separate functions. We save this information to the previously counted calendar file. We have been counting the alarm indicator (a bell to the left of the time) as a field on our displays. We must also count the alarm indicator as a field in the ILF. The resulting count for this EI would be four DETs (date, time, toggle, and command key) and one FTR. If we look at the matrices for applying the weights, we see that a value of low, or three function points, applies.

ALARM MENU SELECTION: CONTROLS

Selecting Controls on the Alarm menu permits setup of the alarm, including the selection of silent alarm and early ring (see Figure 13-14).

FUNCTIONALITY OF CONTROLS: EI

We make and save selections for Alarm Controls. The resulting count for this EI would be three DETs (early ring time selection, sound toggle, and the command key) and one FTR. Note that the alarm controls apply to all alarms and not to

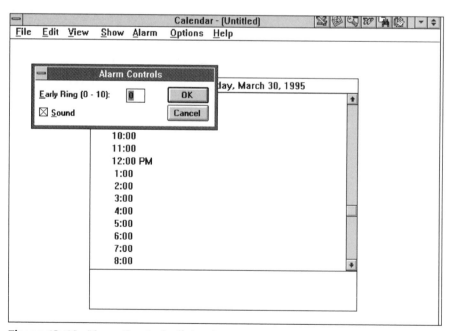

Figure 13-14 Alarm Controls dialog box

specific dates. If we look at the matrices for applying the weights, we see that a value of low, or three function points, applies.

FUNCTIONALITY OF CONTROLS: ILF

Our Alarm Controls selections do not relate directly to a particular date and time; therefore they are saved to a different file. The resulting count for this ILF would be two DETs (early ring time selection and sound toggle) and one RET. If we look at the matrices for applying the weights, we see that a value of low, or seven function points, applies.

FUNCTIONALITY OF SOUNDING ALARM: EO

The alarm goes off at the designated times. The resulting count for this EO would be one DET (the time, regardless of the internal fields read for early ring selection, sound, and so on) and two FTRs (Alarm Controls and Clock). However, the Alarm is recognized as an EO rather than an EQ because computation is required to determine the time of the alarm by calculation based on the early ring selection. If we look at the matrices for applying the weights, we see that a value of low, or four function points, applies.

FUNCTIONALITY OF ALARM ACKNOWLEDGMENT: EI

We must acknowledge and turn off the alarm. The resulting count for this control EI would be one DET and zero FTRs (we are just turning off the view and/or sound and not touching any of the files). If we look at the matrices for applying the weights, we see that a value of low, or three function points, applies.

Action Bar Selection: Options

Selecting Options on the action bar offers the following choices: Mark, Special Time, and Day Settings (see Figure 13-15).

OPTIONS MENU SELECTION: MARK

Selecting Mark on the Options menu permits a date to be marked with up to five symbols (see Figure 13-16).

FUNCTIONALITY OF MARK: EI

We can mark a specific date, but not a time, within the calendar with up to five specific symbols. The resulting count for this EI would be four DETs (date, symbol number, symbol selection, and the command key) and one FTR (Calendar).

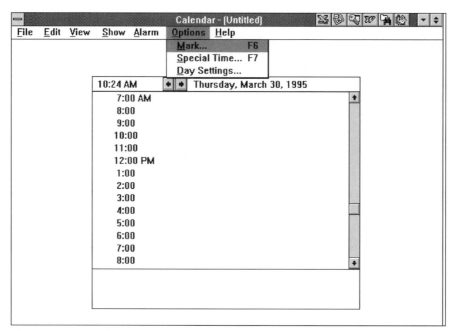

Figure 13-15 Action bar selection: Options

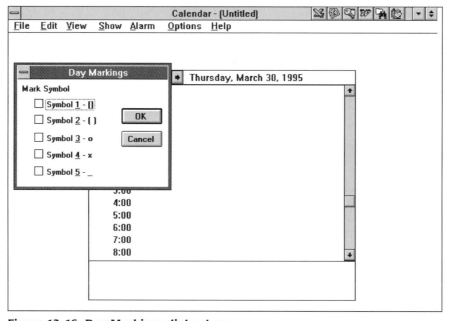

Figure 13-16 Day Markings dialog box

If we look at the matrices for applying the weights, we see that a value of low, or three function points, applies.

OPTIONS MENU SELECTION: SPECIAL TIME

Selecting Special Time on the Options menu permits a particular time to be inserted or deleted (see Figure 13-17).

FUNCTIONALITY OF SPECIAL TIME: EI

We can either enter or delete a specific time on the calendar. Special Time is an update function for updating individual calendar times; it does not represent separate add and delete functions. This is a good example of something called delete that is deleting not a calendar, but an individual field on a calendar. The update is applied to all calendars, not a particular date. The resulting count for this EI would be three DETs (time, AM versus PM, and the command key) and one FTR (Calendar). If we look at the matrices for applying the weights, we see that a value of low, or three function points, applies.

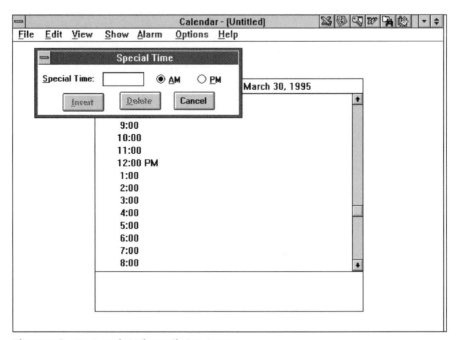

Figure 13-17 Special Time dialog box

OPTIONS MENU SELECTION: DAY SETTINGS

Selecting Day Settings on the Options menu permits appointments to be set at 15-, 30-, or 60-minute intervals based on a 12- or 24-hour format (see Figure 13-18). Starting time may be revised.

FUNCTIONALITY OF DAY SETTINGS: EI

As with the Special Time function, we can modify the calendar to provide different intervals and starting times. The resulting count for this EI would be four DETs (interval, hour format, starting time, and the command key) and one FTR (Calendar). If we look at the matrices for applying the weights, we see that a value of low, or three function points, applies.

5. **Determine the Unadjusted Function Point Count**

The unadjusted function point count is computed from the sum of all the data and transactional function types (see Table 13-1).

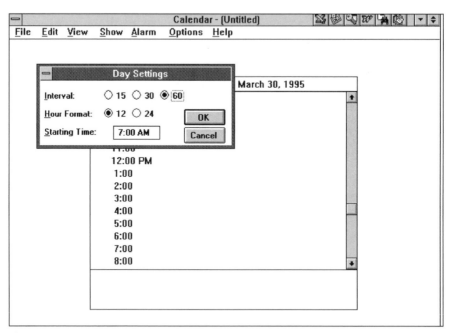

Figure 13-18 Day Settings dialog box

Table 13-1: Calculating the Unadjusted Function Point Count

	Function Levels			
	Low	Average	High	Total
External inputs	9×3	$\times 4$	$\times 6$	27
External outputs	1×4	$\times 5$	$\times 7$	4
External inquiries	5×3	$\times 4$	$\times 6$	15
Internal logical files	2×7	$\times 10$	$\times 15$	14
External interface files	1×5	$\times 7$	$\times 10$	5

Total unadjusted function points (UFP) = 65

Table 13-2: Calculating the Value Adjustment Factor

Characteristic	Degree of Influence	Characteristic	Degree of Influence
1. Data communications	4	8. Online update	3
2. Distributed data processing	0	9. Complex processing	1
3. Performance	3	10. Reusability	2
4. Heavily used configuration	2	11. Installation ease	1
5. Transaction rate	3	12. Operational ease	3
6. Online data entry	5	13. Multiple sites	2
7. End user efficiency	4	14. Facilitate change	2

Total degree of influence (TDI) = 35

6. Determine the Value Adjustment Factor

The value adjustment factor (VAF) is computed on the basis of the 14 general system characteristics as shown in Table 13-2. The formula is: VAF = (TDI × 0.01) + 0.65, where TDI is the total degree of influence of the GSCs. For this example, then, we get the following for the value adjustment factor:

VAF = (TDI × 0.01) + 0.65 = 1.00

7. Calculate the Final Adjusted Function Point Count

In step 7 the final function point count for the installed application is calculated from the unadjusted function point count (step 5) and the value adjustment factor (step 6):

$$\text{Adjusted function point count (FP)} = \text{UFP} \times \text{VAF}$$

Consequently, the

$$\text{Final function point count} = 65 \times 1.00 = 65$$

CHAPTER FOURTEEN

Counting an Object-Oriented Application

Introduction

This chapter will describe function point counting of an object-oriented application, Personnel Query Service, using the International Function Point User Group (IFPUG) definitions, rules, and guidelines. Counting an object-oriented (OO) application often requires a different approach from counting a more traditionally oriented functional specification or requirements document. The function point counter is well advised to first become familiar with all available system documents, including the functional description, object model(s), and system diagram(s). Once an overall understanding has been gained, the function point counting process can begin with a greater assurance of a complete and accurate count. Consequently, we recommend that you review the entire application description that follows before commencing your function point count.

Functional Description of Personnel Query Service

Personnel Query Service is an application used to request information from the personnel information database. It also permits users to change information in the personnel information database.

Principal users of Personnel Query Service can query, create, or delete personnel records and update all personnel information. Principal users also can add or delete Title,

Location, and Organization records. Regular users can query the personnel information database and update limited information about themselves.

Figure 14-1 presents the main window for Personnel Query Service. This window is used for both data entry and data retrieval. The action bar has seven buttons: System, Edit, Object, Special, Operation, Mode, and Help.

- **System** has a pull-down menu that includes an Exit button. By clicking on the Exit button you can quit the application.
- **Edit** has a pull-down menu that includes Cut, Copy, Paste, and Clear buttons. You can use Cut, Copy, and Paste to edit the window contents, or the Clear button to clear the window.
- **Object** has a pull-down menu that includes AddTit, AddLoc, AddGrp, DelTit, DelLoc, and DelGrp buttons. These buttons are used to add or delete Title, Location, and Organization records.
- **Special** has a pull-down menu that includes AddPic and DelPic buttons. These buttons are used to add or delete an employee's picture when records for the employee are being created or updated.

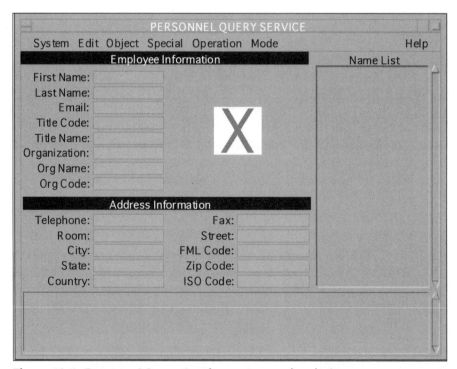

Figure 14-1 Personnel Query Service system main window

- **Operation** has a pull-down menu that includes Query, Update, Create, and Delete buttons. By clicking on one of these buttons, you trigger the query, update, create, or delete operation, respectively.
- **Mode** has a pull-down menu that includes Principal and Regular buttons. A regular user can change to a principal user with proper password information.
- **Help** has not yet been implemented.

The main window displays employee information and address information for a particular employee. Included in the employee information are the fields First Name, Last Name, Email, Title Code, Title Name, Organization, Org Name, and Org Code, as well as a picture display area (marked by the X in Figure 14-1). The name (Last Name, First Name) of each employee will display in the Name List window. Included in the address information are the following fields: Telephone, Fax, Room, Street, City, FML Code, State, Zip Code, Country, and ISO Code.

Starting Personnel Query Service

Personnel Query Service is on the network; users can access the system from their desktops. A password is required for a principal user.

Principal User

Logging on to Personnel Query Service requires the following steps:

1. On the command line, type in "pq-p." A password request window (see Figure 14-2) will pop up.

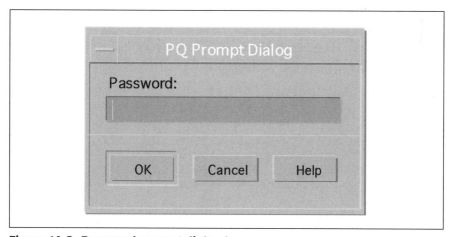

Figure 14-2 Password request dialog box

2. A principal user enters the password (which does not display on the screen). The password can be up to ten characters.

3. Click on the OK button to process, or on the Cancel button to quit the log-on session.

4. If the password is correct, Personnel Query Service will start with a principal user's privileges; otherwise it assumes the user is a regular user.

Regular User

If the user types "pq" on the command line, Personnel Query Service will start without principal user privileges; that is, the Create and Delete buttons in the Operation pull-down menu will be disabled.

Query

Principal users and regular users have the same capability of query, which requires the following steps:

1. Initiate a retrieval of possible employees by entering the Org Code, FML Code, and/or Title Code, or by editing the existing contents of those three fields (on the basis of the previous query) in the window. When Org Code is entered, Org Name and Organization will be displayed. When Title Code is entered, Title Name will be displayed. When FML code is entered, all appropriate Location data will be displayed. These three displays can be accomplished independently or in conjunction with an employee retrieval.

2. Click on the Query button in the Operation pull-down menu to process the query.

3. If there is no match, an error message "No match record" appears in the message window. If there are one or more matches, a message "Query is completed, xx number of records have been retrieved" displays in the message window. The list of employees' names (first and last) will display in the employee Name List (see Figure 14-1). Click on a name in the employee Name List to select an employee and display that employee's information. All information in the main window will display for the employee selected.

Update

Principal users can update the information of any employee; regular users can update limited information for themselves. In both cases the following steps are required:

1. Edit the contents in the main window.
2. Click on the Update button in the Operation pull-down menu, and the Social Security Number input dialog box (see Figure 14-3) will pop up.
3. Enter the social security number. Click on Cancel to cancel the update. A message that says "Record update canceled" will appear in the message window. Click on the OK button to process the update.
4. If the social security number entered does not match the employee's social security number, the message "Invalid social security number" will appear in the message window.
5. If the two social security numbers match, the message "Record update successful" will appear in the message window.

Create

Only principal users can create an employee record, by performing the following steps:

1. Type the information in the information window, or edit the existing contents (on the basis of the previous query) in the information window. Only employee data and Org Code, Title Code, and FML Code may be entered.
2. Click on the Create button in the Operation pull-down menu, and the Social Security Number input dialog box (see Figure 14-3) will pop up.
3. Enter the social security number. Click on Cancel to cancel the creation. The message "Record creation canceled" will appear in the message window. Click on the OK button to process the record creation.

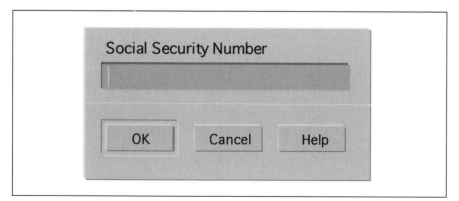

Figure 14-3 Social Security Number input dialog box

4. If the record for the social security number already exists, an error message will appear in the message window that reads as follows: "The record already exists, can't create a new one!"

5. Upon successful creation, the message "Record create successful" will appear in the message window.

Delete

Only principal users can delete an employee record, by performing the following steps:

1. Perform query as described earlier. Select an employee's record.
2. Click on the Delete button in the Operation pull-down menu.
3. The Social Security Number input dialog box (see Figure 14-3) will pop up.
4. Enter the social security number. Click on the OK button to process. Click on Cancel to cancel the creation; the message "Record deletion canceled" will appear in the message window.
5. If the social security number does not match the employee's social security number, the message "Invalid social security number" will appear in the message window.
6. If the two social security numbers do match, a confirmation window will pop up asking the user to confirm the deletion (see Figure 14-4). Click OK to confirm. The message "Record delete successful" will appear in the message

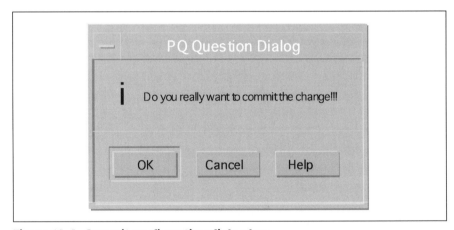

Figure 14-4 Commit confirmation dialog box

window. Click Cancel to cancel the delete; the message "Record deletion can-celed" will appear in the message window.

Add and Delete Title, Location, and Organization Records

Principal users can add or delete Title, Location, and Organization records. These operations can be accessed in the Object pull-down menu. Error messages are returned if data is entered incorrectly.

Add and Delete an Employee's Picture

An employee can enter a picture, together with the social security number and the date of the picture, in the personnel information database. The picture can be deleted if the relevant social security number and the date of the picture are entered. A command key is required, and messages result. These operations can be accessed in the Special pull-down menu.

Exit

Click on the Exit button in the System pull-down menu, and an Exit confirmation window will pop up (see Figure 14-5). Click on the OK button to quit Personnel Query Service; click on the Cancel button to continue using the application.

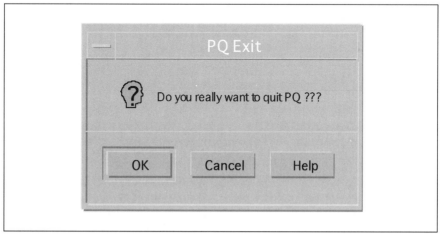

Figure 14-5   Exit confirmation dialog box

Object Model for Personnel Query Service

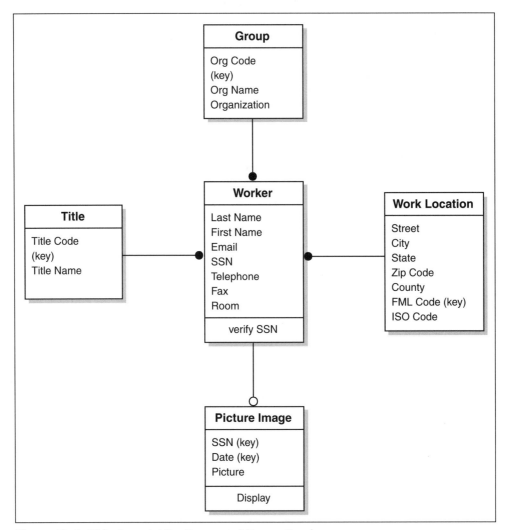

Figure 14-6   Object model for Personnel Query Service

System Diagram for Personnel Query Service

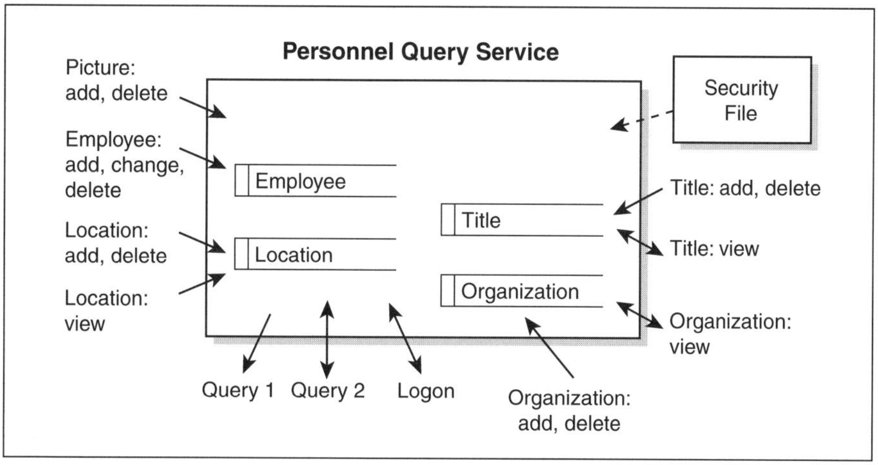

Figure 14-7 System diagram for Personnel Query Service

Function Point Analysis for Personnel Query Service

Function Point Count Summary

Project Number	Project Name Personal Query System
Date of Count	Counter's Name DCG

Instructions: Enter all function types included. For development and initial function point counts, there will not be any entries in the "Before" columns. Annotate all function types added by the conversion. You may wish to use different sheets for files and transactions.

Description	Type[a]	DETs After	RETs/FTRs After	Complexity[b] After	DETs Before	RETs/FTRs Before	Complexity[b] Before
Employee File Employee Info and keys Picture	ILF	12	2	L			

[a] ILF, EIF, EI, EO, or EQ
[b] L = Low, A = Average, H = High   (continued)

Figure 14-8 Function point count summary for Personnel Query Service 1–1

Description	Type[a]	DETs After	RETs/FTRs After	Complexity[b] After	DETs Before	RETs/FTRs Before	Complexity[b] Before
Location File	ILF	7	1	L			
Title File	ILF	2	1	L			
Organization File	ILF	3	1	L			
Security File	EIF	<20	1	L			
Employee: create	EI	12	4	H			
Employee: update	EI	12	4	H			
Employee: delete	EI	3	1	L			
Title: add	EI	4	1	L			
Title: delete	EI	3	2	L			
Location: add	EI	9	1	L			
Location: delete	EI	3	2	L			
Organization: add	EI	5	1	L			
Organization: delete	EI	3	2	L			
Picture: add	EI	5	1	L			
Picture: delete	EI	4	1	L			
Query 1 (Derived Data)	EO	8	1	L			
Logon	EQ	3	1	L			
Query 2	EQ	20	4	H			
View Organization	EQ	5	1	L			
View Title	EQ	4	1	L			
View Location	EQ	9	1	L			

Identification of DETs and RETs/FTRs counted:

Employee file   ILF   12   2   L
- 12 DETs: First Name, Last Name, Email, Social Security Number, Telephone, Fax, Room, Title Code, Org Code, FML Code, Picture, and Date of picture
- 2 RETs: Employee Information/keys and Picture image

Location file   ILF   7   1   L
- 7 DETs: Street, City, State, Zip Code, Country, FML Code and ISO Code
- 1 RET: Location

Title file   ILF   2   1   L
- 2 DETs: Title Code and Title Name
- 1 RET: Title

Organization file   ILF   3   1   L
- 3 DETs: Org Code, Org Name, and Organization
- 1 RET: Group

[a] ILF, EIF, EI, EO, or EQ
[b] L = Low, A = Average, H = High

Description	Type[a]	DETs After	RETs/FTRs After	Complexity[b] After	DETs Before	RETs/FTRs Before	Complexity[b] Before
Security file	EIF	<20	1	L			

- <20 DETs = Social Security Number, designation of security level (principal or regular user), and password plus the possibility of a window ID or function ID
- 1 FTR: Security

| Employee: create | EI | 12 | 4 | H | | | |

- 12 DETs: First Name, Last Name, Email, Social Security Number, Telephone, Fax, Room, Title Code, Org Code, FML Code, command key, and messages
- 4 FTRs: Employee, Location, Title, and Organization

| Employee: update | EI | 12 | 4 | H | | | |

- 12 DETs: First Name, Last Name, Email, Social Security Number, Telephone, Fax, Room, Title Code, Org Code, FML Code, command key, and messages
- 4 FTRs: Employee, Location, Title, and Organization

| Employee: delete | EI | 3 | 1 | L | | | |

- 3 DETs: Social Security Number, command key, and messages
- 1 FTR: Employee

| Title: add | EI | 4 | 1 | L | | | |

- 4 DETs: Title Code, Title Name, command key, and messages
- 1 FTR: Title

| Title: delete | EI | 3 | 2 | L | | | |

- 3 DETs: Title Code, command key, and messages
- 2 FTRs: Title and Employee (to ensure no employee assigned to Title)

| Location: add | EI | 9 | 1 | L | | | |

- 9 DETs: Street, City, State, Zip Code, Country, FML Code, ISO Code, command key, and messages
- 1 FTR: Location

| Location: delete | EI | 3 | 2 | L | | | |

- 3 DETs: FML Code, command key, and messages
- 2 FTRs: Location and Employee (to ensure no employee assigned to Location)

| Organization: add | EI | 5 | 1 | L | | | |

- 5 DETs: Org Code, Org Name, Organization, command key, and messages
- 1 FTR: Group

| Organization: delete | EI | 3 | 2 | L | | | |

- 3 DETs: Org Code, command key, and messages
- 2 FTRs: Group and Employee (to ensure no employee assigned to Organization)

(continued)

[a] ILF, EIF, EI, EO, or EQ
[b] L = Low, A = Average, H = High

Description	Type[a]	DETs After	RETs/FTRs After	Complexity[b] After	DETs Before	RETs/FTRs Before	Complexity[b] Before
Picture: add	EI	5	1	L			

- 5 DETs: Social Security Number, Picture, Date of picture, command key, and messages
- 1 FTR: Employee

Description	Type[a]	DETs After	RETs/FTRs After	Complexity[b] After	DETs Before	RETs/FTRs Before	Complexity[b] Before
Picture: delete	EI	4	1	L			

- 4 DETs: Social Security Number, Date of picture, command key, and messages
- 1 FTR: Employee

Description	Type	DETs	RETs/FTRs	Complexity			
Query 1 (derived data)	EO	8	1	L			

- 8 DETs: First Name, Last Name, and number of records (displayed); and Title Code, Org Code, FML Code, command key, and messages (on the request)
- 1 FTR: Employee

Description	Type	DETs	RETs/FTRs	Complexity			
Logon	EQ	3	1	L			

- 3 DETs: command line together with command key, password, and messages
- 1 FTR: Security

Description	Type	DETs	RETs/FTRs	Complexity			
Query 2	EQ	20	4	H			

- 20 DETs: First Name, Last Name, Email, Title Code, Title Name, Organization, Org Name, Org Code, Picture display, Telephone, Fax, Room, Street, City, State, Zip Code, Country, FML Code, and ISO Code (displayed); and command key for the request (there are no messages, and First Name and Last Name have already been counted on the display)
- 4 FTRs: Employee, Location, Title, and Organization

Description	Type	DETs	RETs/FTRs	Complexity			
Organization: view	EQ	5	1	L			

- 5 DETs: Org Code, Org Name, and Organization (displayed); and command key and messages (on the request)
- 1 FTR: Group

Description	Type	DETs	RETs/FTRs	Complexity			
Title: view	EQ	4	1	L			

- 4 DETs: Title Code and Title name (displayed); and command key and messages (on the request)
- 1 FTR: Title

Description	Type	DETs	RETs/FTRs	Complexity			
Location: view	EQ	9	1	L			

- 9 DETs: Street, City, State, Zip Code, Country, FML Code, and ISO Code (displayed); and command key and messages (on the request)
- 1 FTR: Location

[a] ILF, EIF, EI, EO, or EQ
[b] L = Low, A = Average, H = High

CHAPTER FIFTEEN

Tools

Introduction

The primary purposes of software measurement are to provide meaningful and useful information to the software development organization, and to contribute to the organization's ability to identify opportunities for improvement and ultimately become more productive. Incorporating the use of automated software measurement tools enables the IT organization to collect, analyze, and report measurement-related information more accurately and effectively, thereby improving the efficiency of the metrics program. In addition, metrics tools can provide access to industry data values as they incorporate these values into their proprietary estimating and process evaluation models.

Numerous metrics-related software tools are available. They address a wide range of functionality, including project tracking, estimating, defect tracking, resource planning, and code complexity. However, this is a book about function points; therefore, we will focus on two types of function point–related tools: function point repositories and function point–based project-estimating tools. These are the two most common types of tools used in conjunction with function points.

Having a clear understanding of the organization's specific requirements for a metrics tool is critical to the success of the tool selection and utilization. In this chapter we will address basic tool selection criteria, as well as how to select a repository tool and an estimating tool. In order to more effectively select the proper estimating tool and ensure a proper fit into the organization, we recommend a proof of concept. A proof of concept will provide an organization with practical experience and insights into the performance and accuracy of selected tools.

Basic Tool Selection Criteria

A few basic guidelines apply when you are considering the purchase of an automated measurement tool. A quick review of these general guidelines will help to focus our discussion on selecting function point–specific tools.

The tool selection process should begin with a well-defined requirement—for example, what is driving the need for buying (or building) an automated tool. Selection of a function point repository may be based on the organization's need to record, report, and track the size of applications and associated enhancements or maintenance activities. Selection of an estimating tool may be based on the need to have access to an estimating model that can be applied consistently throughout the development organization. Once we have gained a clear understanding of our measurement tool requirements, the selection of a tool can begin.

A list of vendors and tools is compiled and the selection process begins. The selection of a tool and an appropriate vendor should be based on credibility. Vendor credibility can be judged on various factors, including the length of time in business, the level of subject matter expertise, and reference accounts. In the case of new vendors or start-up vendors, credibility may be based on the experience of those individuals that designed and built the tool. We can assess tool credibility by researching tool certifications and industry reviews and awards. For instance, the International Function Point Users Group (IFPUG) certifies function point–related tools. In addition, several trade magazines review tools and offer awards for tools that are best in their category.

When purchasing a tool, you may be required to provide a cost justification. Justifying the expense of a measurement tool is not typically accomplished with the standard ROI (return on investment) format. There are no measurable improvements in productivity attributed directly to the use of measurement tools; therefore, the benefits of using these tools cannot be directly linked to bottom-line dollar savings. After all, how does one measure the direct benefit of being able to track, monitor, and accurately record function points or justify the cost of the ability to generate a more accurate estimate? Organizations that are not performing measurement activities will most likely experience an increase in cost because of the labor required to learn how to use the tool and to properly use the tool in day-to-day activities.

The expense associated with purchasing a measurement tool is typically accounted for as project management overhead. Expense considerations include maintenance fees, upgrade fees, or additional features, which will need to be purchased. The good news is that these tools are not very expensive; therefore, a rigorous cost justification process is not usually required.

Finally, a tool must be easy to use. Some very sophisticated tools on the market perform very well but have a relatively high overhead cost. An easy-to-use tool does not require a lot of classroom time; it does not take a highly skilled individual to use the tool, nor does it take a great deal of time to put data in and get data out. It is particularly important for an organization just beginning to travel down the software metrics path to choose a set of tools that provide simple, basic functionality.

Selecting a Function Point Repository Tool

Selecting a function point repository tool can be a relatively simple process. There are fewer than a half dozen commercially available tools worth considering. A handful of tools on the market have function point counting components, but they are not suited to the rigorous collection, storing, and tracking of baseline application, enhancement, and project function point counts. These tools are not primarily function point counting tools but have function points as one of the required pieces of input data—for example, an estimating tool that uses function points as an input parameter to generate an estimate. Most tools can be found by a search on the Internet or through IFPUG. IFPUG has a list of available tools and provides information on the tools that have been certified to current counting standards.

The amount of functionality required to make a counting tool robust is not extraordinary; thus the tool review process is quick and easy. The functionality, in addition to the general selection criteria already noted, that is absolutely mandatory when considering the purchase of a function point repository tool includes the ability to

- Enter data at both a project and an application level
- Enter function point data on the basis of current and past function point counting guidelines

- Track data at the project and/or application level
- Allow for the input of detail or summarized complexity data
- Track how enhancement counts affect the baseline application
- Report at a summary and/or detail level
- Access a tutorial-based help function

Sometimes organizations choose to develop an in-house Microsoft Excel–based function point counting tool. These tools usually include the basic functionality for recording counts on a project-by-project or application-by-application basis; however, they are not sophisticated enough to track and automatically update changes to baseline application counts. They perform well on an individual basis but are not robust enough to support division- or organization-wide function point measurement needs.

If an organization is serious about its function point counting activity and about making the investment in resources to count and record function points, then it is easy to justify the purchase of one of the economical tools available on the market today. The International Function Point Users Group has certified three such tools: CHARISMATEK Software Metrics' Function Point WORK-BENCH, DDB Software's COUNTER, and a recent entry from Real Decisions/Gartner Group.

Selecting a Project-Estimating Tool

At the core of an effective estimating process is a set of tools that can be used to collect, analyze, and report project estimates. Currently more than 50 project-estimating tools are available on the market. Which is the best one for your organization?

Commercially available tools typically fall into one of two categories: (1) those that are very sophisticated and complex and (2) basic models with essential features and easy-to-use functions. Both tools have a place in today's software measurement programs. Some of the more common tools in use today include DDB Software's PREDICTOR, Software Productivity Research's Knowledge-PLAN, Quantitative Software Management's SLIM, and Software Productivity Center's ESTIMATE Professional.

High-end, sophisticated estimating tools permit greater flexibility with regard to the amount and the degree to which project variables may be entered. This flexibility allows the user to make numerous adjustments and calibrate the tool to profile the current development environment. These tools also contain a wider selection of output reports and templates, and they have been used effectively in organizations that have a well-established baseline of metrics data and use dedicated resources for internal estimating practices.

The more fundamental tools are easier to use because they do not demand a wide array of input variables. There is less opportunity with these tools to make adjustments and fine-tune your input parameter; however, their results are based on industry profiles that parallel organizational profiles. Because they are easier to use, both project estimators and project managers can use them. In other words, they can be used by a wider variety of personnel. A project manager can quickly assess project risks and perform "what if" scenarios while the estimating manager is performing an in-depth analysis of the same project.

Among the more common features required in an estimating tool include the abilities to

- Conduct "what if" analysis
- Provide repository functions
- Estimate deliverables (effort, duration, productivity, defects, cost)
- Export to project management tools
- Evaluate process strengths and weaknesses
- Store project profile information
- Accept multiple sizing criteria (function points, lines of code)
- Accomplish baseline assessments
- Compare to actual results
- Compare to industry and best-in-class practices
- Interface with a function point tool
- Perform maintenance assessments
- Provide standard reporting
- Enable risk management
- Track the actual process against the development plan
- Track resources
- Track scope creep

Interestingly, the main difference (other than functionality) between the high-end and low-end tools is not the accuracy of the results. The main difference is the cost of the tools. High-end tools may be as much as five to ten times more costly for an organization to fully implement than low-end tools. Granted, high-end tools contain a great deal more functionality, but that does not necessarily equate to added value. As for the accuracy issue, the two types of tools appear to calculate similar results. For example, Software Productivity Research's Checkpoint and DDB Software's PREDICTOR were used in tandem at a large Philadelphia-based insurance company. When they were used on projects of similar size and complexity, the estimated project results for effort and cost of both tools were very similar.

Conducting a Proof of Concept

Organizations that identify the need to improve their estimating practices typically initiate estimating improvement strategies that are doomed to failure. Without fully evaluating the estimating problem domain, the organization embarks on an initiative to improve its estimating practices by quickly selecting a commercially available software product and immediately rolling it out to the entire development organization. Six months later, the product is sitting on the shelf, and the project managers have returned to their previous estimating habits.

In order for an organization to improve its ability to effectively estimate project deliverables, it needs to develop an estimating process that incorporates the use of an automated tool, but more importantly the process needs to direct the project team toward the proper execution of good estimating practices. The selection of a tool alone will not improve an organization's ability to estimate. The selection of the wrong tool will negatively affect an effective estimating process. Get the process right, and an automated tool will be an excellent added value.

To ensure the right selection of an estimating tool, the following proof-of-concept approach is recommended. This approach allows an organization to fully define the estimating problem, discover the proper solution(s), test those solutions, and then proceed with a well-focused and effective estimating process. It can be accomplished in a relatively short time frame, usually 60 to 90 days, which minimizes the initial commitment of an organization.

Someone in the organization must take on the proof of concept as an assigned project and bring the expertise necessary—for example, tool utilization and sizing techniques. The individual(s) assigned to this project will be responsible for the following ten steps:

1. Identification of the current estimating problem
2. Definition of the deliverable
3. Process and tool selection

    4.   Project selection

    5.   Review of the estimating process with the project managers

    6.   Sizing and complexity analysis

    7.   Identification of project variables

    8.   Analysis of the data

    9.   Review of the estimate

   10.   Assessment of the process

1. Identification of the Current Estimating Problem

This step is for improving awareness and setting expectations. It is critical that the organization identify exactly what the problems are with the current estimating process and what its expectations are for an estimating process that works.

Many factors contribute to a successful estimating process, including good requirements, application familiarity, skill levels, and historical and/or industry data. It is critical that an organization recognize these elements as contributing factors that have an impact on the accuracy of a generated estimate. An inaccurate estimate may be the result of shortcomings in any one of these elements, and not the fault of the estimating process or the tools being used.

2. Definition of the Deliverable

What is the set of deliverables that the organization needs to estimate? Many of the commercially available estimating tools compute a variety of basic estimated values—for example, time, cost, defects, and effort. In addition, some of these tools provide a wide range of full lifecycle values, including estimated number of test cases, pages of documentation, and defects by phase. These tool features may seem impressive in a product demo session, but if an organization is not managing at that level of granularity, they are of little benefit to the project team. The primary deliverable of the estimating process must be clearly defined up front. For example, project time and cost estimates may be the primary need, while number of test scripts expected may be a nice-to-have.

3. Process and Tool Selection

An estimating process does not need to be reinvented for each organization. Most organizations subscribe to a development methodology that includes a generically defined estimating process. As long as the process clearly states a project manager's role and responsibility and allows for the use of a generic estimating model, it should be an effective method. The definitive selection of a tool at this point is premature. During the proof of concept, several tools should be tested and run in parallel. This approach has a distinct advantage in evaluating the effectiveness of the tools because they will be demonstrated in a live environment.

4. Project Selection

Next a set of projects to be estimated must be selected. These projects will be used to evaluate the effectiveness of the estimating process and tool(s). Select projects that have been recently completed or are still in progress to enable a wider range of experiences and provide some data values (actual results on completed projects) that can be used for comparison. We often suggest a selection of three to six projects. They should be in varying phases of development activity and of varying sizes.

In all cases the size and complexity must be established. If the project is complete, the size can be accurately assessed from the delivered product. If the project is in progress, the size and complexity must be gleaned from the best information available (usually a requirement or design document).

Naturally, in the case of projects in progress, some assumptions about the requirements and other project risk factors will need to be made. This is precisely what will be experienced in a live situation when estimates are required early in the lifecycle.

5. Review of the Estimating Process with the Project Managers

As you develop and document an estimating process, be sure to review and discuss the process with each project manager whose project has been selected. The project manager is ultimately responsible and must be comfortable with the process and potential benefits. You must also solicit the project managers' participation in the proof-of-concept process. Most project managers and project teams will welcome this approach. They are being invited to participate, not forced to execute a practice to which they don't subscribe. Their commitment per project is, on average, several hours.

6. Sizing and Complexity Analysis

The nature of the sizing activity will depend on where the project is in the development lifecycle and the extent of documentation available. The size may even need to be approximated if the documentation is incomplete or known to be inaccurate.

The project-sizing technique that delivers the greatest accuracy and flexibility is function point analysis. Based on logical, user-defined requirements, function points permit the early and accurate sizing of the software problem domain. If the problem domain is not clearly or fully defined, the project will not be properly sized. When requirements are missing, brief, or vague, a simple process, using basic diagramming techniques with the requesting user, can be executed in order to more fully define the requirements. In addition, the function point methodology presents the opportunity to size a user requirement regardless of the level of detail available. An accurate function point size can be determined from the information in a thorough user requirements document, or an adequate function point size can be derived from the limited information provided in an early proposal.

In addition to size, and as part of the definition element of an estimating model, the complexity values for an application must be assessed to determine their influence on expected delivery rates. Examples of appropriate complexity factors to be assessed include the following:

- **Logical algorithms.** This factor refers to the complexity of the processing logic required by the application. It includes if/then/else logic.
- **Mathematical algorithms.** This factor refers to the complexity of mathematical algorithms required by the application. It includes a range of simple math to differential equations, fuzzy logic, and interpretive decision making.
- **Data relationships.** This factor refers to the complexity of the data relationships required by the application. It recognizes joins, connections, or associations between the data maintained within the application.
- **Functional size.** Some applications have a very small number of data fields in most transactional and data function types in comparison to the function point matrices. Likewise, some applications have a much higher number of data fields than are represented by the function point matrices.
- **Reuse.** This factor extends the potential for reuse to requirements, design, code, test, and documentation phases, or prototyping.
- **Code structure.** Source code structure evaluates the code that will be developed or the code that will be utilized and/or revised during an enhancement.
- **Performance.** This factor relates to the availability and execution frequency of the application.
- **Memory.** Memory requirements restrain the developer to utilize a very restricted amount of core memory in executing the application.
- **Security.** Security is additional to that required to enter the application and may include field sensitivity, as well as provide for audit data.
- **Warranty.** The application must be developed with a sensitivity to the delivery of critical errors based on the critical nature of the application and the responsibility of the developers.

Complexity factors vary from tool to tool. These factors commonly have a high degree of influence in the overall outcome of the estimate and are therefore essential to the process (see Appendix C).

7. Identification of Project Variables

A two-hour session with the project team is necessary to collect information regarding the project variables. This task may also be accomplished by an interview with the project manager.

The capability to deliver software is based on a variety of risk factors that influence a development organization's ability to deliver software in a timely and economical fashion. Risk factors include the software processes to be used, the skill levels of the staff (including user personnel), the automation to be utilized, and the influences of the physical (e.g., development conditions) and business environment (e.g., competition and regulatory requirements). In fact, numerous factors influence our ability to deliver high-quality software in a timely manner. Categorized in the list that follows are some examples of influencing factors that must be evaluated to produce an accurate estimate:

- Team dynamics
- Project management
- Clarity of requirements
- Customer involvement
- Formal design process
- Design reuse
- Formal reviews and inspections
- Staff experience levels
- Test methods
- Quality assurance

Once again, these variables will differ depending on the tool utilized. Most tools will simply ask for a yes-or-no or sliding-scale response to each variable. As with the sizing step, assumptions are often required when a particular variable is either not known or subject to change.

8. Analysis of the Data

Now the results must be analyzed. As with any value-added tool, some calibration of the tool will be necessary in order to fine-tune the results. If you have included a set of projects that are complete and have actual results available, then a quick comparison will indicate how close the tool approximated reality. When there is a difference between the planned and the actual beyond an accepted level of variability, the tool must be calibrated. These tools are set to respond on the basis of a set of experiences that have been converted into a series of algorithms, which drive the end results. Not all experiences are exactly alike; therefore, adjustments can be necessary. Experience with the tool and/or support from the tool vendor may be necessary to make the proper adjustments. The key here is consistency. You do not want to have to make adjustments for each project. Once calibrated, the tool should perform consistently on the majority of projects.

9. **Review of the Estimate**

When you are comfortable with the calibrated result, review the estimate with the project manager(s). This review is critical. The review criteria include accuracy of the estimate and benefit gained from the process. If the project is complete, the level of accuracy will be quickly assessed. The benefit of the process, aside from the accuracy, should be based on the manager's opinion as to whether or not the insights gained from the sizing, complexity analysis, and risk variable assessment yielded additional insights that may not have naturally surfaced. For example, the complexity factor analysis may indicate a high degree of technical complexity that was not apparent from the business requirements. Another example may include a discovery of a certain weakness within the development process that is highlighted by the assessment of the risk variables.

10. **Assessment of the Process**

Remember that the two key criteria are the accuracy of the estimate and the value gained from insights into the project variables. Accuracy will be measurable only when you have the actual results. Hopefully, you will have been able to include at least one project in the proof of concept that was near completion and had actual data available. An assessment of the value gained by the project team can be gathered simply through an interview or survey process.

After you have executed these ten steps, you are ready to review the effectiveness of the estimating tools and process based on a live experience. Perhaps the results will reveal that some adjustments must be made (likely). Perhaps you will realize that the estimating process or tool is not applicable for all project scenarios (less likely). Perhaps you will not have realized any benefit from this proof of concept (unlikely).

Summary

The purchase of a tool must be based on a clearly identified need. Once the need is defined and agreed upon, the selection of a tool should be based on a well-defined set of criteria. The basic elements include vendor and tool credibility, ease of use, and cost.

Commercially available function point repositories contain all the basic features required to support the collection, tracking, and reporting of function point data. Their value-added feature is their ability to organize function point counts and provide an audit trail of historical counts to any given application.

Estimating tools come in two varieties: sophisticated and basic. Both types have their place in supporting an organization's metrics program. The higher-end tools provide a wider variety of options and can be effectively used within organizations that have made a longer-term commitment to measurement and project estimating. The lower-end tools are easier to use and provide greater flexibility in terms of utilization. Both types of tools produce reasonably accurate estimates.

One final note: The practical organization would be wise to consider the selection of more than one tool. We often find that the different tools perform effectively in certain, but not all, scenarios. It may be reasonable to expect that one tool will do well in estimating large mainframe projects, while another tool may have its strengths in estimating client-server and distributed types of projects. Of course, utilization of multiple tools should be weighed against the consequences of having too many unintegrated tool sets.

CHAPTER SIXTEEN

Preparing for the CFPS Exam

Practice Certified Function Point Specialist Exam

The International Function Point Users Group (IFPUG) Certification Committee provides certification of function point counters, training materials, and tools. You can determine who has been certified by calling the IFPUG office or by checking the IFPUG Web site. Counters become certified by passing an IFPUG-sponsored Certified Function Point Specialist (CFPS) examination.

We have designed the following practice exam so that you can determine, on your own, how well prepared you are to take the IFPUG CFPS examination. Our practice exam, in three parts, follows. Use the answer sheet provided at the end of this chapter to record your answers to parts I and II, and Figures 16-1 through 16-4 to record your answers to part III. Answers to the practice exam are provided in Appendix F. You should be able to complete the exam within three hours. Good luck!

Part I

1. The objectives of function point analysis are to
   a. Measure functionality that the user requests and receives
   b. Measure technology used for implementation
   c. Measure resources used for implementation
   d. All of the above

2. An application function point count
   a. Is also referred to as the baseline or installed function point count
   b. Includes the functionality provided by data conversion and associated conversion-reporting requirements
   c. Is altered every time an enhancement alters the application's functions
   d. a and c

3. Internal logical files (ILFs) are
   a. Stored external to the application's boundary
   b. Maintained within the application
   c. Identified as a requirement of the application by the users
   d. b and c

4. An external interface file (EIF) can be
   a. A user-identifiable group of logically related data utilized by the application but maintained by another application
   b. A user-identifiable group of logically related control information maintained by the application
   c. A user-identifiable group of logically related data maintained by the application but referenced in another part of the application
   d. a and c

5. An external input is considered unique if
   a. Data is maintained in different internal logical file(s)
   b. The input data fields are unique
   c. The processing logic is unique
   d. All of the above

6. External outputs can include
   a. Data calculated and sent external to the application's boundary
   b. Control information solely retrieved and sent external to the application's boundary
   c. Help text retrieved and returned to the user
   d. a and b

7. Which of the following could be external inquiries?
   a. Help text
   b. Menu screens that provide only navigation

c. Derived data

d. Calculated data

8. Examples of general system characteristics do *not* include

a. Installation ease

b. Language

c. End user efficiency

d. Data communications

9. Flexible query/report capability is accounted for in which of the following GSCs?

a. Installation ease

b. Facilitate change

c. Performance

d. End user efficiency

10. Which of the following should be counted as a DET on an external input (EI)?

a. Command line(s) or function/action (PF) key(s) that provide the capability to specify the action to be taken by the external input

b. Error messages as a result of the EI transaction

c. Fields relating to the EI transaction

d. All of the above

11. Help within an application includes full screen help, field-sensitive help, and system help. How many EQs are counted?

a. One for the application

b. One for each screen

c. Three for the application

d. One for each occurrence

12. TDI is

a. The sum of the 14 degrees of influence

b. A score between 0 and 70

c. ±35%

d. a and b

13. Internal logical files or external interface files can

a. Be counted in more than one application

b. Contain multiple RETs

   c. Be hard-coded

   d. a and b

14. An application count includes
    a. What is delivered by the application
    b. How something is delivered by the application
    c. User-requested data conversion to populate the application
    d. a and c

15. Boundaries
    a. Identify the border between the software being measured and the user
    b. Define the functionality that will be included in a function point count
    c. Consider the application from a technical point of view
    d. a and b

16. Which of the following can be counted as one or more ILFs in a project?
    a. Application data
    b. Application security data
    c. Control data
    d. All of the above

17. Which of the following can equate to one or more EIFs?
    a. Reference data utilized by the application but maintained elsewhere
    b. Error messages hard-coded into the application
    c. Control data that is not maintained but is utilized by the application
    d. a and c

18. Unique processing logic for EIs includes
    a. Edits
    b. Calculations
    c. Different FTRs
    d. All of the above

19. Which of the following are external outputs?
    a. Data residing in an ILF that is retrieved, processed, and sent for use by an external application
    b. Error or confirmation message reports associated with EIs
    c. Data retrieved, calculated, and displayed to a user
    d. All of the above

20. Which of the following cannot be counted as external inquiries?
    a. Selection of data retrieval based on data input
    b. Data retrieval capabilities prior to change or delete functionality, provided that the inquiry capability can be and is used as a stand-alone function
    c. Data retrieved and displayed to a user, which results in a simultaneous update to an ILF
    d. Full screen help

21. Degrees of influence (DIs) are evaluated
    a. On a scale of 0 to 5
    b. For each transaction
    c. On a scale of ±35%
    d. All of the above

22. Security or timing considerations are accounted for in which of the following GSCs?
    a. Distributed data processing
    b. Heavily used configuration
    c. End user efficiency
    d. Online data entry

23. Which of the following fields on an internal logical file are counted as multiple DETs?
    a. An account number or date that is physically stored in multiple fields
    b. Fields that appear more than once in an internal logical file where they serve as secondary keys
    c. Summary fields at the monthly, quarterly, and annual levels
    d. All of the above

24. When applied, the value adjustment factor adjusts the unadjusted function point count by
    a. ±5%
    b. ±35%
    c. 65%
    d. None of the above

25. Which of the following is *not* an EI?
    a. Unique data used to maintain an ILF
    b. A unique file referenced from another application

  c. A unique batch process that maintains an ILF

  d. A unique screen function that maintains an ILF

26. A file type referenced (FTR) is counted for
  a. Each internal logical file maintained or referenced during the processing of an external input
  b. Each internal logical file maintained or referenced during the processing of an external output
  c. a and b
  d. None of the above

27. A development project function point count
  a. Is associated with the initial installation of new software
  b. Measures the function provided to the end users by the project
  c. Includes the functionality provided by data conversion and associated conversion-reporting requirements
  d. All of the above

28. Which of the following can equate to one or more ILFs?
  a. Work files
  b. Edit data
  c. Sort files
  d. All of the above

29. Which of the following can equate to one or more EIFs?
  a. Data received from another application that adds, changes, or deletes data on an ILF
  b. Edit data used by the application to validate inputs
  c. Data maintained by the application being counted, but accessed and utilized by another application
  d. Data formatted and processed for use by another application

30. Which of the following is an incorrect statement?
  a. An EI processes data or control information that enters the application's external boundary
  b. Control information must directly maintain an internal logical file
  c. Control information is data used by a process within an application boundary to assure compliance with business function requirements specified by the user
  d. Processed data must maintain an internal logical file

31. Multiple external outputs are counted for
    a. Identical reports that have the same format and processing logic but send unique data values to multiple users
    b. Summary fields on a detail report
    c. Identically formatted and calculated reports at the detail and summary levels
    d. a and c

32. An external inquiry (EQ)
    a. Could be a unique input/output combination that results in the calculation of data
    b. Could be a report generated monthly with retrieved data
    c. Does not update an internal logical file
    d. b and c

33. Multilingual support counts as how many items under end user efficiency?
    a. None
    b. Six
    c. Two
    d. One

34. Which of the following are counted as DETs on EOs?
    a. Each user-recognizable, nonrepeating field that appears on the external output
    b. Each unique summary total on a report
    c. Each type of label and each type of numerical equivalent in a graphical output
    d. All of the above

35. The unadjusted function point count is
    a. The sum of the weighted function type values of the application being measured
    b. Multiplied by the value adjustment factor to arrive at the adjusted function point count
    c. The sum of the general application processing complexities based on the 14 general system characteristics
    d. a and b

36. An enhancement function point count
    a. Measures the modifications to an existing application that add, change, or delete user function within the scope of a project

b. Does not include the functionality provided by data conversion and associated conversion-reporting requirements

c. Represents the count of the installed application when completed

d. a and b

37. System files are counted as ILFs if they are
    a. Hard-coded as requested by the user to meet legal requirements
    b. Required for normal backup and recovery procedures
    c. Introduced only because of technology used
    d. None of the above

38. Which of the following are EIs?
    a. External data that maintains internal logical files
    b. Data input used to drive selection for data retrieval
    c. User updates associated with the elementary process of an EO
    d. All of the above

39. An EI can be invoked if a user enters "A" or "Add" on a command line or uses
    a PF key. How many DETs should be counted for the three command keys on
    the EI?
    a. Zero
    b. One
    c. Two
    d. Three

40. If one elementary process—to issue an item from inventory—writes to two
    separate ILFs (Inventory and Department Billing) within the same applica-
    tion, count
    a. One external input
    b. Two external outputs
    c. Two external inputs
    d. b and c

41. Which of the following could be counted as multiple EQs?
    a. Identical queries produced on different windows with identical process-
       ing logic
    b. Different graphical displays with different processing logic
    c. Multiple methods of invoking the same inquiry logic
    d. a and b

42. Extensive logical processing is accounted for in which of the following GSCs?
    a. Transaction rate
    b. Online data entry
    c. Complex processing
    d. Performance

43. Which of the following are counted as DETs on EOs?
    a. Literals on reports
    b. Paging variables or system-generated time/date stamps
    c. Each distinct error or confirmation message available for display on an external input
    d. None of the above

44. An average-complexity EIF has an unadjusted function point value of
    a. 5
    b. 7
    c. 10
    d. 15

45. To assign an unadjusted function point value to each external inquiry,
    a. Calculate the functional complexity on the basis of only the output side of the external inquiry
    b. Calculate the functional complexity on the basis of the total nonrepeated DETs from both the input and output sides of the external inquiry
    c. Select the higher of the two functional complexities on the basis of both the input side and the output side
    d. None of the above

46. An external input may
    a. Display data
    b. Maintain an ILF
    c. Perform calculations
    d. All of the above

47. An external output may
    a. Process data on the basis of user requests
    b. Maintain an ILF
    c. Perform calculation for display
    d. All of the above

48. An external inquiry may
   a. Send data to another application
   b. Display data on the basis of user requests
   c. Result in creation of a diskette
   d. All of the above

49. A user view
   a. Is a description of the business functions
   b. Can be used to count function points
   c. Can vary in physical form
   d. All of the above

50. Function point size can be approximated, but not measured, during
   a. Proposal
   b. Requirements
   c. Design
   d. All of the above

Part II

1. The unadjusted function point value of an ILF with 19 DETs and 5 RETs is
   a. 5
   b. 7
   c. 10
   d. 15

2. The unadjusted function point value for a project that includes 3 low-complexity EIs, 1 low-complexity EQ, 1 average-complexity EQ, and 1 low-complexity ILF is
   a. 23
   b. 24
   c. 25
   d. 27

3. How many EQs are counted on a screen that permits a user to add a customer, view customer information, delete a customer, and change customer information?
   a. One
   b. Two
   c. Three
   d. Four

4. An enhancement is planned for application A. An EI is being revised from 12 DETs and 1 FTR by the addition of 1 DET and 2 FTRs. The EI will now have 13 DETs and 3 FTRs. The unadjusted value of this EI toward the enhancement function point count is

   a. 3

   b. 4

   c. 6

   d. None of the above

5. The increase in the value of the application unadjusted function point count for the preceding question is

   a. 1

   b. 4

   c. 3

   d. 6

6. The Accounts Payable (AP) application sends a transaction to the General Ledger (GL) application, which updates an ILF in the GL. How is the transaction counted?

   a. As an EIF to the AP and an EI to the GL

   b. As an EO to the AP and an EIF to the GL

   c. As both an EIF and an EI to the GL

   d. As an EO or an EQ to the AP and an EI to the GL

7. The Payroll application provides the capability to the user to extract information from two separate ILFs. The user enters an ID number and a function key. One screen display is provided in response, with 19 retrieved fields. There is no derived or calculated information. What is counted?

   a. A low EI and an average EQ

   b. A high EQ

   c. A low EI and a high EQ

   d. An average EQ

8. A screen or window provides 12 different sort selections with the request to print a report. There are neither calculations nor derived data on the report. What is counted?

   a. 1 EQ

   b. 12 EOs or 12 EQs

   c. 1 EI and 12 EOs or EQs

   d. 12 EIs and 1 EO or EQ

9. A screen provides capability for the user to add data to an ILF by completing the data fields Employee ID, Employee Name, Employee Job Title, Employee Job Location, and Employee Phone Number by entering "Add" on the command line and pressing Enter. Either error messages or a confirmation message will appear. How many DETs are counted in the EI?

   a. 1
   b. 6
   c. 7
   d. 8

10. A display is generated internally with retrieved fields from two ILFs; a different ILF is updated with a flag to indicate that the display has been generated. What is counted?

    a. 1 EI and 1 EO
    b. 1 EQ and 1 EI
    c. 1 EO
    d. None of the above

11. An ILF is updated by three separate applications (A, B, and C). Where is it counted?

    a. In the largest application
    b. In the application where it experiences the most use
    c. In all three applications
    d. In the application where most of the data is maintained

12. When counting DETs in an ILF, count

    a. All DETs in the file
    b. Only those DETs maintained
    c. Only those DETs referenced
    d. Only those DETs maintained and/or referenced

13. What is the project unadjusted function point count for an enhancement that includes the following: 1 new high EI, 1 deleted average EO, and 1 ILF revised from low to average?

    a. 21
    b. 16
    c. 11
    d. 14

14. Data is collected upon entry into a temporary file. The temporary file is sorted before being loaded to an employee file. The employee file is maintained. An extract of the employee file is utilized to create reports. How many ILFs are counted?
    a. 4
    b. 1
    c. 2
    d. 3

15. Three user-defined and -maintained groups of data are combined into one physical file. How many ILFs are counted?
    a. 0
    b. 1
    c. 2
    d. 3

16. A user-defined customer file is maintained by the use of three database tables: customer, address, and point of contact. How many ILFs are counted?
    a. 0
    b. 1
    c. 3
    d. 4

17. Users have requested three tabs to accomplish the elementary process of creating a purchase order. What is counted?
    a. 1 EI
    b. 3 EIs
    c. 1 EI and 3 EQs
    d. None of the above

18. Which of the following cannot be ILFs?
    a. Application data
    b. Error messages maintained by users
    c. JCL
    d. Help messages maintained by users

19. An ILF
    a. Is read only within the boundary of the application being counted
    b. Is maintained by the application being counted

    c. May contain control information

    d. b and c

20. Application A maintains an ILF that is also read by application B. Application A should

    a. Get credit for an ILF and an EIF

    b. Get credit for an ILF

    c. Get credit for an EO

    d. b and c

21. Examples of EIs include

    a. Batch input that adds data to an ILF

    b. Control information that initiates a search for data to be printed

    c. Data that is referenced from another application

    d. a and b

22. An input references 2 EIFs in updating an ILF with 5 DETs entered by the user. Count the EI as

    a. Low

    b. Average

    c. High

    d. Insufficient information to complete this statement

23. In a count of DETs in an EO,

    a. Literals in the heading should be counted

    b. System-generated dates in the heading should be counted

    c. Any information in headings should be counted

    d. None of the above

24. The functional complexity of EOs is determined by

    a. The number of DETs and RETs

    b. The number of FTRs and RETs

    c. The number of DETs and FTRs

    d. a and c

25. External inquiries

    a. Always have a user input and an output display

    b. Sometimes have derived fields on the output side

    c. Can output a file to another application

    d. None of the above

26. Which of the following cannot be EQs?
    a. Navigation
    b. Log-on screens with security
    c. Screen displays that contain derived data
    d. a and c

27. The possible range of adjustment to an unadjusted function point count based on the general systems characteristics is
    a. ±35%
    b. 0 to 5
    c. 35%
    d. None of the above

28. Which of the following is an EO?
    a. Error messages displayed online
    b. Error messages printed as a report
    c. Online derived report requested via report selection menu
    d. b and c

29. Which of the following is *not* an EQ?
    a. Field-sensitive help
    b. A log-on screen that does not reference an ILF or EIF
    c. A selection menu screen with no retrieved data
    d. b and c

30. When determining the value adjustment factor for an enhancement project,
    a. Use the value adjustment factor from the previous project
    b. Do not use the value adjustment factor
    c. Evaluate and include the influence of the questions as they apply to a project
    d. Evaluate and include the influence of the questions as they apply to a project within an application boundary after completion of the project

31. To calculate the value adjustment factor (VAF),
    a. Select and total scores for all statements within each general system characteristic that apply to an application; the result is the VAF
    b. Select the statement for each general system characteristic that most clearly describes the application; the total equals the VAF
    c. Total the scores for all 14 characteristics and multiply by the unadjusted function point count to calculate the VAF
    d. None of the above

32. Application A has a master file (Parts) that contains parts inventory informa-
    tion. Application B uses Parts as an external interface file. Application A
    counts Parts as
    a. an ILF and an EIF
    b. an ILF only
    c. an EIF only
    d. None of the above

33. The Marketing System reports sales in detail for the branch managers and,
    using the same format, summary totals for the marketing director. How
    many external outputs are there?
    a. One, the sales report
    b. Two, sales report detail for the branch manager and sales report summary
       for the marketing director
    c. One for each of the branch managers and one for the marketing director
    d. None of the above

34. The Sales System sends a file of completed orders to the Billing System. The
    Sales System counts this file of orders as
    a. an EIF
    b. an EO or an EQ
    c. an ILF
    d. None of the above

35. The Branch Manager Sales Report is calculated and sent by file to three
    branch managers. The data is different, but the fields are identical. How
    many EOs are there?
    a. 1
    b. 2
    c. 3
    d. None of the above

36. System A has four menus of selection functionality for navigation through
    the system. How many external inquiries should be counted?
    a. 0
    b. 1
    c. 4
    d. One for each potential selection

37. The maximum total degree of influence is
    a. 35
    b. 65
    c. 70
    d. 135

38. The unadjusted function points total 100. The total of the 14 general system characteristics is 35. What is the adjusted function point count?
    a. 100
    b. 135
    c. 114
    d. None of the above

39. The original unadjusted function points for an application totaled 400, with a value adjustment factor of 1.10. The first enhancement adds 30 function points and deletes 10. The functions being changed were originally worth 12 function points and are now worth 15. The value adjustment factor will stay the same. What is the size of the enhancement project, in adjusted function points?
    a. 57.2
    b. 60.5
    c. 55
    d. 47.3

40. The original unadjusted function points for an application totaled 400, with a value adjustment factor of 1.10. The first enhancement adds 30 function points and deletes 10. The functions being changed were originally worth 12 function points and are now worth 15. The value adjustment factor will stay the same. What is the size of the application, in adjusted function points, after the enhancement project?
    a. 478.5
    b. 465.3
    c. 462
    d. 463

41. An ILF consisting of 250 DETs has 5 RETs with 20, 110, 60, 50, and 10 DETs, respectively. The file should be counted as
    a. 1 high-complexity ILF
    b. 2 high-complexity ILFs and 3 low-complexity ILFs

   c. 2 average-complexity ILFs and 3 low-complexity ILFs

   d. 3 average-complexity ILFs and 2 low-complexity ILFs

42. An EI has 16 DETs and 2 FTRs. What is its unadjusted function point value?
   a. 6
   b. 5
   c. 4
   d. 3

43. An EO has 16 DETs and 3 FTRs. What is its unadjusted function point value?
   a. 7
   b. 6
   c. 5
   d. 4

44. An ILF has 50 DETs and 1 RET. What is its unadjusted function point value?
   a. 5
   b. 7
   c. 10
   d. 15

45. An EIF has 20 DETs and 2 RETs. What is its unadjusted function point value?
   a. 5
   b. 7
   c. 10
   d. 15

46. A new development project consists of 4 low-complexity EIs, 2 average-complexity EIs, 2 high-complexity EIs, 4 low-complexity EQs, 2 average-complexity EQs, 2 average-complexity EOs, 3 low-complexity EIFs, 2 low-complexity ILFs, 1 average-complexity ILF, and 2 low-complexity EIs (used only for data conversion in developing the application). The project unadjusted function point count is equal to
   a. 101
   b. 107
   c. 109
   d. None of the above

47. For the previous question, the initial application unadjusted function point count is equal to
   a. 101
   b. 107
   c. 109
   d. None of the above

48. Application A maintains a customer file with the following fields: Customer ID (key to file), Customer Name, Customer Street Address (three lines), Customer City, Customer Postal Code, Customer State, Customer Country, Customer Contact, Contact Phone Number, Contact Fax Number, and Contact E-mail Address. How many DETs are counted for the ILF in application A?
   a. 10
   b. 11
   c. 13
   d. 14

49. Application B extracts the customer name, street address, city, postal code, state, and country as a single block of data to be printed on a label using the customer ID. Assuming that this is the only use of the customer file within application B, how many DETs are counted for the EIF in application B?
   a. 2
   b. 6
   c. 7
   d. 11

50. A user enters five different fields on an EI, plus a command key. A verification prompt ("Are you sure?") requires a response. Two different error messages are possible, and a confirmation message confirms update. In addition to the five fields entered by the user, two additional total fields are updated in an ILF. One of these total fields is displayed together with the confirmation message. How many DETs are counted for the EI?
   a. 8
   b. 9
   c. 10
   d. 12

Part III

The following two case studies involve (1) the identification and sizing of a new development project and (2) an enhancement project and the resulting application count.

CFPS Case Study 1

Complete a function point count for the following new development project. Record all data and transactional functions on the function point count summary (see Figure 16-1, page 278). Enter results on the function point calculation worksheet (see Figure 16-2, page 279), and compute the adjusted function point count.

OVERVIEW

Company XYZ plans to automate its accounts payable system. The application will interface with existing banking, help, and purchase order (PO) applications. Determine the development function point count on the basis of the processing requirements indicated in the following paragraphs for the accounts payable system.

This will be a menu-driven system. To enter the accounts payable system, the user must make selections from a main menu. The menu(s) will have the following options:

- Invoices
  1. Add an invoice
  2. Display an invoice
  3. Change an invoice
  4. Delete an invoice

- Payments
  1. Retrieve payments due
  2. Record payments

- Vendors
  1. Add a vendor
  2. Display vendor information
  3. Change vendor information

In addition, some system-generated processing and audits must be performed.

DETAILED REQUIREMENTS

1. Invoice data will be maintained in an Invoice data store utilizing the PO number as the primary key to the file.

    1.1 Invoices will be entered upon receipt with the following data: PO number, vendor name, date of invoice, date invoice received, product/service, terms, payment due date, and amount billed. A function key will initiate the edit and save this data. As part of an audit trail, each invoice record will have a system-generated date stamp to show when it was entered or modified; no other audit data is maintained in the Invoice data store. The PO number, vendor name, and amount billed will be validated against the PO data store (an externally maintained data store within the PO system), the vendor name will be validated against the Vendor data store (internally maintained). Error messages will be returned. The PO data store contains PO number, vendor name, date of PO, maximum PO amount, and department code, some of which are not used by the accounts payable system.

    1.2 There will be drop-down list boxes to display (1) outstanding purchase orders by PO number, vendor name, and maximum PO amount from the PO data store; (2) vendor name and mailing address (street, city, state, and zip code) from the Vendor data store.

    1.3 Invoices may be displayed with the same data as listed in paragraph 1.1. POs will be selected by PO number and a function key. A message will be returned if the PO does not exist in the Invoice data store. The identical drop-down list box will be available to assist in the selection.

    1.4 All data contained in paragraph 1.1 may be changed except the PO number, which is the key required to access and change the proper record in the Invoice data store. The same editing and list boxes provided in paragraphs 1.1 and 1.2 will be available. Error messages will be returned. A function key will initiate the edit and save the data.

    1.5 A user may delete an invoice by selecting the PO number and a function key. A message will be returned if the PO does not exist in the Invoice data store.

2. Payment information will be saved in an optional subgroup (RET) within the Invoice data store that utilizes the PO number and a payment date as the secondary key. The Invoice data store will contain fields from paragraphs 1.1 and 2.1 (including the date stamp, and the previous payment dates and amounts paid on those dates). The entering of payment information is considered a separate business function.

2.1 The user will select payments by scrolling through invoices using the payment date. The payment date must be selected from a hard-coded drop-down list of dates. The user will enter the date and a function key. Invoices with payments due will be displayed with the following data: PO number, vendor name, date of invoice, date invoice received, payment due date, terms, amount billed, previous payment dates, amounts paid on those dates, and current balance due (which is calculated upon display). There are no error messages.

2.2 The user can enter received payment information by selecting the PO number (which must be in the Invoice file) and entering the payment date (which must be a future date), the amount to be paid, and a function key. Error messages are returned.

2.3 At the close of business each day, the system will send a file of all payments received that will be passed to the banking system. This file will contain the payment date, payment amount, PO number, vendor name, and vendor billing street address, city, state, and zip code. All information will be retrieved from the Invoice data store and the Vendor data store.

3. Vendor information will be maintained in a Vendor data store using a vendor name as the primary key.

3.1 A new vendor may be added with the following data: vendor name; vendor billing address (three lines), city, state, and zip code; vendor point of contact; vendor phone number; and a function key. The vendor name distinguishes between vendors with more than one location. Errors are returned. The same vendor drop-down list that is discussed in paragraph 1.2 will be provided.

3.2 Vendor data may be displayed with the same information as contained in paragraph 3.1. Selection will be by vendor and a function key. A message will be returned if the vendor does not exist in the vendor file. The vendor drop-down list will be provided.

3.3 All data contained in paragraph 3.1 may be changed except the vendor name, which is the key required to access and change the proper record in the Vendor data store. The same editing and list box that is provided in paragraph 3.1 will be available. A function key will initiate the edit and save the data. There is no plan to delete vendor information.

4. Two levels of help (window and field) will be available. Both levels of help are from one externally maintained Help data store. There will be one set of help text for each selection, which may be scrollable.

The data files for Case Study 1 are presented in Table 16-1.

Complete Figure 16-1 by entering the data and transactional functions. Utilize the totals of the data and transactional functions and their assigned complexities to complete the function levels in Figure 16-2. Fill in all blanks, and use the degrees of influence for the general system characteristics to complete the adjusted function point count for the new development project.

CFPS Case Study 2

The previous case study indicated that the accounts payable system would interface with existing banking, help, and purchase order applications. No changes

Table 16-1: Data Files, Records, and Fields for Case Study 1

Data File	Fields[a]
Invoice data store Invoice record	**PO Number** Vendor Name Date of Invoice Date Invoice Received Product/Service Terms Payment Due Date Amount Billed Date Stamp
Invoice payment record	**PO Number** *Payment Date* Amount Paid
PO data store[b]	**PO Number** Vendor Name Date of PO Maximum PO Amount Department Code
Vendor data store	**Vendor Name** Vendor Billing Address Vendor City Vendor State Vendor Zip Code Vendor Point of Contact Vendor Phone Number

[a]Fields shown in boldface are primary keys; those in italics, secondary keys.

[b]The fields used from the PO data store are PO Number, Vendor Name, and Maximum PO Amount.

Function Point Count Summary

Project Number CFPS Case Study 1		**Project Name**
Date of Count		**Counter's Name**

Instructions: Enter all function types included. Annotate all function types added by the conversion. You may wish to use different sheets for files and transactions.

Description	Type[a]	DETs	RETs/FTRs	Complexity[b]

[a] ILF, EIF, EI, EO, or EQ
[b] Low (L), Average (A), High (H)

Figure 16-1 Function point count summary for Case Study 1

were required to the help and purchase order systems; however, paragraph 2.3 indicated that a file would be passed to the banking system at the close of every business day. This file contains the payment date required (usually a future date); payment amount; PO number; vendor name; and vendor billing street address,

Function Point Calculation Worksheet

Project Number CFPS Case Study 1	**Project Name**
Type of Count Development Project/Application Counting (circle one)	
Phase of Count Proposal/Requirements/Design/Code/Test/Delivery (circle one)	
Date of Count	**Counter's Name**

IFPUG's Unadjusted Function Point Table*

	Function Levels			
Components	**Low**	**Average**	**High**	**Total**
External inputs	$\times\,3$	$\times\,4$	$\times\,6$	
External outputs	$\times\,4$	$\times\,5$	$\times\,7$	
External inquiries	$\times\,3$	$\times\,4$	$\times\,6$	
Internal logical files	$\times\,7$	$\times\,10$	$\times\,15$	
External interface files	$\times\,5$	$\times\,7$	$\times\,10$	

Total unadjusted function points (UFP) =

*The development function point count includes function types added by the conversion. The application function point count does not include conversion requirements. An application count after an enhancement must include all existing function types, including those unchanged. If information on all existing function types is not available, the application adjusted function point count can be computed by the formula given in the text.

General System Characteristics

Characteristic	Degree of Influence	Characteristic	Degree of Influence
1. Data communications	4	8. Online update	3
2. Distributed data processing	0	9. Complex processing	0
3. Performance	0	10. Reusability	3
4. Heavily used configuration	0	11. Installation ease	0
5. Transaction rate	0	12. Operational ease	3
6. Online data entry	5	13. Multiple sites	2
7. End user efficiency	3	14. Facilitate change	2

Total degree of influence (TDI) =

VAF	Value adjustment factor	$= (\text{TDI} \times 0.01) + 0.65$ =	
FP	Adjusted function point count	$= \text{UFP} \times \text{VAF}$	=

Figure 16-2 Function point calculation worksheet for Case Study 1

city, state, and zip code. The banking system must now be enhanced to process this incoming file and to generate the appropriate checks.

1. The banking system will process the incoming file from the accounts payable system without any edits or validation into two user-maintained data stores: Checking Account and Disbursements.

   1.1 The Checking Account data store previously had 2 RETs and 19 DETs. This change will require the addition of the PO number to the Checking Account data store. All other fields were previously included.

   1.2 The Disbursements data store will not require any changes as a result of this enhancement.

2. The current process to generate checks to pay invoices will be modified. Checks now will be generated with the PO number as a separate memo field by the banking system. Previously, checks contained the following information: preprinted name and address for the company; preprinted check numbers; payment date; payment amount; payee (same as vendor's name); and payee street address, city, state, and zip code. They previously did not include a memo field. These checks reference only the Checking Account data store when they are created. The Checking Account data store is updated internally to indicate payment as part of the check generation elementary process.

3. A printed report will be generated from the Checking Account data store if checks were not produced because of an inadequate balance. The report will appear as shown in Table 16-2.

Table 16-2: Report of Insufficient Funds

Insufficient Funds for Payment Date_____		
Payee	PO Number	Payment Amount
—		
—		
—		
—		
Total number of payees[a] ___		Total payment amount[a] ___

[a]Totals are generated when the report is produced.

4. These transactions will be maintained in a new Suspense data store until cleared. Suspense will contain the original payment date, payee, PO number, and payment amount.

   4.1 There will be a new online inquiry to retrieve information from the Suspense data store. It will display the original payment date, payee, PO number, and next payment amount due, which is calculated from the payment amount from the Suspense data store whenever the user enters the payment date and a function key. An error message may appear.

   b. The Suspense data store must be updated (and simultaneously cleared) by users through an online update transaction that will enter a new payment date. This transaction will pass the original payment date, the PO number, the new payment date, and the payment amount to the Banking, Disbursement, and Suspense data stores using a function key. An error message will be returned immediately to the screen if there are insufficient funds to process the request and the transaction cannot be processed.

5. There will be no changes to the banking system's general system characteristics and associated degrees of influence (shown here in parentheses), which are as follows:

   1. Data communications (4)

   2. Distributed data processing (0)

   3. Performance (3)

   4. Heavily used configuration (2)

   5. Transaction rate (3)

   6. Online data entry (5)

   7. End user efficiency (3)

   8. Online Update (3)

   9. Complex processing (3)

   10. Reusability (3)

   11. Installation ease (2)

   12. Operational ease (3)

   13. Multiple sites (3)

   14. Facilitate change (2)

   Total **degree of influence: 39**

6. The previous unadjusted function point count for the banking system was 330.

7. Calculate the function point count for the enhancement project using the enhancement function point count summary and function point calculation worksheet (see Figures 16-3 and 16-4).

Enhancement Function Point Count Summary

Project Number CFPS Case Study 2   Project Name

Date of Count   Counter's Name

Instructions: Enter all function types included. For development and initial function point counts, there will not be entries in the "Before" columns. Annotate all function types added by the conversion. You may wish to use different sheets for files and transactions.

Description	Type[a]	DETs After	RETs/FTRs After	Complexity[b] After	DETs Before	RETs/FTRs Before	Complexity[b] Before

[a] ILF, EIF, EI, EO, or EQ
[b] Low (L), Average (A), High (H)

Figure 16-3 Enhancement function point count summary for Case Study 2

8. At the bottom of the function point calculation worksheet, indicate the formula that should be used to calculate the new unadjusted function point count for the banking system. Then show your calculations and derive the revised application count.

Enhanced Function Point Calculation Worksheet

Project Number CFPS Case Study 2	Project Name
Type of Count Enhancement Project Count	
Phase of Count Proposal/Requirements/Design/Code/Test/Delivery (circle one)	
Date of Count	Counter's Name

	Function Levels			
* Function Types Added or Modified (Value After)	**Low**	**Average**	**High**	**Total**
External inputs	× 3	× 4	× 6	____
External outputs	× 4	× 5	× 7	____
External inquiries	× 3	× 4	× 6	____
Internal logical files	× 7	× 10	× 15	____
External interface files	× 5	× 7	× 10	____

Unadjusted Added and Modified function points = ____

* Include added function types and modified function types (value after). The enhancement function point count includes function types added by the conversion.

	Function Levels			
* Function Types Deleted	**Low**	**Average**	**High**	**Total**
External inputs	× 3	× 4	× 6	____
External outputs	× 4	× 5	× 7	____
External inquiries	× 3	× 4	× 6	____
Internal logical files	× 7	× 10	× 15	____
External interface files	× 5	× 7	× 10	____

Unadjusted deleted function points = ____

* Includes those function types deleted by the enhancement.

Figure 16-4 Enhancement function point calculation worksheet for Case Study 2

(continued)

General System Characteristics

Characteristic	Degree of Influence Before	After	Characteristic	Degree of Influence Before	After
1. Data communications	___	___	8. Online update	___	___
2. Distributed data processing	___	___	9. Complex processing	___	___
3. Performance	___	___	10. Reusability	___	___
4. Heavily used configuration	___	___	11. Installation ease	___	___
5. Transaction rate	___	___	12. Operational ease	___	___
6. Online data entry	___	___	13. Multiple sites	___	___
7. End user efficiency	___	___	14. Facilitate change	___	___

Total degree of influence (TDI) =

Enhancement project function point count

$[(ADD + CHGA + CFP) \times VAFA] + [DEL \times VAFB] =$ ___

Indicate the formula and calculation for the application adjusted function point count after enhancement.

Figure 16-4 Enhancement function point calculation worksheet for Case Study 2 (*cont.*)

Answer Sheets

Answer Sheet: Part I

Name:

Instructions: Darken your answer to each question. Only one answer is correct. Recommend use of pencil. To delete an answer, cross through with an X.

1. a b c d	8. a b c d	15. a b c d
2. a b c d	9. a b c d	16. a b c d
3. a b c d	10. a b c d	17. a b c d
4. a b c d	11. a b c d	18. a b c d
5. a b c d	12. a b c d	19. a b c d
6. a b c d	13. a b c d	20. a b c d
7. a b c d	14. a b c d	21. a b c d

22. a b c d	32. a b c d	42. a b c d
23. a b c d	33. a b c d	43. a b c d
24. a b c d	34. a b c d	44. a b c d
25. a b c d	35. a b c d	45. a b c d
26. a b c d	36. a b c d	46. a b c d
27. a b c d	37. a b c d	47. a b c d
28. a b c d	38. a b c d	48. a b c d
29. a b c d	39. a b c d	49. a b c d
30. a b c d	40. a b c d	50. a b c d
31. a b c d	41. a b c d	

Answer Sheet: Part II

Name:

Instructions: Darken your answer to each question. Only one answer is correct. Recommend use of pencil. To delete an answer, cross through with an X.

1. a b c d	18. a b c d	35. a b c d
2. a b c d	19. a b c d	36. a b c d
3. a b c d	20. a b c d	37. a b c d
4. a b c d	21. a b c d	38. a b c d
5. a b c d	22. a b c d	39. a b c d
6. a b c d	23. a b c d	40. a b c d
7. a b c d	24. a b c d	41. a b c d
8. a b c d	25. a b c d	42. a b c d
9. a b c d	26. a b c d	43. a b c d
10. a b c d	27. a b c d	44. a b c d
11. a b c d	28. a b c d	45. a b c d
12. a b c d	29. a b c d	46. a b c d
13. a b c d	30. a b c d	47. a b c d
14. a b c d	31. a b c d	48. a b c d
15. a b c d	32. a b c d	49. a b c d
16. a b c d	33. a b c d	50. a b c d
17. a b c d	34. a b c d	

Answer Sheet: Part III

Use Figures 16-1 through 16-4 for the two case studies.

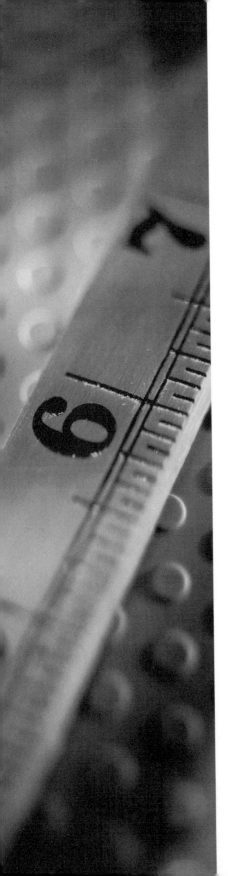

Project Profile Worksheet

PROJECT PROFILE WORKSHEET

Project   _____

Project Managers   _____

Organization   _____

Location   _____

Questionnaire Completed by   _____

Date   _____

The David Consulting Group

TABLE OF CONTENTS

PROJECT CLASSIFICATION   SECTION 1

Project Type   ☐
1.1   New program development
1.2   Enhancement (functions modifying an existing application)
1.3   Maintenance (defect repair to an existing application)
1.4   Data conversion
1.5   Software reengineering
1.6   Migration to different platform

Project Complexity   ☐
1.7   Disposable prototype
1.8   Evolutionary prototype
1.9   Minor coding changes (less than 12 months)
1.10 Major application revision (without significant documentation)
1.11 Small application release (6–18 months)
1.12 Average application release (1.5–5 years)
1.13 Major system release (greater than 5 years)

Expected Application Use (Multiple responses possible)
1.14 Single location   ☐
1.15 Multiple locations   ☐
1.16 Internal program, developed by external contractor   ☐
1.17 Bundled with hardware and marketed as product   ☐
1.18 Commercial contract   ☐
1.19 Government contract   ☐
1.20 Military specifications   ☐

Application Type (Multiple responses possible)
1.21 Nonprocedural (generated, query, spreadsheet) application   ☐
1.22 Batch database application   ☐
1.23 Interactive database application   ☐
1.24 Systems application   ☐
1.25 Communications/telecommunications application   ☐
1.26 Process control application   ☐

1.27	Embedded or real-time application	☐
1.28	Knowledge-based application	☐
1.29	Scientific/mathematical application	☐
1.30	Object-oriented application	☐
1.31	Graphical user interface application	☐
1.32	Client-server application	☐
1.33	Multimedia application	☐

MANAGEMENT   SECTION 2

Performance Measures

PROCESS

2.1	Defect tracking, with plans to correct, during Requirements	☐
2.2	Defect tracking, with plans to correct, during Design	☐
2.3	Defect tracking, with plans to correct, during Testing	☐
2.4	Automated and complete lifecycle productivity measures	☐
2.5	Automated time capture	☐
	Accurate timekeeping, including overtime:	
2.6	To task level	☐
2.7	To phase level	☐

PERSONNEL

2.8	Individual performance goals are linked to team performance	☐
2.9	Personnel reviews are conducted formally	☐

Team Dynamics

2.10	Small team (less than 5 staff)	☐
2.11	Large team with one manager	☐
2.12	Responsibilities are very clear and well documented	☐
2.13	High morale on project	☐
2.14	Good morale on project	☐
2.15	Salaries and benefits are competitive	☐

Project Management

2.16 Agreement on project deliverables, methodologies, and schedule   [ ]

Project management has:

2.17	Significant experience	[ ]
2.18	Average experience	[ ]

Project management methods include:

2.19	Estimates with historical data	[ ]
2.20	CPM, PERT, GANT milestones, and delivery dates	[ ]
2.21	Schedule of phases/tasks with start and end dates	[ ]

Project management activities are:

2.22	Fully automated, integrated, and effective	[ ]
2.23	Partially automated and effective	[ ]
2.24	Manual but effective	[ ]

DEFINITION   SECTION 3

(CUSTOMER QUESTIONS REFER TO THE CUSTOMER,
END USER, AND/OR MARKETING GROUP)

Process

3.1 Customer software requirements are clearly stated and stable   [ ]

Requirements were developed using:

3.2	JAD or equivalent methodology	[ ]
3.3	Formal interviews with customer involvement	[ ]

The definition process involves:

3.4	Prototyping of all major transactions	[ ]
3.5	Prototyping of most transactions	[ ]

3.6	Review process is very rigorous and thorough and involves customers	[ ]
3.7	Review process is mostly rigorous and thorough	[ ]

Experience

3.08	Customers very experienced in their application field	[ ]
3.09	Customers familiar with application field	[ ]

3.10	Customers have significant prior software experience	[ ]
3.11	Customers understand their support roles and responsibilities	[ ]

3.12 Development staff very experienced with type of application
being developed

☐

3.13 Development staff experienced with type of application being developed ☐

3.14 Development staff experienced with the definition process ☐

Business Impact

3.15 No known legal or statutory restrictions ☐

3.16 Limited legal or statutory restrictions ☐

3.17 Conversion or functional repeat of a well-understood application ☐

3.18 Functional repeat, but some new and unique functions ☐

3.19 New application, but some well-understood functions ☐

DESIGN   SECTION 4

Process

4.1 Use of data and/or entity modeling techniques ☐

4.2 Use of structured data analysis ☐

4.3 Formal design methods ☐

4.4 Formal design reviews are very rigorous and thorough ☐

4.5 Formal design reviews are consistently conducted ☐

4.6 Extensive design reuse ☐

4.7 Customers very involved during design reviews ☐

4.8 Customers involved during design reviews ☐

Experience

4.9 Development staff very experienced with application type ☐

4.10 Development staff experienced with application type ☐

4.11 Development staff experienced in the tools and methods
being utilized

☐

4.12 New tools and methods being introduced, but with adequate
training

☐

4.13 Development staff experienced in analysis and design methods
utilized

☐

4.14 Analysis/design methods being introduced, but with adequate training ☐

4.15 Development staff very experienced in design reviews ☐
4.16 Development staff experienced in design reviews ☐

Automation
4.17 Design-to-code automation with reusable code library ☐

BUILD   SECTION 5

Process
5.1 Code review and inspection is very rigorous and thorough ☐
5.2 Code review and inspection is mostly rigorous and thorough ☐

5.3 Extensive use of reusable code ☐
5.4 Reusable code used ☐
5.5 Data administration and active data dictionary available ☐
5.6 Computer support is very reliable and effective ☐
5.7 Computer support is usually reliable and effective ☐

Experience
5.8 Development staff very experienced in language(s) used for the project ☐
5.9 Development staff familiar with languages used ☐

5.10 Development staff very experienced in code inspections and reviews ☐
5.11 Development staff experienced in code inspections and reviews ☐

Automation
5.12 Full (tracking and management) source code library with automated support ☐
5.13 Partial (tracking or management) source code library with automated support ☐

5.14 All support tools and software very effective ☐
5.15 Most support tools and software effective ☐
5.16 Support software is familiar and well understood ☐
5.17 Executable code is generated ☐

TEST   SECTION 6

Process

6.1	Outside development testing, plus development and user testing
6.2	Outside development testing, plus development testing
6.3	Development and user testing

6.4	Test plans developed and formally reviewed
6.5	Test plans developed and informally reviewed

6.6	Testing is very rigorous and thorough
6.7	Testing is rigorous and thorough

Experience

6.8	Development staff very experienced in software test methods
6.9	Development staff experienced in test methods

6.10	Development staff very experienced in testing this type of application
6.11	Development staff experienced in testing this type of application

6.12	Training available and utilized in testing procedures
6.13	Training adequate in testing

Automation

6.14	All test tools and software are very effective
6.15	Most test tools and software are effective

6.16	Fully automated test bed facilities
6.17	Effective manual test bed

ENVIRONMENT   SECTION 7

Technology

7.1	The project is introducing new technology with adequate training
7.2	New technology is being applied for part of the project

7.3	Automated and effective system development methodology
7.4	No automation, but effective system development methodology

Resources

7.5   Workstations available to all personnel   ☐
7.6   Adequate office space and team meeting rooms   ☐
7.7   Significant software development training   ☐
7.8   Adequate software development training   ☐

Organizational Factors

7.9   Single department, single-site development project   ☐
7.10 Multiple development departments within same site   ☐

7.11 Organizationwide ISO certification of some types of work   ☐
7.12 Awaiting final ISO certification   ☐

7.13 Complete organizationwide deployment of TQM   ☐
7.14 Complete I/S organization deployment of TQM   ☐
7.15 Responsibility for the project is outside of IT   ☐
7.16 Contract programmers are more than 50% of total staff   ☐

Project Profile
Worksheet Guidelines

The Project Profile Worksheet (see Appendix A) provides project managers with a tool to assist them in identifying areas that could affect a project team's ability to deliver a particular software solution. The process involves answering questions relative to the project's attributes. Once the type of application, type of methodology, and application use have been identified, specific questions regarding basic software development phases are reviewed. The guidelines in this appendix provide insights to project managers as they complete a project worksheet for each project being analyzed.

Section 1: Project Classification

Each of these selections provides input into the estimating formula. Enter the data as shown in Table B-1.

Table B-1: Project Classification Data

Project Attributes	Selection Options
Project type	Make a selection from the list box. This represents the **majority or significant portion** of the release or project if there are multiple descriptions of the project. The choices are as follows: • **1.1 New program development.** Developing a new software system • **1.2 Enhancement.** Changing, adding, or deleting functionality in an existing system • **1.3 Maintenance.** Correcting software defects, bugs in the production system • **1.4 Data conversion.** Converting databases in an existing system • **1.5 Software reengineering.** Modifying an existing system through the introduction of new technology, not changing the functionality of the system as a whole. • **1.6 Migration to different platform.** Migrating functionality from one technical environment to another.
Project complexity	Make a selection from the list box. The choices are • **1.7 Disposable prototype** • **1.8 Evolutionary prototype** • **1.9 Minor coding changes** (less than 12 months) • **1.10 Major application revision** (without significant documentation) • **1.11 Small application release** (6–18 months) • **1.12 Average application release** (1.5–5 years) • **1.13 Major system release** (greater than 5 years)
Expected application use	Make a selection from the list box. Where is the system functionality deployed? The choices are • **1.14 Single location, single city** • **1.15 Multiple locations: single city, multiple cities, or international** • **1.16 Internal program, developed by external contractor**

Project Attributes	Selection Options
Expected application use (*continued*)	• **1.17 Bundled with hardware and marketed as product** • **1.18 Commercial contract** • **1.19 Government contract** • **1.20 Military specifications**
Application type	Make a selection from the list box. The choices are • **1.21 Nonprocedural (generated, query, spreadsheet)** • **1.22 Batch database** • **1.23 Interactive database** • **1.24 Systems** • **1.25 Communications/telecommunications** • **1.26 Process control/operating system** • **1.27 Embedded or real-time** • **1.28 Knowledge-based** • **1.29 Scientific/mathematical decision support** • **1.30 Object-oriented** • **1.31 Graphical user interface** • **1.32 Client-server** • **1.33 Multimedia**

Section 2: Management

This section identifies factors of management that contribute to a project's success. Three dimensions are considered: performance measures, team dynamics, and project management.

Performance Measures

2.1–2.3 Defect Tracking

Defect tracking is the formal and rigorous process of defect detection, removal, analysis, and tracking. Defects are detected through a formal inspection process, such as following Fagan or Gilb methodology. Defects are recorded relative to type, origin, and severity. Defects are analyzed throughout the lifecycle.

2.4 Automated and Complete Lifecycle Productivity Measures

This question is a test to see if the project team is doing extensive measuring—for example, tracking defects, counting function points, and estimating using historical data.

2.5–2.7 Accurate Timekeeping

These questions assess the degree of detailed recording of effort associated with the project. *Overtime must be included.* The accurate recording of time is a critical success factor in future estimating activities.

2.8 Individual Performance Goals

This question addresses some project motivation and awards factors that affect the performance of a team.

2.9 Personnel Reviews

This question addresses a basic project management issue that affects the performance of individuals, which ultimately affects the performance of the team.

Team Dynamics

2.10–2.11 Team Size

Select "Small team (less than 5 staff)" if the entire development team consists of only five members or less. Select "Large team with one manager" if the entire development team is managed by only one individual.

2.12 Responsibilities

Do all members of the project team know what they are responsible for? If responsibilities are clearly understood, documentation is not necessary and you may select this box.

2.13–2.14 Morale

Select "Good morale on project" unless otherwise stated.

2.15 Salaries and Benefits

This question is really a test to see if the organization is retaining its people.

Project Management

2.16 Agreement

Make sure the project wasn't delayed because of lack of agreement on schedule, deliverables, and so on.

2.17–2.18 Project Management Experience

Select "Significant experience" if the project manager has more than five years experience managing projects. Select "Average experience" for one to four years of experience.

2.19–2.21 Project Management Methods

These questions identify the tools used to communicate effectively with the project team, and the project manager's experience and comfort level with these tools.

2.22–2.24 Project Management Activities (Use of Tools)

Select "Fully automated, integrated, and effective."

Section 3: Definition

This section identifies factors of effective requirements definition that contribute to a project's success. Three dimensions are considered: process, experience, and business impact.

Process

3.1 Software Requirements

This is really two questions: whether the requirements are *clearly stated* and whether they are *stable.* It measures a sense of how disruptive changes were to a project.

3.2–3.3 Requirements Developed

These questions address the various practices and processes used within the project team or expected to be followed within the project team to gather effective software requirements.

3.4–3.5 Definition Process

One of the most effective methods in advancing the understanding of requirements is through the use of prototyping. These questions assess the extent of prototyping in the project.

3.6–3.7 Review

The question of review process addresses formal inspection methodology (Fagan or Gilb method), with strict adherence to roles, process, tracking flaws, and so on. The process must be documented and well understood.

Experience

3.8–3.9 Customer Experience with the Business

These questions address the customer's business knowledge. If the customer doesn't know the business, the level of risk is higher. Does the customer understand the business side of the process that is being automated by the project?

3.10–3.11 Customer Experience with IS and Projects

These questions address the significant role of the customer as a business partner within a software development project. Do the customers understand what they are supposed to do to engage in the project, and do they realize that their contribution to the project can have a significant impact on the success of the project?

3.12–3.13 Development Staff Experience

These questions address the people involved with requirements and definition; it is a measurement of their business knowledge—for example, subject matter experts. The question does not address technical expertise.

3.14 Definition Process

This question measures the requirements team's knowledge of the software development methodology (SDM) process being used in the organization.

Business Impact

This section identifies additional project risks that are often overlooked during the planning of successful software projects.

3.15–3.16 Legal Impact

These questions address any state, federal, or legal impacts that were *not* part of the original requirements, but were added later and interfered with the project.

3.17–3.19 Functional Impact

If any description applies, select the most appropriate for the project.

Section 4: Design

This section identifies factors of effective design methodology that contribute to a project's success. Three dimensions are considered: process, experience, and automation.

Process

4.1 Data Modeling

Select this if the development staff is using data entity diagrams—that is, developing a logical data model to support the business requirements.

4.2 Data Analysis

This question addresses the best practices of analyzing the data required to support the system.

4.3 Design Methods

This question assesses the impact of methods being used (e.g., if this is an OO application, is the team using Schlear-Mellor, Raumbaugh, or Bachman?).

4.4–4.5 Design Reviews

These questions address formal inspection methodology (Fagan or Gilb method), with strict adherence to roles, process, tracking flaws, and so on. The process must be documented and well understood.

4.6 Design Reuse

Select this if there is any design reuse.

4.7–4.8 Customer Participation

Is the customer involved in the design? These questions address both the logical and the physical design, and often it is not applicable to both designs.

Experience

4.9–4.11 Development Staff

These questions measure the level of business knowledge by the IS organization.

4.12 Tools

This question is looking at case tools and design methods the team is using; for example, if this is an OO application and the team is using an automated tool, measure the team's competence in the tools being used.

4.13–4.14 Methods

These questions assess the team's experience in methodology.

4.15–4.16 Design Reviews

These questions assess the design team's depth and breadth of knowledge relative to formal inspection methodology. How long have they been doing the reviews?

Automation

4.17 Tools

This question really addresses case tools and possibly code generators being used. Otherwise leave it blank.

Section 5: Build

This section identifies factors of effective coding and unit-testing methodology that contribute to a project's success. Three dimensions are considered: process, experience, and automation.

Process

5.1–5.2 Code Inspections

These questions address formal inspection methodology (Fagan or Gilb method), with strict adherence to roles, process, tracking flaws, and so on.

5.3–5.4 Reuse

These questions address reusable code from a library; however, this does *not* include macros.

5.5 Data Administration

Select this *only* if you have a *true* data administration function or maintain a *true* data dictionary; otherwise leave blank.

5.6–5.7 Environment

These questions address the computer support environment for the development team during the processes of coding and compiling.

Experie**n**ce

5.8–5.9 Developer Experience

These questions address the technical experience of the team.

5.10–5.11 Reviews

These questions address the skill level of the development team while performing (or not performing the task), as opposed to the process questions regarding code review (5.1 and 5.2), which address whether the process is even being done.

Automa**t**ion

5.12–5.13 Libraries and Tracking

Select if any source control, configuration management, or version control for software is being used.

5.14–5.15 Tools

These questions assess tools used (compilers, debuggers, and so on) by the software developers.

5.16 Support Systems

If new tools are being introduced in the project, leave this blank.

5.17 Case Tool

This question addresses the use of case tools that create executable code from design to code automatically. This is "generated" code rather than "developed" code.

Sectio**n** 6: Test

This section identifies factors of effective system-testing methodology that contribute to a project's success. Three dimensions are considered: process, experience, and automation.

Process

6.1–6.3 Test Team Composition

These questions measure the scope of the test team. Is the test team an outside group, separate from the development group? Who tests the software (after the unit test)?

6.4–6.5 Test Plans

Are test plans *written*?

6.6–6.7 Testing Level

These questions address a sense of the amount of testing done for the project—that is, whether there was extra time and additional tests were run.

Experience

6.8–6.9 Test Methods

Does the test team have professional software testers? Have the testers attended formal testing training (via STAR, ASM, ASQC, and so on)?

6.10–6.11 Experience

These questions measure the technical experience level of the testing team for the application.

6.12–6.13 Training

This question assesses the training necessary for the testing team.

Automation

6.14–6.15 Tools

This is a judgment call based on the system test team's response and perception of the tools they use.

6.16–6.17 Test Bed

Select if automated test beds of data are used or if manual regression testing is *formally* done.

Section 7: Environment

This section identifies factors of the environment that contribute to a project's success. Three dimensions are considered: technology, resources, and organizational factors.

Technology

7.1–7.2 New Technology

These questions assess the impact that new technology and the training team has had on the development of the application; we must consider the risk to the project.

7.3–7.4 Development Methodology

These questions address the impact of case tools on methodology in order to facilitate effective software development.

Resources

7.5 Workstations

Do people have to share PCs to get their work done?

7.6 Space

Is there sufficient space for both work and meetings?

7.7–7.8 Training

Do the members of the project team feel they have had the training needed?

Organizational Factors

7.9–7.10 Location

Is the project being developed at the same physical location, or are the teams separated geographically?

7.11–7.12 ISO

Is the organization required to maintain ISO compliance with this project?

7.13–7.14 Total Quality Management

Is the organization or IT pursuing a specific Total Quality Management (TQM) initiative?

7.15 Responsibility

Is the project management for the project done by the business partner?

7.16 Contracts

To compute this number, assess the total number of contractors for all phases in the project, including design, coding, and testing.

Complexity Factors
Project Worksheet

COMPLEX FACTORS
PROJECT WORKSHEET

Project   _____

Application   _____

Version   _____

Project Type   _____

Application Type   _____

Platform   _____

Expected Use   _____

Project Manager   _____

Organization   _____

Questionnaire Completed by   _____

Logical Algorithms

This factor refers to the complexity of the processing logic required by the application. This includes If, Then, Else logic.

Identification of Values	Select	Score
1.0 to 1.2 Simple logical algorithms.	○	☐
1.3 to 1.5 Many logical algorithms, some complex.	○	☐
1.6 to 1.8 Many complex logical decisions.	○	☐
1.9 to 2.1 Many complex nested algorithms.	○	☐
2.2 to 2.4 Most complex decision support system.	○	☐
2.5 to 2.7 Extremely complex nested and embedded algorithms; Very significant logical decisions throughout.	○	☐
2.8 to 3.0 Most advanced applications ever produced.	○	☐

Mathematical Algorithms

This factor refers to the complexity of mathematical algorithms required by the application. This includes a range of simple math to differential equations, fuzzy logic, and intepretative decision making.

Identification of Values	Select	Score
1.0 to 1.2 Simple addition, subtraction, division and multiplication.	○	☐
1.3 to 1.5 Many calculations in series, more difficult calculations.	○	☐
1.6 to 1.8 Significant calculations with derivation, smoothing or regression analysis.	○	☐
1.9 to 2.1 Mathematical formula based system.	○	☐
2.2 to 2.4 Complex differential equations common throughout.	○	☐
2.5 to 2.7 Numerous mathematical calculations, most of which would include hundreds of equations and many unknowns.	○	☐
2.8 to 3.0 Most complex mathematical algorithms ever utilized.	○	☐

Data Relationships

This factor refers to the complexity of the data relationships required by the application. This would include the potential for different updates to different files, based upon processing logic, for the same transactional function or message. It also recognizes joins, connections or associations between the data maintained within the application.

Identification of Values	Select	Score
1.0 to 1.4 Simple data relationships; simple edits and validations.	○	☐
1.5 to 1.9 Multi-dimensional data relationships; extensive edits and validations.	○	☐
2.0 to 2.4 Multi-dimensional and relational data with significant attributive and associative relationships. Complex edits and validations resulting in multiple error conditions.	○	☐
2.5 to 3.0 Processing includes extremely complex data and data relationships. Inputs occur selectively or continuously with different processing.	○	☐

Functional Size

The fundamental size of an application is calculated using Function Points. However, some applications have a very small number of data fields in most transactional and data function types in comparison to the Function Point matrices. Likewise, some applications have a much higher number of data fields than represented by the Function Point matrices.

Identification of Values	Select	Score
1.0 to 1.4 Small number of data fields and data relationships.	○	☐
1.5 to 1.9 Small number of data fields or data relationships.	○	☐
2.0 Functionality can be adequately sized using the Function Point matrices.	○	☐
2.1 to 2.5 Much higher number of data files or data relationships.	○	☐
2.6 to 3.0 Much higher number of data files and data relationships.	○	☐

ReUse

Reuse is an often cited advantage of utilizing pre-existing code in order to reduce development effort and standardize applications. This factor extends that potential for reuse to Requirements, Design, Test and Documentation Phases or Prototyping.

Identification of Values		Select	Score
1.0 to 1.4	Essentially a data conversion or re-engineered application; extensive reuse.	◯	☐
1.5 to 1.9	Average benefit greater than 20% in all phases of development. Usually achieved from extensive automated library or existing object oriented warehouse.	◯	☐
2.0 to 2.4	10 to 20% benefit within all phases of Requirements, Design, Build, Test and Documentation. This score can also be achieved by extensive prototyping.	◯	☐
2.5 to 2.9	Reuse planned but less than 10% benefit or limited prototyping.	◯	☐
3.0	No reuse within application development.	◯	☐

Code Structure

Source Code structure refers to both the code which will be developed or code which will be utilized and/or revised during an Enhancement.

Identification of Values		Select	Score
1.0	Generated Code.	◯	☐
1.1 to 1.5	Simple, easy to read and maintain. Fourth generation language.	◯	☐
1.6 to 2.0	Average, typically third generation language.	◯	☐
2.1 to 2.5	Typical legacy application; many previous revisions.		
2.6 to 3.0	Very poorly structured existing application; very difficult to read and maintain.	◯	☐

Performance

Performance relates to the availability and execution frequency of the application.

Identification of Values		Select	Score
1.0	No performance or execution frequency impact on application development.	○	☐
1.1 to 1.5	Minor performance and execution frequency impact on application. Typical of batch or stand-alone PC.	○	☐
1.6 to 2.0	Average performance and execution frequency impact in order to fulfill on-line processing commitments. Typical of client-server development.	○	☐
2.1 to 2.5	Significant performance and execution frequency impact, most frequently found in real-time systems.	○	☐
2.6 to 3.0	On-line, continuously available, critically timed application which executes almost instantly. Inputs could occur at either fixed or variable intervals, but require interruption in order to process input of a higher priority.	○	☐

Memory

Memory requirements restrain the developer to utilize a very restricted amount of core memory in executing the application.

Identification of Values		Select	Score
1.0	No memory requirements.	○	☐
1.1 to 2.0	Memory requirements for a portion of the application.	○	☐
2.1 to 3.0	Severe memory restrictions across the entire application.	○	☐

Security

Security for use of the application is an important consideration. Security is additional to that required to enter the application and may include field sensitivity as well as provide audit data.

Identification of Values		Select	Score
1.0	Application does not require specific screen/window or field level security.	○	☐
1.1 to 1.5	Application contains security restrictions on the entry/update of data into certain fields within the application or to view specific screens/windows.	○	☐
1.6 to 2.0	Application contains security restrictions on both the entry/update in and the retrieval of data from numerous fields. This factor should also be selected for a government application classified as confidential.	○	☐
2.1 to 2.5	Application contains not only severe security restrictions, but maintains audit data on the date, time and identity of those individuals who access the application and the specific data to which they had access. This factor should also be selected for a government application classified as secret.	○	☐
2.6 to 3.0	Highly sensitive, top-secret government applications.	○	☐

Warranty

The application must be developed with a sensitivity to the delivery of critical errors.

Identification of Values		Select	Score
1.0	Application is not of a critical nature. Although it is a goal to reduce delivered bugs, there is no significant penalty.	○	☐
1.1 to 1.5	Application is being developed and delivered with implied warranty that defects will be corrected by the developer.	○	☐
1.6 to 2.0	Application developer will be rewarded by quality levels prescribed in the contract.	○	☐
2.1 to 2.5	Application developer will suffer severe penalties by quality levels prescribed in the contract. Likely to result in severe cost to users.	○	☐
2.6 to 3.0	Application is critical. Failure is likely to cause loss of life of individual or organization.	○	☐

Sample Project Analysis

Project Estimate

Project   : ISBSG Project - ISBSG Project
Application : ISBSG Appl - ISBSG Application
Version   : First - One
Project Type : New Development
Platform   : Client Server
Productivity : 13.29
Staff Months : 26.34
Cost / FP   : 753

Application Type : Interactive Database
Expected Use   : Multiple Locations, International
Function Points : 350
Calendar Months : 10.97
Defects   : 44

Productivity

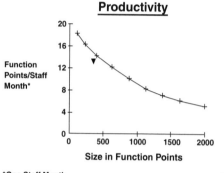

Function
Points/Staff
Month*

Size in Function Points

*One Staff Month
  = 120 Hours

Effort

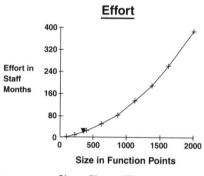

Effort in
Staff
Months

Size in Function Points

ISBSG Values   Size   Elapsed Time
Min - 321   11 Months
Avg - 336   11 Months
Max - 350   10 Months

Defects

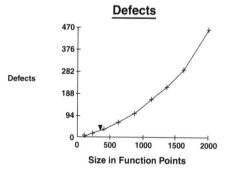

Defects

Size in Function Points

Productivity

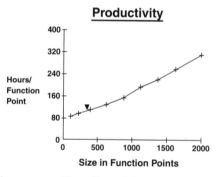

Hours/
Function
Point

Size in Function Points

ISBSG Values   Size   Elapsed Time
Min - 321   3.4 Hrs/FP
Avg - 336   2.5 Hrs/FP
Max - 350   1.6 Hrs/FP

Project Estimate   01/28/2000   Page 2

Project   : ISBSG Project - ISBSG Project
Application   : ISBSG Appl - ISBSG Application
Version   : First - One
Project Type : New Development   Application Type : Interactive Database
Platform   : Client Server   Expected Use   : Multiple Locations, International
Productivity : 13.29   Function Points   : 350
Staff Months : 26.34   Calendar Months : 10.97
Cost / FP   : 753   Defects   : 44

Category Risk Analysis

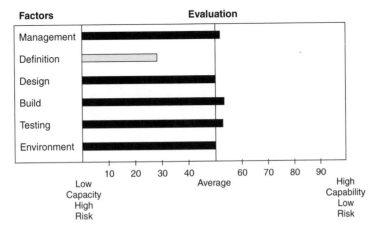

Category Scoring

Category	Score	Category Maximum	Percent within Category
Management	4.6	8.8	52.27
Definition	6.6	23.4	28.21
Design	11.0	22.0	50.00
Build	8.4	15.6	53.85
Testing	11.9	22.4	53.13
Environment	3.9	7.8	50.00
Total	**46.4**	**100.0**	

Project Estimate

Project   : ISBSG Project - ISBSG Project
Application : ISBSG Appl - ISBSG Application
Version   : First - One
Project Type : New Development   Application Type : Interactive Database
Platform   : Client Server   Expected Use   : Multiple Locations, International
Productivity : 13.29   Function Points   : 350
Staff Months : 26.34   Calendar Months : 10.97
Cost / FP   : 753   Defects   : 44

Category Strengths and Weakness

Strengths	Weakness
Management	
Responsibilities Very Clear, Well Documented	
Definition	
Requirements Clear, Stable	Requirements Definition Process
	Lack of Prototyping
	Limited Formal Review Process
	Customers Inexperienced in Application Field
	Customers Inexperienced in Software Definition
Design	
Structured Data Analysis	
Formal Design Methodology	
Code Generation	
Build	
Developers Experienced in Code Reviews	
Developers Experienced in Support Software	
Test	
Environment	
Effective System Development Methodology	Inadequate Office Space

---

Project Estimate   01/28/2000   Page 4

Project   : ISBSG Project - ISBSG Project
Application : ISBSG Appl - ISBSG Application
Version   : First - One
Project Type : New Development   Application Type : Interactive Database
Platform   : Client Server   Expected Use   : Multiple Locations, International
Productivity : 13.29   Function Points   : 350
Staff Months : 26.34   Calendar Months   : 10.97
Cost / FP   : 753   Defects   : 44

Phase Breakdown

Methodology : Traditional

Phase	Percent of Effort	Staff Months
Requirements/Review	20	5.27
Design/Review	25	6.59
Build/Unit Test	15	3.95
Integration/Test	5	1.32
System Testing	20	5.27
Project Management	10	2.63
Installation	5	1.31
Total	100	26.34

Frequently Asked Questions (FAQs)

How to Identify the Scope and Boundary of a Count

The counting scope is determined by the purpose of the count; it identifies all of the systems, applications, and/or subsets of an application that will be sized. The application boundary indicates the border between the application being measured and external applications or the user domain.

Question

When performing a function point count, how do you determine the scope and application boundary when the system to be counted includes multiple but separate applications?

Answer

The scope may include an entire project, but function points are counted separately by application. Development projects and enhancement projects often include more than a single application. In these cases, the multiple application boundaries would be identified within the counting scope, but they would be separately counted by application.

Question

When performing a function point count, how do you determine the application boundary when the system to be counted includes several platforms?

Answer

In a function point count, the application should be counted from the perspective of the business solution versus the technical solution. The platforms are part of the physical environment and not part of the functional requirements. As an example, the application boundary of a client-server application consists of all components that collectively meet the business requirements, regardless of physical implementation or platform.

Question

When performing a function point count, how do you count reusable components that may be used in multiple applications?

Answer

We count the functionality in each application where it is used. Function points do not directly equal effort; consequently, project attributes (e.g., skills, tools, and reuse) aid in the productivity of projects but do not change the size. Chapter 12 discusses both object-oriented development and data warehouses, which are costly to build but easy to reuse.

Question

When performing a function point count, how do you decide on the scope and application boundary for GUI front ends or report generator back ends?

Answer

The development or enhancement project could build these components separately, but they probably will belong to the applications they were intended to support. This is particularly true if they are supporting only one application.

Question

When performing a function point count, how do you determine the scope and application boundary when the system to be counted includes a vendor package? What should be counted when you purchase a package?

Answer

There are many potential counts relating to the purchase of a package. First, when you shop for a package you have a group of requirements that can and should be sized; this is the functionality you need. A potential vendor may already have an application count, but do you care about the functionality you do not intend to use? Next, you should be interested in the enhancement project count to make necessary changes to the package and satisfy interfacing requirements. Finally, you need an application count to measure the functionality that will be used after the enhancement and thus must be supported.

How to Count ILFs and EIFs

Internal logical files (ILFs) and external interface files (EIFs) are commonly over-counted. They should be counted as logical groupings of data and not physical representations or tables of those groupings of data. An ILF must not be dependent on or attributive to another ILF in order to maintain its existence. Optional or mandatory subgroups (e.g., multiple types of payments with different fields for each payment type, but additional common fields) and attributive groups (e.g., address tables or contact tables that could belong to one or more higher-level groupings) must be merged with their parents. It is possible, but very unlikely, that the logical grouping will match the physical implementation. ILFs and EIFs should be counted in a logical manner regardless of the database structure. An application should be counted with the same number of ILFs and EIFs whether the physical file structure consists of flat files, an IDMS database, an IMS database, a relational database, DB2 tables, or objects.

Question

A particular application contains ten identical databases to handle ten different sales regions. The databases are identical in format, but the users want them maintained separately. How many internal logical files (ILFs) should be counted?

Answer

One. Although it takes extra effort to maintain ten different databases, logically the data is the same regardless of whether it is maintained in separate physical files or in a single file.

How to Count Tables

Question

If error or edit criteria are embedded in the code, no internal logical files (ILFs) are counted. If the criteria are maintained by the user in a table through a standardized process of the application, they are counted as an ILF. In the former case, the application's function points are fewer because of a physical design decision. So if the idea is to get as many function points as possible, the messages and/or edit criteria simply need to be stored in tables. Is this correct?

Answer

It is not just a matter of placing something in a table and therefore getting credit for it. If the messages and/or criteria are maintained in a table, the table must meet all of the criteria of an ILF (i.e., it must be stored inside the application boundary, required by the user, and maintained by an elementary process of the application). We typically have hard-coded tables where we expect data changes to be infrequent. Remember that when those hard-coded tables require revision, the enhancement project will recognize and count the transactional functions that utilize those tables as a result of any changes in processing logic.

Some Typical Errors in Identifying ILFs and EIFs

- Various iterations of the same file (e.g., multiple months, quarters, years, quartiles, payment types, insurance types) are only records within the same ILF or EIF and should not be counted as separate ILFs or EIFs.
- JCL, trigger files, and static tables should not be counted; count only maintained dynamic data.
- Various sorts of the same file belong to one ILF, and the repeating fields are counted only once for their DETs.
- Extract files, or view files, that contain data extracted from other ILFs or EIFs prior to display should not be counted; the source of the data is counted, and the external output or external inquiry is counted.
- Files introduced because of technology should not be counted.
- Alternative indices, joins, relationships, or connections should not be counted unless they contain additional and separately maintained non-key attributes.
- ILFs maintained by other applications and "read or referenced" should be counted as EIFs; the same file cannot be both an ILF and an EIF.
- Backup data used for backup and recovery should not be counted.
- Incoming files and outgoing files are typically EIs, EOs, or EQs and not ILFs; an EI can create an ILF.
- An extract from another application that is loaded (and refreshed on a regular basis) and not further maintained or updated by additional input transactions

should not be counted as an EI or an ILF; this data should be counted as one or more EIFs.

How Is the Complexity Assigned for Data Functions?

Each identified ILF and EIF must be assigned a functional complexity based on the number of data element types (DETs) and record element types (RETs) associated with the ILF or EIF.

How Should RETs Be Counted for an ILF or EIF?

Record element types (RETs) are user-recognizable subgroups (optional or mandatory) of data elements contained within an ILF or EIF. Subgroups are typically represented in an entity relationship diagram as entity subtypes or attributive entities, commonly called parent-child relationships. The user has the option of using one or none of the optional subgroups during an elementary process that adds or creates an instance of the data; the user must use at least one of the mandatory subgroups. If there are no subgroups, count the ILF or EIF as one RET. Tables often equate to RETs and not separate ILFs or EIFs.

How Should DETs Be Counted for an ILF or EIF?

Data element types (DETs) are unique user-recognizable, nonrepeating fields or attributes, including foreign key attributes, maintained on the ILF or EIF. An ILF containing 12 monthly amount fields and an annual total would be credited with two DETs, one for the repetitive monthly amounts and one to identify the total; one additional DET would undoubtedly be provided to identify the month. Text counts as one DET regardless of the number of words. DETs are typically overcounted.

How to Count EIs

An external input (EI) consists of an elementary process that is the smallest unit of activity that is meaningful to the end user in the business. This elementary process must be self-contained and leave the business of the application being counted in a consistent state. For example, an input form for mortgage coverage could consist of three screens; if the form were incomplete until all three screens were completed, the elementary process would require the completion of all three screens. We would not question this decision if the form were to be completed manually; we would just hand it back to the individual and request that the entire form be completed. Completing some of the fields, even those on one screen, would neither be self-contained nor leave the business in a consistent state. If all information, recognizing that some of the fields may not be mandatory and could be left blank, were completed, this transaction would be complete and the business would be left in a consistent state. In a Windows environment we can save data at any time, but we don't count each save as a separate EI; we count only the completed transaction that is saved.

Question

The Summary of Functions Performed table in the Counting Practices Manual says that an external input (EI) can present information to a user, but not as the primary intent. Can you provide an example?

Answer

A sales transaction is entered, and the resulting total cost of the sale is returned to the screen (calculations internal). The total is part of the elementary process of the sales transaction.

Question

In the Summary of Processing Logic table of the Counting Practices Manual, an external input (EI) can prepare and present information outside the boundary, but it is not mandatory. Can you provide an example?

Answer

An EI's primary purpose is to save data or to control system functionality. An error or confirmation message or some other data may be sent outside, such as system calculations (x transactions processed, y transactions failed, z transactions for a type of vehicle, and so on) as a part of the elementary process of performing the EI.

Question

How can the behavior of a system be altered by an EI? Can you provide an example?

Answer

In response to reading sensor data, we turn on the heater, change a light from green to red, or fire a missile. This is what we previously called a control EI. Within windows, zoom and minimize are examples.

How to Count Transactions

Question

A Daily Data Input file maintains internally stored data. The file has 36 different records (besides header and trailer information) representing different types of transactions—for example, debits, credits, updates. How would you go about determining the unique external inputs (EIs) to be counted?

Answer

Count an EI for each unique transaction. Each unique transaction represents different processing requirements. Make sure that identical transaction types are counted only once. You can determine unique transaction types by examining the specifications, physical file layouts, and/or code.

Be sure that all of the following criteria are met when you are identifying unique EIs:

- Data is received from outside the application boundary.
- Data in at least one ILF is maintained through an elementary process of the application (unless data is control information that alters the behavior of the application).
- For the identified process, one of the following rules applies:
  - Processing logic is unique from that of other EIs
  - Data elements are different from those of other EIs
  - ILFs or EIFs referenced are different from those of other EIs

Some Typical Errors in Identifying EIs

- Windows and buttons do not count as EIs; buttons are usually command keys to initiate an EQ or EO or to commence or save an EI (the transaction is counted, but not the button, which is a DET on the EI or on the input side of an EO or EQ).
- There may be no EI transactions on a screen or window; the window may be a navigational menu (not counted), display only (an EO or EQ), or one in a series of windows necessary to create the EI.
- Reference data that is read by the application from data stored in another application, but is not used to maintain an ILF in the counted application, is counted not as an EI, but as an EIF.
- The input or request side (consisting of one or more parameters) of an EO or EQ is *not* also counted as an EI.

- Menu screens used for navigation or selection that do not maintain an ILF are not counted.
- Log-on screens are not counted as EIs; they might be counted as EQs.
- Multiple methods of invoking the same logic (e.g., two action keys that perform the same function or the same transaction on the same or multiple screens) should be counted only once with the transaction itself.
- Point-and-click of data on a screen in order to fill field(s) on the screen should not be counted as separate EIs, but the data field will be counted with others as DETs when you are determining the complexity of EIs.
- Refresh or cancel of screen data is not counted; it doesn't store data.
- Deletes of fields on a window, or moving data on a window, are not separate EIs.
- Responses to messages that request a user to confirm a delete or any other transaction are not EIs.
- Data passed between online and batch within the same application should not be counted; it doesn't cross the boundary.
- Data passed between client and server within the same application should not be counted; it doesn't cross the boundary.

How to Count EQs

An external inquiry (EQ) is an elementary process that retrieves information from an ILF or EIF and sends it outside the application boundary. The processing logic contains no mathematical formulas or calculations, creates no derived data, does not maintain an ILF during processing, and does not alter the behavior of the application. Although there may not be an input side to an EQ (i.e., it could be generated internally), an output result (in any media, including files, diskettes, and e-mails) must exit the application boundary. Data must be retrieved from one or more ILFs or EIFs. Traditionally, EQs are user functions such as view, lookup, display, browse, or drop-down list boxes that retrieve dynamic (not hard-coded static) data. Each level of help (e.g., system, field, or window/screen) retrieved from one or more ILFs or EIFs is counted once per level per application.

Question

Users of a tracking system within the Department of Motor Vehicles have the ability to inquire on an eight-digit license number and state. The output side of the inquiry displays information about the registered owner record. On the input side, users can enter up to eight digits of a license number and state, if known. If the user (e.g., a state police officer) recalls only a portion of the number (e.g., K U K ? ? ? ? ?), pick lists are available to help identify colors of the license plates and model codes for the vehicles.

The following pick lists are available:

• State abbreviations
• Color codes
• Model codes

How many EQs would you count?

Answer

Count one EQ for the return of the entire registered owner record. In a situation such as this, the input side may actually have more DETs than the output display. Count each pick list that contains dynamic (user-maintained) information the first time it appears within an application. The state pick list probably contains static information and, if so, should not be counted as an EQ.

Some Typical Errors in Identifying EQs

• Multiple sorts of the same data do not count as additional EQs.
• Different "and/or" parameter selections for the retrieval process do not count as additional EQs.
• Multiple versions of the same retrievals, even if requested from different screens or windows or via different buttons or keys, do not count as additional EQs.
• Menu screens used for navigation or selection should not be counted.
• Log-on screens that facilitate user entry into an application, but do not invoke security, should not be counted.
• Derived or calculated data, versus retrieval of data, should be counted as an EO.
• Data passed between online and batch within the same application should not be counted; it doesn't cross the boundary.
• Data passed between client and server within the same application should not be counted; it doesn't cross the boundary.
• Data that is not retrieved from maintained data (e.g., hard-coded or static data) should not be counted even if retrieved via a list box.

How to Count EOs

An external output (EO) is an elementary process that sends data or control information outside the application boundary. Unlike an EQ, an EO's processing logic must contain mathematical formulas or calculations, create derived data, maintain an ILF during processing, or alter the behavior of the application; only one of these distinctions is necessary.

Some Typical Errors in Identifying EOs

- EOs should be counted only when there is unique processing.
- A report may consist of numerous topics and pages, but if the pages are not independently required and separately produced, the entire report counts as only one EO.
- A physical file sent to multiple locations with exactly the same data but different routing (addresses) is counted as one EO (or one EQ).
- Each EO or EQ reflects separate and additional processing required by the application and not just available from Windows.
- Multiple versions of the same views (same fields and DETs, but different months, quartiles, locations, and so on) without any unique processing should be counted only once.
- Identical reports with different data values, such as a geographical or sales report, are counted only once.
- Summary fields contained on a detail report should be counted, together with the detail information, as one EO.
- Re-sorting or rearrangement of a set of data without other processing logic is not counted.
- Reference data that is read by another application from data stored in the application being counted is not counted as an output.
- Don't confuse EQs with EOs; EOs require additional processing logic.
- Confirmation messages acknowledging that the data has been processed are not EOs, but are counted as one extra DET.
- Messages that request a user to confirm a delete or any other external input are not EOs.
- Identical data fields sent to more than one application or even different organizations are counted as only one EO.

- Data passed between online and batch within the same application should not be counted; it doesn't cross the boundary.
- Data passed between client and server within the same application should not be counted; it doesn't cross the boundary.

How Is the Complexity Assigned for Transactional Functions?

Each identified EI, EO, and EQ must be assigned a functional complexity based on the number of data element types (DETs) and file types referenced (FTRs) associated with the transaction.

How to Count DETs for an EI, EO, or EQ

Data element types (DETs) are usually unique user-recognizable, nonrecurring fields or attributes, including foreign key attributes, that cross the boundary of the application. Some other specific characteristics of a transaction are also counted as DETs; these include the counting of one DET for any number of error and confirmation messages and another DET for any number of command and action keys. Recurring fields, even though they contain different data, should not be counted.

Question

A report of GM vehicles indicates the following production numbers:

Chevy Blazer	9999
Chevy Camaro	9999
Pontiac GP	9999
Olds Cutlass	9999

How many DETs should be counted?

Answer

Two—one for vehicle identification and one for production numbers.

How to Count FTRs for an EI, EO, or EQ

File types referenced (FTRs), or more simply files referenced, are the total number of internal logical files (ILFs) maintained, read, or referenced and the external interface files (EIFs) read or referenced by the transaction. Source files are not to be counted as FTRs on an EI, nor should destination files be counted on an EO.

What Is Application Maintenance?

Application maintenance is an element of the systems production support. The definition of application corrective maintenance is any activity initiated by a customer or developer for fixes or repairs to correct an application not believed to be in conformance to application specifications. Maintenance includes the general support and upkeep of the installed application base but does not add functionality to the application. Enhancements add or change functionality to an application.

The following application maintenance items are classified in the corrective maintenance category:

- Abends
- Incorrect results
- Screen and report formatting errors
- Incorrect calculations
- Incorrect sequence of processing
- Missing data
- Run time improvements required to meet application specifications
- Usability problems

The following application maintenance items are classified in the perfective maintenance category:

- Changes, not required by customer, to avert foreseeable problems
- Application and database changes to improve performance.

A third category of application maintenance items includes the following:

- Package and system software upgrades
- Maintenance of existing support levels
- Ad hoc reporting

Other responsibilities that might be categorized outside of application maintenance into the broad area of production support, include the following:

- Maintenance and monitoring of operations, including the data center, servers, PCs, telecommunications, middleware, and so on
- Support of customers, including help desk and training

What Major Companies Are Using Function Points to Size Their Software?

The International Function Point Users Group has over 600 corporate members. A detailed listing of those organizations is available through IFPUG to its members.

APPENDIX F

Answers to the CFPS Practice Exam

Answer Sheet: Part I

Name: David Garmus

Instructions: Darken your answer to each question. Only one answer is correct. Recommend use of pencil. To delete an answer, cross through with an X.

1. **a** b c d	18. a b **c** d	35. a b **c** d
2. a b c **d**	19. a b **c** d	36. **a** b c d
3. a b c **d**	20. a b **c** d	37. a b c **d**
4. **a** b c d	21. **a** b c d	38. **a** b c d
5. a b c **d**	22. a **b** c d	39. a **b** c d
6. **a** b c d	23. a b **c** d	40. **a** b c d
7. **a** b c d	24. **a** b c d	41. a **b** c d
8. a **b** c d	25. a **b** c d	42. a b **c** d
9. a **b** c d	26. a b **c** d	43. a b c **d**
10. a b c **d**	27. a b c **d**	44. a b c **d**
11. a b **c** d	28. a **b** c d	45. a **b** c d
12. a b c **d**	29. **a** b c d	46. a b c **d**
13. a b c **d**	30. **a** b c d	47. a b c **d**
14. **a** b c d	31. a b **c** d	48. a b c **d**
15. **a** b c d	32. a b c **d**	49. a b c **d**
16. a b c **d**	33. a **b** c d	50. **a** b c d
17. **a** b c d	34. a b c **d**	

Answer Sheet: Part II

Name: David Garmus

Instructions: Darken your answer to each question. Only one answer is correct. Recommend use of pencil. To delete an answer, cross through with an X.

1. a **b** c d	18. a b **c** d	35. **a** b c d
2. **a** b c d	19. a b **c** d	36. a b c **d**
3. **a** b c d	20. a **b** c d	37. a b **c** d
4. a b **c** d	21. **a** b c d	38. a b c **d**
5. a b **c** d	22. a b **c** d	39. a **b** c d
6. a b c **d**	23. a b c **d**	40. a **b** c d
7. a **b** c d	24. a b **c** d	41. **a** b c d
8. **a** b c d	25. a b **c** d	42. **a** b c d
9. a b **c** d	26. a b c **d**	43. a b **c** d
10. a b **c** d	27. **a** b c d	44. a **b** c d
11. a b **c** d	28. a b **c** d	45. a **b** c d
12. a b c **d**	29. a b c **d**	46. a **b** c d
13. **a** b c d	30. a b c **d**	47. **a** b c d
14. a **b** c d	31. a b c **d**	48. a **b** c d
15. a b c **d**	32. a **b** c d	49. **a** b c d
16. a **b** c d	33. a **b** c d	50. **a** b c d
17. **a** b c d	34. a **b** c d	

Answer Sheet: Part III

The answers for the two case studies are given in Figures F-1 through F-4.

Function Point Count Summary

Project Number Answers to CFPS Case Study 1   **Project Name** Accounts Payable
Date of Count   **Counter's Name** DCG

Instructions: Enter all function types included. Annotate all function types added by the conversion. You may wish to use different sheets for files and transactions.

Description	Type[a]	DETs	RETs/FTRs	Complexity[b]
Add Invoice	EI	10	3	H
List Boxes				
Outstanding POs	EQ	4	1	L
Vendor	EQ	6	1	L
Display Invoice	EQ	10	1	L
Change Invoice	EI	10	3	H
Delete Invoice	EI	3	1	L
File to Banking System	EQ	8	2	A
Retrieve Payments Screen	EO	11	1	L
Receive Payments	EI	5	1	L
Add Vendor	EI	9	1	L
Display Vendor	EQ	9	1	L
Change Vendor	EI	9	1	L
Field Help[c]	EQ	4	1	L
Window Help	EQ	3	1	L
Invoice Data Store	ILF	11	2	L
PO Data Store	EIF	3	1	L
Vendor Data Store	ILF	7	1	L
Help Data Store	EIF	3	1	L
Drop-Down List of Dates	NC[d]	--	--	--

[a] ILF, EIF, EI, EO, or EQ
[b] Low (L), Average (A), High (H)
[c] (DETs: Window, Field, Text, and Action Key)
[d] (NC = Not Counted)

Figure F-1 Function point count summary answers for Case Study 1

Function Point Calculation Worksheet

IFPUG's Unadjusted Function Point Table*

	Function Levels			
Components	**Low**	**Average**	**High**	**Total**
External inputs	4×3	$\times 4$	2×6	24
External outputs	1×4	$\times 5$	$\times 7$	4
External inquiries	6×3	1×4	$\times 6$	22
Internal logical files	2×7	$\times 10$	$\times 15$	14
External interface files	2×5	$\times 7$	$\times 10$	10

Total unadjusted function points (UFP) = 74

*The development function point count includes function types added by the conversion. The application function point count does not include conversion requirements. An application count after an enhancement must include all existing function types, including those unchanged. If information on all existing function types is not available, the application adjusted function point count can be computed by the formula given in the text.

General System Characteristics

Characteristic	Degree of Influence	Characteristic	Degree of Influence
1. Data communications	4	8. Online update	3
2. Distributed data processing	0	9. Complex processing	0
3. Performance	0	10. Reusability	3
4. Heavily used configuration	0	11. Installation ease	0
5. Transaction rate	0	12. Operational ease	3
6. Online data entry	5	13. Multiple sites	2
7. End user efficiency	3	14. Facilitate change	2

Total degree of influence (TDI) = 25

VAF	Value adjustment factor	$= (TDI \times 0.01) + 0.65$	$= 0.90$
FP	Adjusted function point count	$= UFP \times VAF$	$= 67$

Figure F-2 Function point calculation worksheet answers for Case Study 1

Enhancement Function Point Count Summary

Project Number Answers to CFPS Case Study 2   **Project Name** Banking
Date of Count   **Counter's Name** DCG

Instructions: Enter all function types included. For development and initial function point counts, there will not be entries in the "Before" columns. Annotate all function types added by the conversion. You may wish to use different sheets for files and transactions.

Description	Type[a]	DETs After	RETs/FTRs After	Complexity[b] After	DETs Before	RETs/FTRs Before	Complexity[b] Before
Accounts Payable File	EI	8	2	A	(new)		
Checks	EO	8	1	L	7	1	L
Printed Report	EO	6	1	L	(new)		
Retrieve Suspense File	EO	6	1	L	(new)		
Update Suspense File	EI	6	3	H	(new)		
Checking Account Data Store	ILF	20	2	A	19	2	L
Suspense Data Store	ILF	4	1	L	(new)		

[a] ILF, EIF, EI, EO, or EQ
[b] Low (L), Average (A), High (H)

Figure F-3 Enhancement function point count summary answers for Case Study 2

Enhancement Function Point Calculation Worksheet

Project Number Answers to CFPS Case Study 2   Project Name Banking
Type of Count Enhanced Project Count
Phase of Count Proposal/Requirements/Design/Code/Test/Delivery (circle one)
Date of Count   Counter's Name

	Function Levels			
* Function Types Added or Modified (Value After)	Low	Average	High	Total
External inputs	× 3	1 × 4	1 × 6	10
External outputs	3 × 4	× 5	× 7	12
External inquiries	× 3	× 4	× 6	
Internal logical files	1 × 7	1 × 10	× 15	17
External interface files	× 5	× 7	× 10	

Total unadjusted function points (UFP) = 39

* Include added function types and modified function types (value after). The enhancement function point count includes function types added by the conversion.

	Function Levels			
* Function Types Deleted	Low	Average	High	Total
External inputs	× 3	× 4	× 6	____
External outputs	× 4	× 5	× 7	____
External inquiries	× 3	× 4	× 6	____
Internal logical files	× 7	× 10	× 15	____
External interface files	× 5	× 7	× 10	____

Unadjusted deleted function points = 0

* Includes those function types deleted by the enhancement.

Figure F-4 Enhancement function point calculation worksheet answers for Case Study 2

(continued)

General System Characteristics

Characteristic	Degree of Influence Before	After	Characteristic	Degree of Influence Before	After
1. Data communications	4	4	8. Online update	3	3
2. Distributed data processing	0	0	9. Complex processing	3	3
3. Performance	3	3	10. Reusability	3	3
4. Heavily used configuration	2	2	11. Installation ease	2	2
5. Transaction rate	3	3	12. Operational ease	3	3
6. Online data entry	5	5	13. Multiple sites	3	3
7. End user efficiency	3	3	14. Facilitate change	2	2
			Total degree of influence (TDI) =	39	39

Enhancement project function point count

$[(ADD + CHGA + CFP) \times VAFA] + [DEL \times VAFB] = 41$

Revised application count: $[(UFPB + ADD + CHGA) -$
$(CHGB + DEL)] \times VAFA$
$[(330 + 25 + 14) - (11)] \times 1.04 =$
$[358] \times 1.04 = 372$

Figure F-4 Enhancement function point calculation worksheet answers for Case Study 2 (*cont.*)

Bibliography

Web Connections

aligne: www.aligne.com

The David Consulting Group: www.davidconsultinggroup.com

DDB Software, Inc.: www.ddbsoftware.com

CHARISMATEK Software Metrics: www.charismatek.com

Function Point FAQ: http://ourworld.compuserve.com/homepages/softcomp/fpfaq.htm

International Function Point Users Group (IFPUG): www.ifpug.org

International Software Benchmarking Standards Group (ISBSG): www.isbsg.org.au

Netherlands Software Metrics Users Association (NESMA): www.nesma.nl/english

Software Engineering Management Research Laboratory, University of Quebec: www.lrgl.uqam.ca

Software Metrics: A Subdivided Bibliography: http://irb.cs.uni-magdeburg.de/sw-eng/us/bibliography/bib_main.shtml

Additional Readings

Abran, Alain, and Pierre N. Robillard. "Function Points: A Study of Their Measurement Processes and Scale Transformations." *Journal of Systems and Software* 25, no. 2 (1994): 171–184.

Albrecht, Allan J. *Application Development and Maintenance Measurement and Analysis Guideline.* White Plains, NY: IBM Corporate Information System and Administration, 1981.

Albrecht, Allan J. "Measuring Application Development Productivity." In *Proceedings of the Joint SHARE/GUIDE IBM Applications Development Symposium,* Monterey, CA, October 14–17, 1979. Monterey, CA: IBM, 1979, 83–92.

Albrecht, Allan J. "Measuring Application Development Productivity." In *Tutorial: Programming Productivity: Issues for the Eighties.* Los Alamitos, CA: IEEE Computer Society, 1986, 35–44.

Banker, Rajiv D., and Chris F. Kemerer. "Scale Economies in New Software Development." *IEEE Transactions on Software Engineering* 15, no. 10 (1989): 1199–1205.

Bock, Douglas B., and Robert Klepper. "FP-S: A Simplified Function Point Count Method." *Journal of Systems and Software* 18, no. 3 (1992): 245.

Boehm, Barry W. *Software Engineering Economics.* Englewood Cliffs, NJ: Prentice-Hall, 1981.

Boehm, Ray. "Counting Data Warehouse Applications." *Voice* 1, no. 2 (1997): 4–5.

Bradley, M., and C. Dekkers. "'You Can't Measure Us'—The Truth behind Developers' Measurement Myths." *Managing System Development* February 1996: 1–5.

Brooks, Irwin L. "Engineering Function Points and Earned Value Tracking Systems," *CrossTalk Journal* 7, no. 11 (1994).

Brown, Darlene. "Productivity Measurement Using Function Points." *Software Engineering* July–August 1990.

Coad, Peter, and Edward Yourdon. *Object-Oriented Analysis.* Englewood Cliffs, NJ: Prentice-Hall, 1991.

Connolley, Michael J. *An Empirical Study of Function Point Analysis Reliability.* Cambridge, MA: MIT Sloan School of Management, 1990.

Connolley, Michael J. *Summary of Microcase Results* (IFPUG/MIT Function Point Reliability Study). Cambridge, MA: MIT Sloan School of Management, 1990.

Dekkers, C., and M. Bradley. "It's the People Who Count in Measurement." *Voice* 1, no. 1 (1996): 25–26.

DeMarco, Tom, and Timothy Lister. *Peopleware.* New York: Dorset House, 1987.

Dreger, J. Brian. *Function Point Analysis.* Englewood Cliffs, NJ: Prentice-Hall, 1989.

Emrick, Ronald D. "Software Development Productivity—Second Industry Survey" (paper presented at the IFPUG Spring Conference, Dallas, TX, May 1988).

Garmus, David. "Function Point Counting." *Software Development* September 1993: 67–69.

Garmus, David. "Function Point Counting in a Real-Time Environment" *CrossTalk Journal* 9, no. 1 (1996): 11–14.

Garmus, David. *Huron Function Point Counting Guide.* Sunnyvale, CA: Amdahl, 1992.

Garmus, David, ed. *IFPUG Counting Practices Manual,* Release 3.4. Westerville, OH: International Function Point Users Group, 1992.

Garmus, David. "Introduction to Function Point Counting in a Real-Time Environment." *Voice* 1, no. 1 (1996): 27–29, 34.

Garmus, David. "Software Project Estimation Principles." *Data Manager* February 1998: 8–10.

Garmus, David, and David Herron. "Accurate Estimation." *Software Development* July 1996: 57–65.

Garmus, David, and David Herron. "Estimating Software Earlier and More Accurately." *Methods & Tools* July 1997: 2–7.

Garmus, David, and David Herron. "Estimating Time, Effort, and Cost." *Software Testing & Quality Engineering* November/December 1999: 30–36.

Garmus, David, and David Herron. *Measuring the Software Process: A Practical Guide to Functional Measurements.* Englewood Cliffs, NJ: Prentice-Hall, 1995.

Garmus, David, and Walter Paskey. *Use of Software Metrics within CACI Information System Development Projects.* Arlington, VA: CACI, 1991.

Grady, Robert B. *Practical Software Metrics for Project Management and Process Improvement.* Englewood Cliffs, NJ: Prentice-Hall, 1992.

Grupe, F. H., and Dorothy F. Clevenger. "Using Function Point Analysis as a Software Development Tool." *Journal of Systems Management* 12 (1991): 23–26.

Heemstra, F. J., and R. J. Kusters. "Function Point Analysis: Evaluation of a Software Cost Estimation Model." *European Journal of Information Systems* 1 (1991): 229–237.

Henderson, Garland S. "The Application of Function Points to Predict Source Lines of Code for Software Development." Master's thesis, Air Force Institute of Technology, 1992.

Herron, David. "Achieving Continuous Process Improvement." *Knowledge Base* 2, no. 1 (1993).

Herron, David. "Function Points." *Data Manager* September 1997: 6–8.

Herron, David. "A Measure of Success." *siliconindia* July 1998.

Hetzel, Bill. *Making Software Measurement Work—Building an Effective Measurement Program.* Boston: QED Technical Publishing Group, 1993.

Hill, Peter, ed. *Software Project Estimation: A Workbook for Macro-estimation of Software Development Effort and Duration.* Melbourne, Australia: ISBSG, 1999.

Hooft, Martin. "The Application of Software Metrics in Cost Accounting." *Voice* 1, no. 1 (1996): 16, 30–31.

Humphrey, Watts S. *A Discipline for Software Engineering.* Reading, MA: Addison-Wesley, 1995.

Humphrey, Watts S. *Managing the Software Process.* Reading, MA: Addison-Wesley, 1989.

IBM. *AD/M Productivity Measurement and Estimate Validation.* Armonk, NY: IBM Corporate Information Systems and Administration, IBM Corporation, 1984.

International Function Point Users Group. *Case Study 1 (ANALYSIS—ERD, Process Hierarchical Model; CONSTRUCTION—DB2 Data Base, Graphical User Interface (GUI) Windows),* Release 1.1. Westerville, OH: IFPUG Standards, 1996; Release 2.0, 2000.

International Function Point Users Group. *Case Study 2 (ANALYSIS—ERD, DFD; CONSTRUCTION—IMS Data Base, Text Base Screen Implementation),* Release 1.0. Westerville, OH: IFPUG Standards, 1994 (in the process of revision).

International Function Point Users Group. *Case Study 3 (ANALYSIS—Object Oriented Analysis; CONSTRUCTION—Object Oriented Design),* Release 1.0. Westerville, OH: IFPUG Standards, 1996 (in the process of revision).

International Function Point Users Group. *Case Study 4 (TRACS—A Traffic Control System with Real-Time Components),* Release 1.0. Westerville, OH: IFPUG Standards, 1998 (in the process of revision).

International Function Point Users Group. *Function Point Counting Practices Manual,* Release 4.0. Westerville, OH: IFPUG Standards, 1994.

International Function Point Users Group. *Function Point Counting Practices Manual,* Release 4.1. Westerville, OH: IFPUG Standards, 1999.

International Function Point Users Group. *Function Points as an Asset—Reporting to Management.* Westerville, OH: IFPUG Standards, 1990.

International Function Point Users Group. *Guidelines to Software Measurement,* Release 1.1. Westerville, OH: IFPUG Standards, 1999.

International Software Benchmarking Standards Group (ISBSG). *Repository Data Disk,* Release 6. Melbourne, Australia: ISBSG, 1999.

International Software Benchmarking Standards Group (ISBSG). *Worldwide Software Development—The Benchmark,* Release 5. Melbourne, Australia: ISBSG, 1998.

Jeffery, D. R., G. C. Low, and M. Barnes. "A Comparison of Function Point Counting Techniques." *IEEE Transactions on Software Engineering* 19, no. 5 (1993).

Jones, Capers. *Applied Software Measurement, Assuring Productivity and Quality.* New York: McGraw-Hill, 1991.

Jones, Capers. *Applied Software Measurement,* 2nd ed. New York: McGraw-Hill, 1996.

Jones, Capers. *Assessment and Control of Software Risks.* Englewood Cliffs, NJ: Prentice-Hall, 1994.

Jones, Capers. "Function Points: A New Way of Looking at Tools." *Computer* August 1994: 66–67.

Jones, Capers. *Metric with Muscle—Measuring Software Productivity in Economic Terms.* Phoenix, AZ: System Development, Applied Computer Research Publishers, 1989.

Jones, Capers. "The Role of Function Point Metrics in the 21st Century." *Voice* 1, no. 1 (1996): 32–34.

Jones, Capers. "A Short History of Function Points and Feature Points," technical paper, Software Productivity Research, Cambridge, MA, 1988.

Jones, Capers. "Should the 'Lines of Code' Metric be Viewed as Professional Malpractice?" *Voice* 1, no. 2 (1997): 10–14.

Kemerer, Chris F. "An Empirical Validation of Software Cost Estimation Models." *Communications of the ACM 30,* no. 5 (1987): 416–429.

Kemerer, Chris F. "Reliability of Function Points Measurement: A Field Experiment." *Communications of the ACM 36,* no. 2 (1993): 85–97.

Kemerer, Chris F., and Benjamin S. Porter. "Improving the Reliability of Function Point Measurement: An Empirical Study." *IEEE Transactions on Software Engineering* 18, no. 11 (1992): 1011–1024.

Keuffel, Warren. "Predicting with Function Point Metrics." *Software Development* July 1994: 27.

Keyes, Jessica. *Software Engineering Productivity Handbook.* New York: McGraw-Hill, 1993.

Low, Graham C., and Jeffery D. Ross. "Function Points in the Estimation and Evaluation of the Software Process." *IEEE Transactions on Software Engineering* 16, no. 1 (1990): 64–71.

Lundquist, G., and Dekkers, C. "The Proof Is in the Ratios: Turning Raw Data into Meaningful Software Metrics." *Journal of the Quality Assurance Institute* July 1996: 1–5.

Matson, Jack E., Bruce E. Barret, and Joseph M. Mellichamp. "Software Development Cost Estimation Using Function Points." *IEEE Transactions on Software Engineering* 20, no. 4 (1994): 275–287.

Netherlands Software Metrics Association (NESMA). "Definitions and Counting Guidelines for the Application of Function Point Analysis," Version 2.0. Amsterdam: NESMA, 1997.

Putnam, Lawrence H., and Ware Myers. *Industrial Strength Software.* IEEE Computer Society Press, 1997.

Putnam, Lawrence H., and Ware Myers. *Measures for Excellence.* New York: Yourdon Press, 1992.

Rask, R., P. Laamanen, and K. Lyytinen. "Simulation and Comparison of Albrecht's Function Point and DeMarco's Function Bang Metrics in a CASE Environment." *IEEE Transactions on Software Engineering* 19, no. 7 (1993): 661–671.

Roman, David. "A Measure of Programming: Function Point Analysis Offers MIS Managers a Reliable Way to Measure Programmer Productivity—And to End Beat-the-Clock Development. *Computer Decisions* 19, no. 2 (1987): 32.

Rubin, H. *Software Engineer's Benchmark Handbook.* Phoenix, AZ: Applied Computer Research, 1992.

Symons, Charles R. "Function Point Analysis: Difficulties and Improvements." *IEEE Transactions on Software Engineering* SE-14, no. 1 (1988): 2–11.

Symons, Charles R. *Software Sizing and Estimating. Mk II Function Point Analysis.* Chichester, England: John Wiley & Sons, 1991.

Van Solingen, Rini, and Egon Berghout. *The Goal/Question/Metric Method.* New York: McGraw-Hill, 1999.

Whitmire, Scott A. "An Introduction to 3D Function Points." *Software Development* April 1995: 43–53.

Yourdon, Edward. *Decline and Fall of the American Programmer.* Englewood Cliffs, NJ: Prentice-Hall, 1994.

Zuse, Horst. *A Framework of Software Measurement.* Berlin, NY: Walter de Gruyter, 1997.

Index

Register
Your Book
at www.aw.com/cseng/register

You may be eligible to receive:
- Advance notice of forthcoming editions of the book
- Related book recommendations
- Chapter excerpts and supplements of forthcoming titles
- Information about special contests and promotions throughout the year
- Notices and reminders about author appearances, tradeshows, and online chats with special guests

Contact us

If you are interested in writing a book or reviewing manuscripts prior to publication, please write to us at:

Editorial Department
Addison-Wesley Professional
75 Arlington Street, Suite 300
Boston, MA 02116 USA
Email: AWPro@aw.com

Addison-Wesley

Visit us on the Web: http://www.aw.com/cseng